THIS BOOK BELONGS TO

MARTHA STEWART'S
Encyclopedia
of Crafts

An A-to-Z guide with
detailed instructions
and endless inspiration

MARTHA STEWART'S
Encyclopedia of Crafts

An A-to-Z guide with
detailed instructions
and endless inspiration

7455

D&C
David and Charles

A DAVID & CHARLES BOOK

Copyright © Martha Stewart Living Omnimedia, Inc. 2009

Originally published in the United States by Potter Craft
an imprint of the Crown Publishing Group
a division of Random House, Inc., New York
www.clarksonpotter.com
www.pottercraft.com

First published in the UK in 2009 by David & Charles
David & Charles is an F+W Media Inc. company
4700 East Galbraith Road
Cincinnati, OH 45236

A catalogue record for this book is available from the British Library.

ISBN-13: 978-0-7153-3635-9 hardback
ISBN-10: 0-7153-3635-5 hardback

Printed in China
for David & Charles
Brunel House, Newton Abbot, Devon

Visit our website at www.davidandcharles.co.uk

David & Charles books are available from all good bookshops;
alternatively you can contact our Orderline on 0870 9908222
or write to us at FREEPOST EX2 110, D&C Direct, Newton Abbot,
TQ12 4ZZ (no stamp required UK only); US customers call
800-289-0963 and Canadian customers call 800-840-5220.

Bubble petal flowers, made out of tissue
paper (see page 260 for instructions).

To all crafters and artisans,
who keep valued traditions alive

A variation of the shell-covered pot on page 204. These terra-cotta pots are adorned with scallop, white cay cay, violet clam, and tiny white cap shells.

ACKNOWLEDGMENTS

This book represents the creative genius, hard work, and tireless efforts of many talented people at Martha Stewart Living Omnimedia.

The brilliant crafts editors at *Martha Stewart Living* deserve high praise and thanks for creating the content that appears within these pages. The editors continue to inspire and delight us with each new issue, and they conceived, created, and produced the craft projects in this book.

Marcie McGoldrick, editorial director of holiday and crafts, and Jodi Levine, a longtime MSLO editor and crafter, carefully reviewed every page of this book to make sure it is accurate and useful. Laura Normandin, long-standing member of our crafts department, also lent her expertise. Of course, we are indebted to our executive editorial director of crafts and original crafts editor, Hannah Milman, who currently oversees the practical and popular crafts merchandise for the company, along with Megen Lee, another very talented crafter. We'd like to thank current members of the crafts department, including Nicholas Andersen, Marissa Corwin, Corinne Gill, Morgan Levine, Athena Preston, Blake Ramsey, and Silke Stoddard, as well as past crafts editors whose contributions appear in these pages, including Anna Beckman, Shannon Goodson Carter, Bella Foster, Katie Hatch, Sophie Mathoulin, Charlyne Mattox, Shane Powers, and Kelli Ronci.

Our special projects group wrangled 17 years of crafts content into one concise, well-written volume; for that we are grateful to editors Amy Conway, Ellen Morrissey, Sarah Rutledge, Kimberly Fusaro, Christine Cyr, and Stephanie Fletcher, as well as interns Megan Rice and Gillian Mohney. A note of thanks, as well, to Jessica Cumberbatch.

As much as it is thoughtfully organized and written, this book is beautifully designed, thanks primarily to Amber Blakesley. Amber worked under the guidance of William van Roden and Eric A. Pike, and was dutifully assisted by Aimee Epstein and intern Eleanor Kramer. Thank you to George D. Planding, Dora Braschi Cardinale, and Gael Towey for their help, as well.

Photographer Ditte Isager captured the beautiful cover image, and many other photographers (too many to name here) also contributed their work (a complete list appears on page 416). Thank you as well to Heloise Goodman and Alison Vanek Devine of our photography department.

We have worked for many years with our original book publisher, Clarkson Potter, a division of Random House, to produce our cookbooks and other lifestyle books, but this is our first joint venture with the enthusiastic team at Potter Craft; they are Rosy Ngo, Erica Smith, Chi Ling Moy, Marysarah Quinn, Derek Gullino, and Thom O'Hearn. Many thanks to them, as well as to Jenny Frost, President and Publisher of The Crown Publishing Group, and Lauren Shakely, Senior Vice President and Publisher of Potter Craft.

CONTENTS

OPPOSITE **Lacquered wooden cubbyholes provide storage space for many supplies in Martha's craft room at her home in Bedford, New York. All of the desks are topped with a pressed-linseed material that absorbs nicks and scratches.**

INTRODUCTION

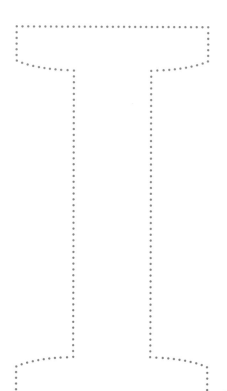n 1988 I had what I thought was a brilliant idea to create a series of beautiful how-to books on a wide assortment of practical, useful, and inspiring topics for the homemaker. I envisioned tomes on flower arranging, on collecting, on every holiday, on gardening, on sewing, on embroidery, and on a vast number of crafts, beautiful crafts.

Understanding that almost each and every one of us is interested in some or all of these subjects, I thought that most publishers would jump at the chance to work with me on this series. Well, like many good ideas, even though the basic concept was sound, the project was rejected. I was told that my concept was too expansive, too all-encompassing, too ambitious for one author to undertake.

After returning to the drawing board, I revised my plan and created not books, but a beautiful how-to magazine, the ubiquitous *Martha Stewart Living*.

It has consistently provided some of the best content on myriad how-to subjects for almost eighteen years, and each story and project has been enjoyed and attempted by many thousands of readers.

Crafts has been an extremely popular area, and our crafts editors have developed an amazing library of projects that clearly display our talent for adopting and adjusting historical and established techniques. Quilling, marbleizing paper, candlemaking, block printing, botanical pressing, silkscreening, and soap making—each is an ancient craft that has been practiced by professionals and amateurs alike. Today, with our ideas and our creativity, and with modern tools and materials, we have brought these crafts into the twenty-first century. Now they have a more contemporary feel, a more modern perspective, and a more pleasing aesthetic, making them appropriate for inclusion in this wonderful encyclopedia.

Whether you wish to craft from paper and glue, or shells, or wax, or paint and canvas, or any other materials, you will find hundreds of wonderful, instructive, and endearing ideas in this book. Many of the projects are directed at adults, but quite a few can be enjoyed by children, too.

At Martha Stewart Living Omnimedia, crafting is inherent in our DNA, as you will certainly realize when turning the pages of this book. We hope that you will love using all of these ideas as much as we loved developing them.

Martha Stewart

how to use this book

This book is divided into 32 chapters of individual crafts techniques. Within each chapter, you will find an overview of the particular technique, including brief descriptions of the basic supplies you will need. Generally, step-by-step instructions follow, then several pages of projects. The projects cover a wide range of skill levels: potato stamp T-shirts can be easily mastered by children, whereas calligraphed labels and note cards admittedly require a bit of practice.

For those new to home crafting, however, keep in mind that practice is often the most important first step. Whether you are dot-painting patterns or monograms onto china and porcelain, rubber stamping a set of stationery, or carefully folding origami paper to make a delicate crane, you may not achieve the intended result on the first try. Practice a bit and soon you will get the hang of it. With each project you complete, you will gain confidence and an eagerness to tackle something new.

Most individual projects will contain a short list of supplies that are in addition to the basic supplies at the front of the chapter. Toward the end of the book, you will find a section called XYZ, with illustrated glossaries and descriptions of our favorite tools and materials, templates to help you complete many of the projects, and lists of trusted vendors and other sources to help you find everything you need. Happy crafting!

Fabric-covered boxes contain a variety of scrapbook papers. Martha stores the boxes in a row on a bookshelf.

ALBUMS, SCRAPBOOKS, AND MEMORY BOXES

If a picture is worth a thousand words, an album filled with photographs and mementos is worth many more. It offers tangible links to the past: The viewer has the chance to unfold a crinkled letter, trace the surface of a punched train ticket, or read a faded newspaper clipping. The scope can be small or large, focused or loose, a chronological narrative or a visual montage. An album or scrapbook is a place to gather anything you don't want to lose, from musings on a particular experience to family recipes to souvenir postcards.

Family history is always an engaging subject for an album. But more current topics, such as a vacation, a wedding, or a baby's first months, are rich in material and possibilities; a scrapbook, after all, provides a way to bring labels, sketches, cards—all the little items that evoke moments past—out of the shoebox and onto display. Try to capture events and emotions while you're experiencing them or soon afterward, rather than waiting until the memories have faded. You can embellish the pages with homemade and store-bought flourishes. Even so, the best part of the scrapbook will still be the photographs and trinkets you've gathered, and the story they combine to tell.

ABOUT THE MATERIALS

ALBUMS AND PAGES Look for acid-free, archival materials. A scrapbook's shape, size, and style are integral to its message: A luxurious 12-by-12-inch (30.5cm x 30.5cm) cloth- or leather-covered album suits a collection of wedding photos, while a small journal might seem right for commemorating a new baby. You can choose a decorative cover or one meant to be embellished. Post-bound and binder-style albums let you add and remove pages so you can expand or edit as you go; they also offer the flexibility needed for bulky pages, displaying three-dimensional objects. Pages can have pockets or be designed for writing and affixing decorations. Page protectors are worth using. Some

pages let you punch your own holes; for those that are prepunched, make sure the holes in the album and pages match up precisely.

PHOTOGRAPHS AND CLIPPINGS You may want to display copies of truly valuable or irreplaceable items in the scrapbook, and tuck the originals away someplace safe. Old photographs can be scanned and printed. Newspaper clippings and documents can also be scanned and printed, or simply photocopied onto acid-free paper.

PAPERS Use decorative papers for backgrounds, borders, trimmings, and more. Look for patterns, colors, and textures that suit the theme of your scrapbook.

CUTTING TOOLS AND PUNCHES Good, sharp scissors and a craft knife are necessary for making clean cuts. Use decorative paper edgers and craft punches to make custom decorations for pages.

GLUES AND TAPES Archival glue sticks, photo adhesive tape (which is double-sided), lay-flat paste, and white craft glue should suffice for most memory-keeping jobs.

EMBELLISHMENTS Scrapbooks often include much more than photographs and mementos—you can use ornaments and trimmings to decorate pages and communicate your theme. See page 16 for more details.

BASIC SUPPLIES

albums and pages

photos and mementos

papers

cutting tools and punches

glues and tapes

embellishments (page 16)

OPPOSITE **Sorting through memorabilia is one of the most enjoyable steps in making a scrapbook.**

EMBELLISHMENTS GLOSSARY

Here's a sampling of the products available (as shown opposite) to customize your creations.

1. RUB-ON LETTER AND NUMBER TRANSFERS These come in a range of fonts and sizes. Easy to apply (rub them with a craft stick or stylus, and the characters will transfer to the paper underneath), the letters and numbers can be used to affix names, dates, and more onto pages.

2. STORE-BOUGHT SCRAPS Scraps come in all forms. Maps and printed papers can be used as backgrounds or to create pockets. Old-looking scraps (such as the seed label shown), postcards, and other ephemera are available from scrapbook stores, flea markets, and online auction sites.

3. TAGS Transform these stationery-store supplies into tiny frames for photographs (color-photocopy the pictures, then cut to size, and glue to surface). You can also use the tags as write-on labels. Fasten them to pages with brads or eyelets.

4. RUB-ON BORDERS These decorative imitations of sewing-machine stitching and calligraphic flourishes can keep pages looking lively. Apply them around photos and scraps, following package instructions.

5. PHOTO ADHESIVE TAPE AND PHOTO CORNERS Acid-free, double-sided photo tape is safe to use on photos. Photo corners provide another way to mount pictures without damaging them, and they give a scrapbook a vintage look.

6. BASIC TOOLS Keep a pencil on hand to make marks, a white (or other light-colored) gel pen to label dark pages, a bone folder to neatly score and fold pages or inserts, and a ruler to take measurements and neatly position scraps.

7. LABELS AND AIRMAIL ENVELOPES Frames for small photos can be created by cutting out the decorative borders of labels. Airmail envelopes can be used to create evocative mini albums for travel souvenirs (page 22).

8. RUBBER STAMPS AND INK PADS Press the stamps into colorful or metallic inks and use them to add words, numerals, or artistic details to album pages.

9. VINTAGE-STYLE PAPERS Faded papers are available at scrapbook stores; these can be used as backgrounds for smaller scraps and to make pockets. You can also make your own antique-looking paper by dipping it in tea or coffee for 10 seconds (longer for darker shades). Look for old, falling-apart books and magazines at tag sales and used bookstores.

10. EYELETS, SETTER, AND HAMMER These metal rings can be used to secure tags, pockets, and other sturdy scraps to pages permanently (follow package instructions to set them), or to make reinforced holes for threading twine or ribbon.

11. BRADS AND JUMP RINGS These familiar fasteners come in traditional brass, and in bright colors and even whimsical shapes. They can be used in the same way as eyelets but are removable. Jump rings are little metal loops that can be used to suspend items from eyelets.

caring for photographs and vintage albums

Photographs are fragile things. In the wrong environment, they deteriorate, becoming brittle, yellowed, and faded. Once the damage is done, you can't undo it. To prevent such damage, keep the original versions of photos in the very best condition, and make copies for scrapbooks and display.

Store photographs in a dark, dry, cool spot where conditions are fairly stable (avoid attics and basements). Handle photos gently, by their edges; dirt and oils from fingers can damage photos. When handling photos with significant value (either sentimental or monetary), wear white cotton gloves; this might sound extreme, but it's better to be safe than sorry.

Look for archival-quality products, including inks and adhesives, that are photo-safe and acid-free. For paper items, seek out lignin-free products; lignin is a chemical compound derived from wood that is used to strengthen paper. It gradually breaks down and releases acids that can cause photos to deteriorate. Pure polyethylene, polypropylene, or polyester plastics (such as Mylar®) are safer choices for albums. Do not write on photos, even on the backs.

Many of the items in old albums are now yellowed and brittle, and, unfortunately, there's no good way to remove the photos from the pages without doing more damage. Newsprint is even more delicate and likely to be destroyed if you try to remove it from an album page. A professional can do the job for you with much better results. (Visit the website of the American Institute for Conservation of Historic & Artistic Works, aic.stanford.edu, to search for photo restorers.) However, it's a time-consuming, and therefore expensive, process, and you may lose more than you gain. Lots of old albums have inscriptions under the photos, and they are as much a part of a family's history as the photos. And unless you have good plans for them once they're out of the album, they're more likely to get lost. Instead, leave them in the album, and handle it carefully. If the pages are falling out, dismantle the album and slip each page into an archival-quality clear sleeve. As for photos, keep albums and album pages in stable conditions.

FAMILY MEMORY ALBUMS

Most households have boxes of photos and memorabilia tucked away in closets and attics. Gather all these gems and organize them so they are ready to enjoy in an album like one of these.

PROJECT: brag books

Keep a few family photos handy, to show off or to admire on your own, in an easy album. It's a cinch to make, so you can create several for yourself and to give as gifts.

PROJECT SUPPLIES Basic Supplies (page 15), plastic binder sheets, wool felt or other heavy fabric (including oilcloth or leather), fabric glue (optional), sewing machine, eyelet, elastic cord

HOW-TO For a small album, use double-sided plastic binder sheets made to hold sports cards. To create a 12-photo book, trim 3 sets of side-by-side pockets from 1 double-sided pocket or binder sheet; each resulting sheet will hold 4 photos, 2 on each side. To make the cover, cut a rectangle from fabric, making it 1/8 inch (3mm) larger on all sides than photo sleeves. (Reinforce oilcloth or leather by cutting 2 rectangles and gluing the wrong sides together. Let them dry before proceeding.) Center and stack the sleeves inside the cover. Sew along the middle seam that divides the 2 sides of the photo pockets, attaching the sleeves to the cover. Attach an eyelet to the front cover, following package instructions. Slip the ends of a length of elastic cord, about the same length as the book's perimeter, through the eyelet, knotting the loop on the inside of the cover to make a band closure. Slip snapshots in sleeves. For a larger book, use sheets made to hold 4-by-6-inch (10cm x 5cm) photos, and repeat the steps above.

Wool felt is more durable and luxurious than synthetic versions. It can be harder to find and more expensive, but it's worth both the search and the cost for keepsake projects.

PROJECT: school days pocket scrapbook

A scrapbook can help you organize—and proudly display—the steady stream of photographs, artwork, awards, and other keepsakes that accrue during a young person's school years. Ideally, this would be made year by year; when a child starts school, buy a scrapbook with enough pages (removable ones are best) to chronicle his or her progression through the grades.

PROJECT SUPPLIES Basic Supplies (page 15), notebook and graph papers, ruler, bone folder, sewing machine (optional), rubber stamps, stamp pad

HOW-TO Cut notebook paper or graph paper to fit your scrapbook pages; affix it with an archival glue stick. To make the pockets, tape together 2 pieces of notebook paper (this one is 7 ½ by 8 ½ inches [19cm x 21.5cm]), short end to short end. Trim width, if necessary, to fit the scrapbook pages. With the bone folder, fold the paper up from the bottom as shown, making pockets in desired depths (above). Stitch the sides to the scrapbook pages with a sewing machine to secure, or glue with an archival glue stick. Mark the years with rubber stamps. Add photos and scraps, tucking them into pockets or gluing them to the outside. Glue on tabs of more notebook paper. Cut out adhesive labels to frame portraits. Add texture with embellishments, such as a school flag made from card stock and a composition book (made from a reduced color photocopy of a real one). On the last page of this album, the graduate is awarded a mini diploma—the crafts store variety.

scrapbooks as workbooks

Not all scrapbooks conjure up the past. Many function in the present, as resource guides or workbooks. You might, for example, document a renovation, with "before" pictures, fabric swatches, sketches of plans, names of tradespeople, and sources of hardware and other fixtures. You can then refer to the book when you're trying to recall the color of the kitchen trim, or when a friend is looking for a tile manufacturer.

And if you're only at the dreaming stage, use the scrapbook as a place to gather ideas: photos, paint chips, magazine clippings. When the time comes to renovate, you won't be starting from scratch. Create a similar working binder for parties you'd like to throw, gardens you want to plant, vacations you plan to take, recipes you intend to try, and even books you keep meaning to read.

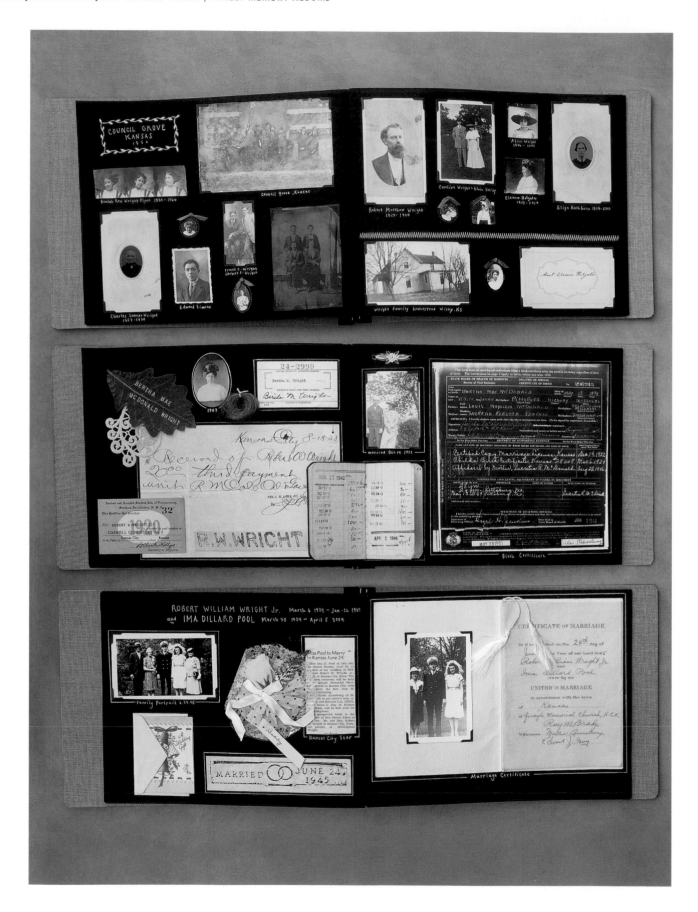

PROJECT: generations album

Part scrapbook, part genealogical record, a family album can commemorate several generations. If you can't find the perfect album, create it. Here a plain new album is given the look of an heirloom. It is covered with book cloth (cloth that has been treated or bonded to paper so it won't unravel), and a vintage-inspired label. The black pages are inscribed with a white gel pen, echoing the tones of old albums. Rub-on borders, some of which resemble sewing-machine stitching, are used to set off text and create dividers between snapshots. Plastic charm frames are topped with ribbons. Along with a lock of hair, an old ledger, and other tokens, they make the book a trove of familial treasures.

PROJECT SUPPLIES Basic Supplies (page 15), pencil, plain paper, book cloth, double-sided adhesive sheets (positional mounting adhesive), "Album" template (page 369), photocopier, craft knife, antique-look paper, archival glue stick, black card stock, hole punch, photo corners, charm frames, white gel pen, rub-on borders

HOW-TO To decorate the cover, trace the album's covers to make paper templates in the shape of the front and back covers, both inside and outside. Trace around templates onto the book cloth and double-sided adhesive sheets (positional mounting adhesive); cut out, so you have 4 pieces each of the cloth and the adhesive sheets. Use the adhesive sheets to attach the cloth to the cover, front and back, inside and outside. Photocopy the "Album" template; cut it out with a craft knife. Trace it onto paper with an antiqued look; cut out. Glue it to the album with an archival glue stick; let it dry. To make the pages, remove the original pages. Using originals as a guide, cut the black card stock to size. Punch holes through the new pages; insert them into the album. (Reserve the originals for another use.) Use photo corners, charm frames, and archival glue stick to mount photos and other items. Label pages with a white gel pen; decorate with rub-on borders.

PROJECT: recipe tin

Keep treasured dishes in the family. Begin by collecting the recipes of a single beloved cook or favorites from a group of relatives.

PROJECT SUPPLIES recipes, lidded tins, baker's twine, patterned paper or vintage kitchen linens (optional), photo, label

HOW-TO Photocopy or scan and print the original recipes onto heavy paper, enlarging or reducing as desired. Cut to size, and place in tins. Wrap tins with a wide band of pretty paper (try copying or scanning vintage kitchen linens); add a photo and label, if desired. Give the boxes as holiday gifts or hand them out to family members at a reunion.

TRAVEL SCRAPBOOKS

When you're on vacation, don't just take a lot of pictures. Save evocative scraps, such as business cards, tickets, maps, even food packaging. Then you can relive your trip through photos and mementos organized in a creative way.

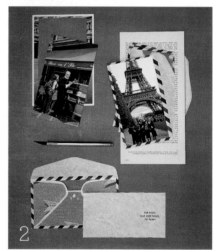

PROJECT: guidebook albums

A guidebook's pages make natural backdrops for photographs of the locales you've visited. For these two albums, out-of-date travel books from destination cities (found at used bookstores) were taken apart, then reassembled into accordion books using the original covers, a few of the pages, and maps. Postage stamps are cut in half and glued to photo corners to create decorative holders for snapshots. You can also insert a miniature album of favorite sights, using your own snapshots and airmail envelopes. A pocket added to the inside back page adds another interactive element.

PROJECT SUPPLIES Basic Supplies (page 15), hardcover travel book, craft knife, ruler, photo corners, photo adhesive tape, airmail envelopes, card stock, postage stamps, rubber stamps

HOW-TO 1. Using a craft knife and ruler, cut off the covers of the book, keeping 1/8 inch (3mm) of the spine intact; set the covers aside, and discard the spine. Cut out the pages (this one has 12) to use as backgrounds (you can also use scraps such as maps). Attach photos and mementos to the pages, using photo adhesive tape, an archival glue stick, or photo corners. Lay out 6 pages, right sides down. Join the pages with photo adhesive tape. Back them with the remaining 6 pages (the wrong sides of the first 6 and the second 6

together), using photo adhesive paper. Use photo adhesive tape to attach the left side of the first page to the right side of the front cover. Attach decorative paper to the inside of the cover, using photo adhesive paper to create an endpaper and to hide the tape. Repeat for the back cover.
2. To make the airmail envelope mini album: Slip a piece of heavy card stock into an airmail envelope. Using a craft knife, cut out the face of the envelope, leaving the backing and border intact; repeat with 4 more envelopes. Cut photos to size; insert them into the envelopes. Stack the envelopes; glue all the flaps together using an archival glue stick. Cut 1 envelope-length slit along 1 edge of each scrapbook page. Slip the flaps through; fold over, and tape to the opposite side to secure.

PROJECT: souvenir binder

The receipts, ticket stubs, maps, and postcards you gather on a trip make a practical and pretty collective; here's a sensible way to retain them. It doesn't involve gluing them into place, so you can still access all the bits and pieces, should you want to pull out business cards, for example, on a return trip to the destination.

PROJECT SUPPLIES Basic Supplies (page 15), 3-ring binder with a clear plastic cover, plastic sleeves with compartments for cards, paper clips, maps

HOW-TO Fill a 3-ring binder with plastic sleeves designed to hold business and baseball cards. Slide souvenirs into the compartments, or if they don't fit, use a paper clip to attach them to a pocket. To decorate the binder's cover, measure the front, back, and spine. Trim maps (or photocopies of them) to those sizes, and slide them into the binder's clear cover.

PROJECT: postcards scrapbook

Design a scrapbook just for postcards, complete with windows revealing the front and back of each card. These are framed, labeled, and dated.

PROJECT SUPPLIES Basic Supplies (page 15), colored and white paper, double-sided tape, border template (page 370), pencil, clear photo corners, label template (page 369)

HOW-TO Remove pages from a post- or ring-bound scrapbook. Cover pages with colored paper (acid-free blue paper was used here), securing with double-sided tape. Photocopy one border template per postcard. Cut out the center of each with a craft knife, keeping the border intact. Position one on the scrapbook page; trace the window inside, and cut out. Glue a border around the window; flip the page over. Attach clear adhesive photo corners around the window; insert a postcard. Repeat with each postcard. Photocopy the label template; trim around the border of the labels. Fill in dates and locations, or other information, as desired. Add labels to pages using an archival glue stick.

BABY ALBUMS

While they're happening, the milestones of parenting—from the pregnancy to the trip home from the hospital to the first birthday party—seem indelible. Parents learn, however, how quickly these moments fade. But a single precious image or keepsake can recall a flood of memories. Be judicious about what to save; keep one special outfit, for example, not all of them. The items will be all the more meaningful (not to mention easier to organize and enjoy).

PROJECT: **pocket-page scrapbook**

Preserve a favorite outfit—on its own "hanger"—and other three-dimensional items in a large album that you customize. Easily misplaced items, such as newborn caps, hospital ID bracelets, cards of congratulations, and birth announcements, can be tucked neatly into pockets you add to the pages.

PROJECT SUPPLIES Basic Supplies (page 15), baby-size clothes hanger, acid-free art paper, needle and thread, cutting mat, ruler, acid-free glassine sheets and envelopes (these are business size), archival tape, double-sided archival tape

HOW-TO Trace a small clothes hanger onto acid-free art paper. (Or trace a larger one, reduce its size on a photocopier, and then trace the shape onto the paper.) Cut it out with a craft knife, and attach it onto the page with archival glue stick. Cut out a paper monogram and glue it to the hanger. Use a needle and thread to tack clothing to the page at strategic spots. **1.** For the pockets, place the cutting mat underneath one page. Using the ruler, draw horizontal lines where pockets will go (the bottom line must be far enough from the page edge to accommodate one of the envelopes). Cut slots, leaving about ½ inch (13mm) of paper uncut at each end. Turn the page over. Cut the flaps off the envelopes (one side will be slightly lower; it will face the page). **2.** Starting at the bottom, place the open edge of one envelope just above a slot. Tape the top of the envelope in place. Turn the page back over and check the pocket's position; adjust if necessary. Use double-sided tape to affix the low side of the envelope to the back of the page below the slot. Repeat for the remaining slots. To protect items that will go into the pockets, lay a sheet of acid-free glassine over the page, fold the top over the edge, and tape it to the back.

PROJECT: covered binder memory book

A vinyl loose-leaf binder can be remade into a sumptuous baby book with felt, rickrack, paper, and your imagination. Keep a three-hole punch on hand for adding papers, such as crayon rubbings of spoons and combs on tissue paper (to make them, just lay tissue over the item and rub gently with the side of a crayon; see Botanical Pressing, page 46, for more details). Use zipper sleeves to hold small treasures. Make dividers from pretty papers to further personalize the book.

PROJECT SUPPLIES Basic Supplies (page 15), vinyl loose-leaf binder, wool felt, ruler, rickrack, pins, pinking or scalloping shears, needle and thread, heavyweight decorative paper, 3-hole punch or regular hole punch

HOW-TO Lay the open book on the felt and measure, wrapping felt around both covers so that it abuts metal binder. Allow ³/₈ inch (9mm) extra on top and bottom for seam allowance. Cut the felt to size. Cut 2 pieces of rickrack, each as long as the open binder. Position the rickrack, centered, on the 2 long edges of the felt as shown above (so the rickrack pieces are peeking over the edge of the felt), and pin or glue it in place and stitch to inside face. To add an interior pocket, use scalloping or pinking shears to cut a piece of felt about ³/₄ inch (1.8cm) narrower and half as high as the cover. Reposition felt across binder, pin pocket in place, and slip binder out. Stitch pocket inside cover. To assemble cover, wrap around binder and pin into place. Slip out binder and sew a continuous seam ¹/₈ inch (3mm) from edge.

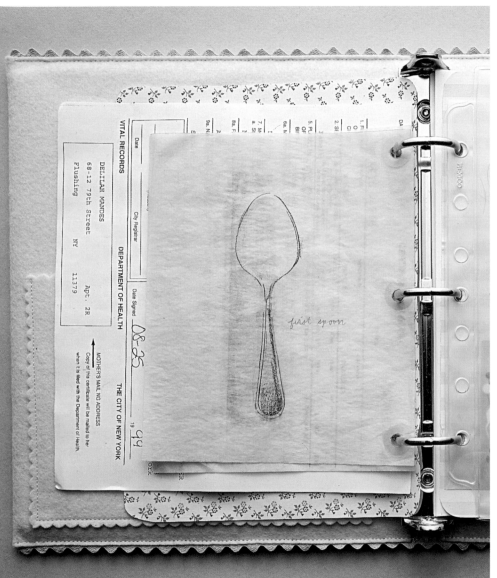

WEDDING ALBUMS

A wedding isn't just a day. It's an accumulation of separate events and small decisions that have to be made: the decorations for an engagement party, the menu for the rehearsal dinner, the favors for the reception. Along the way, the bride and groom acquire mementos of it all, such as guest lists, response cards, swatches of wedding dress fabric, poems, napkins scrawled with notes for a toast, pressed flowers, ceremony programs, and wine labels. Choose the things that mean the most, and then figure out how to best present them—starting with the following ideas.

PROJECT: photo flip book

This mini scrapbook captures a single memorable moment, such as the cake cutting or first dance steps, and sets it in motion. It makes a fun keepsake and a great little gift for parents and bridal party attendants.

PROJECT SUPPLIES Basic Supplies (page 15), photos, photocopier, waxed paper, pencil, ruler, card stock, bone folder, mini hole punch, thin ribbon, large needle

HOW-TO Have a guest or the wedding photographer shoot a rapid succession of images from a stationary position; photocopy the resulting pictures. Place waxed paper over the first photocopy in the photo sequence; draw a frame around the central part of the action, and outline a component that is present and stationary in each image (such as the cake's top tier, here). Cut out a waxed-paper frame; use this as a guide to crop the remaining images, positioning the outline over the image each time. Trim all photos to size. For the cover, cut card stock the same height as the image and wide enough for a front, back, and a spine that's as wide as the stack of pictures. To fold the cover, line up the edge of the images on the cover's left side, and score with the bone folder; repeat on the right side. With a mini hole punch, punch 3 evenly spaced holes along the left side of the first page. Use the punched page to mark remaining pages and covers; punch. Assemble the book; thread thin ribbon through each set of holes, using as large a needle as necessary. Knot ribbon ends, then make a bow. If the right edges of the pages are not aligned, trim them with a craft knife.

PROJECT: pocketed keepsake book

This handmade book provides a way to store keepsakes that need a little breathing room, along with letters and notes that you'll want to pull out and read again. The pockets are strips of cotton organdy that are divided with vertical seams where needed. No hemming is required. This book has ten pages, but you can add a few more as long as they will all fit under the foot of your sewing machine.

PROJECT SUPPLIES Basic Supplies (page 15), 65-pound card stock, rotary cutter, cotton organdy, paper clips, sewing machine, organdy bindings, iron, 300-pound card stock

HOW-TO Note that the thread and paper shown here are different colors for visibility, but you will likely want them to match. For pages, cut 10 sheets of 65-pound card stock. For pockets, use a rotary cutter to cut 20 pressed cotton-organdy panels twice as wide as the pages and as high as you want the pockets to be. **1.** Wrap 2 panels around the left side of the page as shown (align the bottom panel with the edge of the page, and position the top panel 1 inch [2.5cm] from top); use a paper clip to secure the layers. **2.** Top-stitch along the bottom of the panels, sewing through all 3 layers. To join the left- and right-hand pages, cut five 1-inch (2.5cm) wide organdy bindings twice the height of the pages; wrap them over the inside edges of the pages, trapping the raw edges of the pockets under the binding; clip. Sew the binding to both pages from top to bottom. For divided pockets, sew vertical seams from the top edge to the bottom seam of the strips. For covers, cut 300-pound card stock 1 inch (2.5cm) wider and ½ inch (13mm) taller than pages. Cut organdy the same height as the covers and twice the width of open book plus 3 inches (7.5cm); center covers 1 inch (2.5cm) apart on organdy; fold extra fabric over the covers (ends will overlap at center), and press. Stitch around all sides of the covers. Stack the joined pages on the open cover; sew the spine down the center.

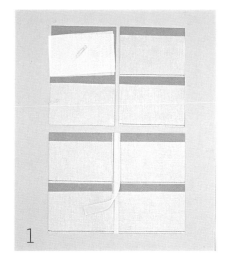

1

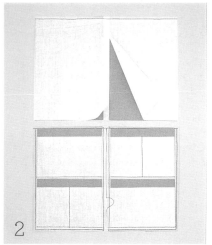

2

MEMORY BOXES

BASIC SUPPLIES

wooden or cardboard box
or deep picture frame

craft knife

adhesive, such as white
craft glue or spray
adhesive

items for display

paint, paper, and other
embellishments (see
individual projects)

Some souvenirs just won't fit in a scrapbook, but that doesn't mean they need to be hidden away. Instead, exhibit them as art in a shadow box, which is essentially a deep picture frame, or a specimen box, similar to those that scientists use to display their findings. First decide on a theme, such as a recent vacation, and gather your items. Then create a three-dimensional display that you can enjoy every day.

PROJECT: shadow box

This technique involves giving a frame a new backing that is not flush against the glass. Choose a frame deep enough to accommodate your collection, such as these seashells.

PROJECT SUPPLIES Basic Supplies (above), balsa wood, ruler, double-sided tape, pencil, paper label (optional), brown-paper tape

HOW-TO Remove cardboard or pressboard backing of frame. Discard clips, if any. With craft knife, cut 4 pieces of balsa wood to fit inside the frame (resting on its inside ridge, 1/8 inch [3mm] shallower than its sides) to create a place for the backing to rest; 2 pieces of balsa wood should be the length of the frame's interior and 2 slightly shorter than the width. Using double-sided tape, attach the 4 pieces inside the frame, starting with the longer pieces (see below). Cut a piece of decorative paper the size of the frame's backing. Working in a well-ventilated area, affix the paper to the backing with spray adhesive. Arrange your display items on this surface; use small pencil dots to indicate their placement. Secure shells to the paper with glue or wax. Let them dry. If you like, use glue to affix a label that identifies the items and indicates where and when they were collected. Insert the backing into the frame, resting on the balsa wood. Affix the backing to the frame with brown-paper tape.

A shadow box filled with seashells shows off their nuances of color and shape. Bivalve sunray and coquina shells (above left) suggest butterflies; rows of scallops (above right) look modern and iconic.

These cases can evoke natural settings (clockwise from top left): a sampling of twigs and stones; a cactus, desert sand, and a tiny landscape image; seaworn clamshells and pressed leaves; and sea glass, driftwood, a vintage postcard, and a map re-creating a journey to Maine.

PROJECT: specimen boxes

Unlike shadow boxes, these are made to be set flat on a surface and viewed from above. You can purchase premade specimen boxes at some crafts stores and nature stores, or you can make your own from a standard lidded box, as described below. Have a glazier cut glass or Plexiglas® for the top.

PROJECT SUPPLIES Basic Supplies (opposite), sturdy gift box with lid, glass or Plexiglas cut to fit inside box lid, fine sandpaper, scissors, map or decorative paper, bone folder, contact cement, colored paper, white craft glue or museum wax, jewelry boxes (optional), paper label (optional)

HOW-TO 1. Remove the box lid. To create a frame for a glass insert, draw a rectangle in the center of the lid (this one has a 1 ½-inch [3.8cm] border). Carefully cut out the rectangle with a craft knife; smooth any rough edges with sandpaper. **2.** To cover the box lid, cut a map or a piece of decorative paper to the size of its width and length plus its depth and an additional ½ inch (13mm) on all sides. Working in a well-ventilated area, coat the top and sides of the lid with spray adhesive. Place paper wrong side up, and center the lid upside down on top; then cut out a rectangular window with the craft knife. At each of the 4 outer corners of the paper, mark and cut out a square that's even with the lid's edge on 1 side and that will leave a flap extending past the lid's edge on the other side, as shown. **3.** Fold the long sides up and over box edge, smoothing with a bone folder; press around the corners. Fold the short sides up and over; smooth with bone folder. Use contact cement to secure the glass pane in the box lid; weigh down with a book. Let it dry according to instructions. Cut colored paper to fit the box bottom; secure it with spray adhesive. Affix items in position with glue or wax. You can also line and mount small jewelry boxes and label them.

BEADING

Stringing beads onto wires and fashioning them into sparkling shapes is a hobby that can be enjoyed over a lifetime. Children often learn the basics in art class or at camp, and adults can appreciate the tactile pleasure of the craft, not to mention the surprisingly sophisticated results. Tiny, glistening beads, after all, can bloom into lush, long-lasting flowers that seem as if they were cultivated in a magical garden. The tradition of making beaded flowers is believed to date back to medieval Europe, where artisans created the blooms for altars, banquet tables, and gravesites. During the Victorian era, ladies whiled away hours beading lampshades and other decorative items. In the 1950s and '60s, a resurgence of interest in home crafts turned beading flowers and baskets into a popular pastime, and do-it-yourselfers took up the craft, following instructions in pattern books and kits. These decades-old creations are now sought-after collectibles, and their bright beauty can add a cheerful touch to almost any room.

The projects on the following pages begin with making those enchanted flowers. Despite their diversity, they are all made using a single technique. Several of the ideas here are for wedding accents (everlasting blooms are a romantic notion for a bride), but they could be translated easily into gifts, everyday accessories, and decorations for the home. The same technique is used to make the winsome beaded bugs that follow; they would be perfect easy projects for children interested in learning how to bead. The hardest part of beading may be deciding what to start with—or when to stop.

ABOUT THE MATERIALS

BEADS You'll find a dazzling array of beads at crafts stores and specialty bead stores. But most of the projects here use tiny, glass round seed beads (2.5-3mm is a good size range; you can add slightly larger ones for accents). Two-cut or three-cut faceted glass beads are particularly shimmery,

as are color-lined beads. Plastic beads are also available. You can also use bugle beads, which are straight-cut tubes. If you buy the beads in prestrung strands called hanks, it's easy to thread them from the strings right onto your wire.

WIRE Wire comes in different thicknesses (known as the gauge—the higher the number, the thinner the wire), and different metals, as well as colorful coated versions. Whatever you prefer, choose wire that's thin enough to pass through the bead's hole twice. For the flowers, 30-gauge

galvanized wire is used. For the bugs, it is 26-gauge copper wire, which comes coated in different colors.

FLORAL TAPE To assemble the flowers, use floral tape. Wrap it around the wire "stem" of each petal and the stamens, gathering these components into blossoms.

BASIC SUPPLIES

seed beads and bugle beads

wire

wire cutters

floral tape

OPPOSITE **Once you get the hang of this craft, you'll probably start to acquire a collection of beads for future projects. Keep your beads—whether loose or prestrung in strands or hanks—separated and organized by color for easy access.**

HOW TO MAKE BEADED FLOWERS

Just one technique is used to create these varied flowers. The number of beads per petal, the number of petals, and the way you shape those petals—rolling, bending, or cupping—will differ for each bloom.

BEADED FLOWERS SUPPLIES Basic Supplies (page 31)

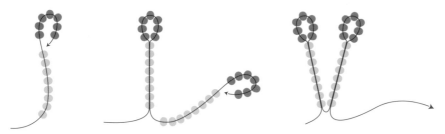

MAKING STAMENS All the stamens for one flower are threaded onto a 1-yard (91cm) length of 30-gauge galvanized wire. Thread wire through the beads for the base of the first stamen, and slide the beads to about 5 inches (12.5cm) from the other end. Add beads for the loop, then send the wire back through the beads of the base; pull taut. Continue, adding stamens. After the last stamen, twist the wire ends together to secure.

 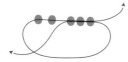    

MAKING PETALS Refer to the formulas on page 35 for the numbers of rows and beads for each flower petal. Cut 1 piece of wire for each petal (about 1 foot [30.5cm] for the smallest petals and 1 yard [91cm] for larger petals; see flowers on page 34 for reference). String beads for the first 2 rows onto the wire, and center them. Send 1 end of the wire around and back through only the beads for the second row; pull taut. Continue adding beads and threading both ends of wire through each row. After the last row, twist the wire ends together.

beading pointers

Work in a bright spot. Cover a tray or table with a towel or felt to prevent beads from rolling. Keep beads separated by color in shallow dishes, jar lids, or other containers.

Beads can be hard to grasp with fingers—before you know it, they're bouncing all over the floor. To avoid this, lift beads by poking the end of your wire into the hole, then use your fingers to slide the bead up the wire. Or buy beads in hanks (already strung), and slide them from their string directly onto your wire.

Wire is stiff enough to pick up beads on its own. But if you use elastic cord (not called for in these projects, but popular for kids' jewelry), you will need a beading needle and a needle threader.

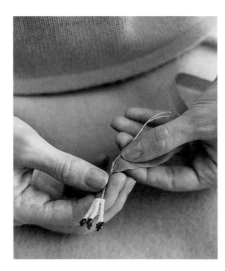

ASSEMBLNG FLOWERS Start by wrapping green floral tape around the stamen wires. Add petals, one at a time, wrapping the stem with tape as you go. Wrap the tape down the combined stems to the desired length, then trim.

Shape the petals with your fingers, rolling or bending the petals as desired. To make a bouquet, wrap the stems of several flowers together with floral tape, and then wrap ribbon around the bundle of stems. Tie to secure.

PROJECT: flower corsage

A large camellia crafted from beads and strung on a velvet ribbon exudes an opulent feel. It can be worn around the neck or the wrist.

PROJECT SUPPLIES Basic Supplies (page 31), 18mm double-face velvet ribbon, pin backing

HOW-TO Make a camellia according to the formula on page 35, and trim the stem. Cut velvet ribbon to desired length, depending on whether you'll be wearing the flower as a necklace or bracelet; cut the ribbon ends on the diagonal. Pin the flower to the ribbon.

PROJECT: blooming slippers

A pair of pale pink anemones makes a sparkling embellishment for a little girl's ballet slippers (and would be particularly fitting for a flower girl).

PROJECT SUPPLIES Basic Supplies (page 31), needle and thread or pin backing (optional), ballet slippers

HOW-TO Make 2 anemones according to the formula on page 35, and trim the stems. Hand-stitch to the ballet slippers, or wire the flower to a pin backing and pin to slippers.

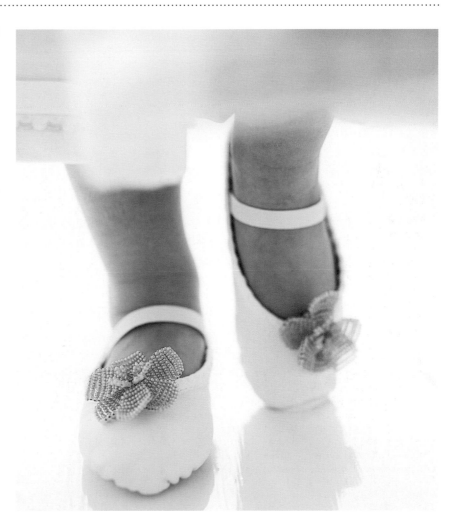

SMALL
CAMELLIA

SWEET
WILLIAM

LARGE
CAMELLIA

LARGE ANEMONE

LARGE AZALEA

SMALL
AZALEA

SMALL
ANEMONE

DOGWOOD
BLOSSOMS

LARGE
DAFFODIL

ROSE

FORGET-
ME-NOT

SMALL
DAFFODIL

FLOWERS GLOSSARY

If you find that you like beading flowers, these are only the beginning. Study pictures and illustrations of flowers you love, and translate them into beaded beauties yourself.

flower formulas

Don't be daunted by all the numbers! Just follow along, taking your time and improvising as you wish.

small camellia

SIX PETALS

ROW 1 21 BEADS; **R2** 20; **R3** 18; **R4** 16; **R5** 15; **R6** 14; **R7** 13; **R8** 12; **R9** 11

THIRTEEN STAMENS

BASE 12 BEADS; **LOOP** 6

large camellia

NINE OUTER PETALS

ROW 1 16 BEADS; **R2** 18; **R3** 20; **R4** 20; **R5** 20; **R6** 19; **R7** 18; **R8** 16; **R9** 14; **R10** 12; **R11** 10; **R12** 8

FIVE MIDDLE PETALS

R1 10; **R2** 12; **R3** 14; **R4** 14; **R5** 14; **R6** 13; **R7** 12; **R8** 11; **R9** 9; **R10**:7

SIX INNER PETALS

R1 8; **R2** 10; **R3** 12; **R4** 12; **R5** 12; **R6** 11; **R7** 10; **R8** 9; **R9** 7

THREE CENTER PETALS

R1 4; **R2** 6; **R3** 8; **R4** 8; **R5** 8; **R6** 6

small azalea

FIVE PETALS

ROW 1 4 BEADS; **R2** 5; **R3** 6; **R4** 5; **R5** 4; **R6** 3; **R7** 2; **R8** 1

THREE STAMENS

BASE 4 BEADS; **LOOP** 5

large azalea

FIVE TO THIRTEEN PETALS

ROW 1 5 BEADS; **R2** 6; **R3** 7; **R4** 8; **R5** 7; **R6** 6; **R7** 5; **R8** 4; **R9** 3; **R10** 2; **R11** 1

FIVE STAMENS

BASE 10 BEADS; **LOOP** 5

sweet william

SIX PETALS

ROW 1 5 BEADS; **R2** 5; **R3** 4; **R4** 3

STAMEN

BASE 2 BEADS; **LOOP** 2

dogwood blossoms

FOUR PETALS

ROW 1 4 BEADS; **R2** 6; **R3** 10; **R4** 12; **R5** 14; **R6** 16; **R7** 16; **R8** 14; **R9** 14; **R10** 11; **R11** 10; **R12** 9; **R13** 6; **R14** 5

SEVEN STAMENS

LOOP 1 LARGE AND 1 SMALL BEAD

rose

ELEVEN OUTER PETALS

ROW 1 21 BEADS; **R2** 21; **R3** 21; **R4** 19; **R5** 18; **R6** 17; **R7** 16; **R8** 15; **R9** 14

FOUR MIDDLE PETALS

R1 20; **R2** 19; **R3** 18; **R4** 17; **R5** 16; **R6** 15; **R7** 14

THREE INNER PETALS

R1 10; **R2** 9; **R3** 8; **R4** 7; **R5** 6; **R6** 5; **R7** 4; **R8** 3

large daffodil

SIX PETALS

ROW 1 1 BEAD; **R2** 3; **R3** 5; **R4** 7; **R5** 9; **R6** 11; **R7** 11; **R8** 10; **R9** 9; **R10** 8; **R11** 7; **R12** 5; **R13** 3

FIFTEEN STAMENS

BASE 8 BEADS; **LOOP** 3

small daffodil

SIX PETALS

ROW 1 1 BEAD; **R2** 3; **R3** 5; **R4** 7; **R5** 9; **R6** 9; **R7** 8; **R8** 7; **R9** 5; **R10** 3

TWELVE STAMENS

BASE 6 BEADS; **LOOP** 3

forget-me-not

FOUR TO SIX PETALS

ROW 1 3 BEADS **R2** 4; **R3** 4; **R4** 2

ONE STAMEN

LOOP 1 LARGE BEAD

small anemone

SIX PETALS

ROW 1 9 BEADS; **R2** 11; **R3** 12; **R4** 12; **R5** 11; **R6** 10; **R7** 9; **R8** 8; **R9** 7

SIX STAMENS

BASE 3 BEADS; **LOOP** 5, PLUS 1 LARGER BEAD FOR CENTER (OPTIONAL)

large anemone

SEVEN OR EIGHT PETALS

ROW 1 10 BEADS; **R2** 11; **R3** 12; **R4** 12; **R5** 11; **R6** 10; **R7** 10; **R8** 9; **R9** 8; **R10** 7; **R11** 6; **R12** 6

SEVEN STAMENS

BASE 2 BEADS; **LOOP** 7, PLUS 1 LARGER BEAD FOR CENTER

PROJECT: **beaded flower bobby pins**

Here's an even simpler way to make a beaded flower. Attach an open-petaled flower shape to a bobby pin for a sweet hair accessory.

PROJECT SUPPLIES Basic Supplies (page 31), chain-nose pliers, bobby pin

HOW-TO Cut a 12-inch (30.5cm) length of 30-gauge wire. Thread 20 seed beads onto the middle of the wire, then bend and twist the wire 1 rotation, using pliers to isolate the petal. Thread 20 more beads, and twist again. Repeat until you have 5 petals. For the center, thread 1 slightly larger seed bead in a contrasting color onto 1 of the 2 remaining ends of wire. Twist petals around the bead, and thread the wire through the petals to secure. Use the remaining wire to attach the flower to the curved end of a bobby pin. Trim the excess wire.

PROJECT: **boutonniere**

A tiny bouquet of seven forget-me-not blooms looks dashing on a lapel (and makes a nice groom's keepsake).

PROJECT SUPPLIES Basic Supplies (page 31); pin (optional)

HOW-TO Make 7 forget-me-nots according to the formula on page 35. Trim their stems, and bundle them together with floral tape. Pin to a jacket from behind the lapel, or tuck the bouquet stem into a buttonhole.

PROJECT: **floral "bows"**

Use a flower or two to add romance to a simple hairstyle. These large dogwood blossoms look chic against a sleek, looped ponytail.

PROJECT SUPPLIES Basic Supplies (page 31); hairpin, comb, or barrette

HOW-TO Make 2 dogwood blossoms according to the formula on page 35, and trim stems. Wire to a hairpin, comb, or barrette.

PROJECT: **beaded letters**

A large sparkling letter is a great way to personalize a present. Use a pretty script, either drawn yourself or copied from the templates on page 371 (enlarge or reduce it to the size you want). Twenty-gauge wire will hold the shape of the letters well; choose seed beads with a hook large enough to string onto the wire. These beads are silver-lined, for extra shimmer.

PROJECT SUPPLIES Basic Supplies (page 31; use 20-gauge and 30-gauge wire, and silver-lined beads), string, round-nose pliers, letter templates

HOW-TO Lay a piece of string along the outline of your letter form to see how much wire you'll need. Cut 20-gauge wire to that length plus about 6 inches (15cm). Make a loop at one end with round-nosed pliers. Transfer beads onto the wire, leaving 3 inches (7.5cm) of wire unbeaded (to allow for sharp turns in the shape), and loop the other wire end so the beads don't slide off. Following your letter template, shape the beaded wire. Cut off excess beads and wire at 1 end, using wire cutters, leaving ½ inch (13mm) of exposed wire, and loop it. For 2-piece letters (like P), wrap pieces together at intersections using 30-gauge wire.

HOW TO MAKE BEADED BUGS

Although their characters are very different, these little insects were made with the same method as the beaded flowers (page 32).

BEADED BUGS SUPPLIES Basic Supplies (page 31), jump rings (optional)

Rather than counting the beads, as for the flowers, use the templates opposite to make the ladybug, dragonfly, butterfly, and bumblebee. Change bead colors to make stripes, dots, and eyes. Start with about 26 inches (66cm) of 26-gauge colored wire for each bug. Follow the instructions below for adding wings. When you're finished beading, slip the extra lengths of wire back through the previous row of beads. Pull tight, then snip off excess wire.

ADDING WINGS Begin beading the body using the "Making Petals" method shown on page 32 and referring to the formulas on page 35 for numbers of beads. Once you've finished beading the body row where the wings should be attached, slip the wing beads onto 1 end of the wire. Loop the wire, then pass the end back through the first wing bead. Tug on the wire until the beads are snug. Make another wing on the opposite side with the other end of the wire. Then continue to bead the rest of the body, adding other pairs as necessary.

ADDING A JUMP RING Little loops, called jump rings, turn a bug into a charm to hang from a zipper pull or necklace.

1. Bend your wire in half. Place the wire's loop behind the ring.

2. Pass the loose ends of the wire first through the ring, then through the loop.

3. Pull the ends down in front of the ring to tighten. If the first row has one bead, follow the template. If it has more, thread them on alternating sides of the ring; proceed by following the template, threading the second row to the right of the ring. To add a ring on the side, pass the wire through before starting a row.

Kids (okay, grown-ups too) will have fun making a bevy of bugs. Create them using the colors found in nature, or wing it, improvising with any favorite shades. Instead of clipping the wire ends flush with the bug, leave them a little long and curl them with pliers to make antennae. Add a jump ring (see how-to, opposite) to turn the bug into a charm. To make the little orange daisy, see the how-to for the beaded bobby pin on page 35.

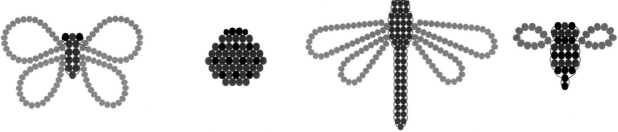

BUTTERFLY   LADYBUG   DRAGONFLY   BUMBLEBEE

thank you

Merci

SOPHIE
&
JASON

Mr. Christopher Smith
1889 Fairview Lane
Wichita, KS
66207

Thanks

Thank you

thank you

thanks

BLOCK PRINTING

Here's one way to make an impression: Carve one-of-a-kind designs to create custom prints. The images for these projects were chiseled from soft, rubbery blocks that are similar in texture to white art erasers—think of the carvings as rubber stamps that you make yourself. Historically, block printing dates to ninth-century China, when blocks of wood were carved and coated with ink to reproduce Buddhist texts. In Europe, six centuries later, block prints were used to make book illustrations, playing cards, and religious images. As the craft evolved, people engraved clay, metal, and, more recently, linoleum. The rubbery blocks that many crafters favor today are flexible and easy to cut into. A finished carving can be used to make an unlimited number of prints, so it's easy to create invitations, place cards, and party menus. Experiment with different inks and paints on different surfaces. A print on a thin paper with watery ink will look very different from a print on heavily textured paper with an opaque ink; prints will also vary depending on the amount of pressure you use. (For a kid-friendly take on this craft, try printing with potatoes, also covered in this chapter.) If you're creating a series, don't worry about making each one identical to the last—slight nuances add charm and character.

ABOUT THE MATERIALS

SOFT-CARVE BLOCKS You'll find these sold under a variety of brand names at art-supply stores. Experiment with different brands to decide which you like best. The blocks can be carved on opposite sides, and cut into sections for smaller prints. For very small prints, you can use a flat white art eraser.

LINOLEUM CUTTER AND BLADES Linoleum cutters were initially used, as the name implies, for carving linoleum; they're ideal for cutting into soft-carve blocks, which have a similar texture. Their long blades are U-shaped (picture a metal straw, divided in half lengthwise), or V-shaped for a finer line. Their shapes allow you to carve long, continuous strips from a block. Cutters with wooden handles are the most comfortable to grasp. Look for one with a removable blade; this will allow you to change blades if the original gets dull, or if you need a wider or narrower blade.

RUBBER BRAYER A rubber brayer works like a paint roller, allowing you to easily—and evenly—spread ink over your carving.

INK There are two types of ink for block printing: oil-based and water-soluble. Both are available in a wide array of colors. Oil-based inks are waterproof and less prone to fading, but dry more slowly. Water-soluble inks are nontoxic and faster-drying; spatters can be wiped away with a damp cloth.

BASIC SUPPLIES

tracing paper

pencil

soft-carve block

tape

spoon

cutter blades

linoleum cutter

block printing ink

paper plate

rubber brayer

scrap paper

OPPOSITE **How best to express the depth of your gratitude? A handmade card is a wonderful way to start.**

HOW TO CARVE AND PRINT

1. Choose a design (see templates, pages 372–373) or pick a photograph, magazine cutout, pattern, or leaf. Photocopy the design, enlarging or reducing it as desired. Lay a sheet of tracing paper over the design. Trace the design with a pencil. (For a mirror-image print, flip the tracing paper over and retrace the image onto the other side.) Shade the areas you'll carve out. Arrange a soft-carve block on a flat surface, and position the tracing paper, design-side down, on top of it. Secure the paper to the block with tape. To transfer the pencil marks to the block, use the back of a spoon to rub the entire surface of the tracing paper against the block. Remove the paper and tape. Secure a linoleum-cutter blade into place on the handle. Hold the cutter like a pencil, with the hollow side of the blade facing up, and cut away from yourself. Use your other hand as a guide, keeping it clear of the blade's path. Begin with shallow cuts; if you dig the cutter down into the block, it could cut all the way through. Work slowly, carving the marked areas.

2. Deposit a small dollop of ink onto a paper plate. Roll the brayer over the ink to spread it. The brayer should be thoroughly covered with a thin, even layer of ink. Using a clean piece of scrap paper, make a light initial roll to blot excess ink, then roll the brayer over the block to coat the uncarved surface.

3. Place a piece of paper facedown over the ink-coated block. Lightly rub the back of the paper with the back of a spoon, then gently pull the paper away from the block. Let the print dry overnight.

PROJECT: greeting cards

A simple line drawing is easy to reproduce; look for a high-contrast image with no shadows. Stamp greeting cards (page 40), envelopes, party invites, and stationery to make a suite.

PROJECT SUPPLIES Basic Supplies (page 41); store-bought note cards, postcards, or envelopes; kraft paper; glue stick

HOW-TO Engrave your design in a soft-carve block (see "How to Carve and Print," left). Print on note cards, post-cards, or envelopes. (You can also make cards from card stock.) To mimic the design shown, print on kraft paper, then cut out the print. Glue it to the front of a note card.

TIP Make an unlimited number of prints from one block; simply reapply ink for each print. After making three consecutive prints, wash the block with warm water and soap, and dry it with a clean, lint-free cloth.

PROJECT: wrapping paper and gift tags

One-of-a-kind paper—with a matching tag—is perfect for any gift-giving occasion. Rice paper, which is thin and accepts the print nicely, works best for wrapping paper.

PROJECT SUPPLIES Basic Supplies (page 41), template (page 372), rice paper, gift tags

HOW-TO Using the template, engrave your design in a soft-carve block (see "How to Carve and Print," opposite) and print on rice paper. You can also experiment with other thin papers, such as kraft paper or newsprint. For gift tags smaller than your carving, print part of the design onto precut or homemade gift tags. Handwrite a greeting on the back.

POTATO PRINTING

BASIC SUPPLIES

baking potato

cookie cutter

paper plate

craft stick

fabric paint

paper towels

Kids don't need fancy tools to print a pattern on a T-shirt—they don't even need to know how to paint. Adding a print to a plain top is simple with ordinary potatoes. Thanks to their firm texture, raw spuds can be easily shaped into sturdy stamps, and their smooth interiors are perfect for coating with paint. Help kids get started, but let them dream up their own designs with stamps in a variety of shapes and sizes.

1. Slice a potato in half lengthwise. Place cookie cutter on cut side of one half. Push cutter through potato, keeping potato flat.

2. Break away and discard excess potato; set aside other potato half to make another stamp.

3. Poke shape out of cutter; blot away any moisture with a paper towel.

4. Spread a thin layer of fabric paint on a paper plate using a craft stick. Dip shape, white side down, into paint a few times, moving it around for an even coat.

5. Wipe off paint on sides of stamp with a paper towel, then stamp the shape onto fabric, pressing down firmly for five seconds.

PROJECT: **tulip t-shirt**

A plain cotton shirt is instantly upgraded with a bright, cheerful motif.

YOU WILL NEED Basic Supplies (opposite), cardboard, cotton T-shirt

HOW-TO Prepare potato stamps (see instructions opposite, and glossary below). Slip a piece of cardboard inside a cotton T-shirt, then follow the instructions to stamp a trio of tulips, then a pair of leaves and a stem for each. Let the paint dry, then follow the package instructions to set it.

shapes glossary

Each part of an item can be made with a separate stamp. Top to bottom: for this flower, the blossom was cut with a tulip-shaped cookie cutter, leaves with an aspic cutter (normally used for shaping jellied garnishes), and a stem with a knife. A large, simple stamp, like a star, is easiest for younger kids to work with. For letters or numbers, place the cutter on potato so character is backward and cut out; turn the stamp over, and dip into paint. A fingerling potato is great for making small polka dots—just cut off the tip.

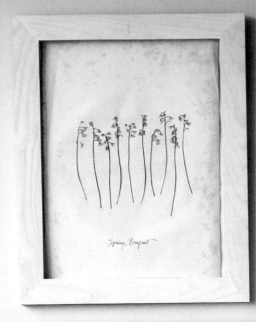

Spring, Bouquet

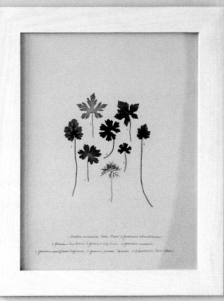

Pressed plants can have a place in any room. A collection in matching wooden frames is just one decorative possibility.

BOTANICAL PRESSING

Nature is in the habit of offering up ready-made artwork. The flowers in your garden, the leaves in the forest, and the ribbons of seaweed that wash ashore each day are just a few examples. Capturing these works for your permanent collection is as easy as gathering and pressing them. The Victorians were fond of doing just that. In botanical collections of that era, plants of all kinds were gathered to aid scientific investigation, a practice botanists still use today to create herbariums—organized collections of preserved plant specimens. Herbariums can last hundreds of years, the specimens providing a more accurate record than even the best camera. Scientists use the dried flowers, leaves, and seaweed to create a monograph (a paper describing all the species of a particular group of plants), or a flora (a record of all the plants growing in a particular region). Yet you needn't be a scientist to get excited about collecting and pressing botanicals. An herbarium can be as simple as a record of all the different varieties of pansies and violets you grew last year, or a sampling of the seaweed you found on vacation. Pressed flowers, leaves, and seaweed also make wonderful additions to cards, pictures, and even window dressings. A properly pressed plant can last a lifetime, tucked into the pages of a diary, or mounted, framed, and hung on the wall. What garden, forest, or vase of flowers can offer that?

ABOUT THE MATERIALS

BOTANICALS Find specimens still rich with color, and moist so they won't break or crack when pressed. Gather fresh specimens in full sunlight, when leaves and flowers are not wet from rain or dew. Never gather species that are protected or endangered; if in doubt, check local regulations. Recently fallen autumn leaves will be at their height of color, but will not have had time to dry out. Snip flowers at their base, or leave a bit of stem attached. Keep fresh seaweed in salt water until you're ready to press.

PLANT PRESS Plant presses come in many sizes, some small enough to carry in your backpack on a hike, and others big enough to dry large pieces of seaweed or flowers with their stems intact. Small plant presses are generally made with two thin pieces of plywood as an exterior frame. Larger presses are constructed from strips of wood that are connected in a crosshatch formation, which allows moisture to evaporate out of the press. Sheets of corrugated cardboard, blotting paper, and plain newsprint are layered within the frame. The newsprint, which you may have to buy separately, will keep the plants from staining the more expensive blotting paper. Use Velcro® straps or a stack of heavy books (such as phone books) to keep the press tightly closed. If one end of the press is higher than the other after filling it with botanicals, turn a few of the layers around in a group to even them out. This will ensure even pressure on the specimens as they dry. Make sure that any sharp edges don't pierce the blotters. Do not allow the press to get wet or rained on, and do not place the press in an oven—even the lowest temperature is too hot.

GLUE White craft glue is often the best choice for attaching dried leaves, flowers, and seaweed to paper. For more delicate dried flowers—especially those with papery or brittle textures—use spray adhesive.

TWEEZERS Keep a set of tweezers on hand to lift delicate botanicals from the press, or to help glue them to paper or other surfaces.

PRESSED FLOWERS AND LEAVES

BASIC SUPPLIES

plant press or phone book (with paper towels for layering)

flowers or leaves

A home gardener may not have to stray far to collect beautiful leaves and flowers for pressing. If you plan to collect botanicals beyond the boundaries of your own property, ask for permission from the landowner, whether a municipality, a county, or an individual. But even in the confines of a suburban yard, or in the weed-filled cracks of a short stretch of urban sidewalk, slowing down enough to take an inventory of what lives there will quickly reveal some lovely botanicals to press.

HOW TO PRESS FLOWERS AND LEAVES

As botanicals dry, the height of the press will shrink and the straps will loosen; check them and retighten as necessary. The drying time will vary depending on the thickness of the item. Delicate wildflowers dry in about three days; roses and other large specimens may take up to three weeks. If you are not going to use your dried botanicals right away, remove them from the press and store them between layers of tissue or newsprint in a flat box or between the pages of a heavy book.

1. Place leaves or flowers in a plant press between layers of blotting paper and newsprint. Arrange the items so they do not touch one another, then use Velcro straps to close the press. If your press does not have straps, weigh it down with heavy books.

2. If you don't have a flower press, place the leaves or flowers between the pages of a phone book or another sturdy book. Sandwich the botanicals between layers of paper towels—these will help absorb moisture. (You may need to replace the paper towels after a few days.) Weigh down the book with other heavy books.

PROJECT: autumn-leaf curtain

Creating translucent material for a window covering is easy with waxed paper and a few leaves.

PROJECT SUPPLIES Basic Supplies (above), waxed paper, leaves, kraft paper, iron, tape, thread, needle

HOW-TO Measure the area you want to cover, then cut out squares of waxed paper to fit the window (you'll need two squares for each panel). Sandwich each leaf in waxed paper squares, and place between 2 pieces of kraft paper. Iron at low temperature, melting edges of waxed paper to form swatches. Tape swatches on a table in the order they'll hang. Sew swatches together, pulling needle and thread from back to front, connecting them at the middle point of each edge; tie knot in the back. Secure curtain to window by stitching thread through top, from back to front; tie knot in back, and tape long ends to top of window frame.

Capture a moment in time: With this lovely window decoration, fallen leaves look as though they're drifting by your window all season long.

PROJECT: plant cards

Send spring notes or invitations on cards decorated with dainty ferns and flowers (opposite). This drying technique skips the step of using a book or press to flatten the botanicals; instead, thin, delicate cuttings—including maidenhair fern, goldenrod, and hydrangea—are quickly dried and pressed with a hot iron.

PROJECT SUPPLIES ironing board, ferns or other thin botanicals, plain newsprint, iron, card stock or small blank cards, spray adhesive

HOW-TO Working on an ironing board, place leaves and petals on top of 3 layers of plain newsprint. Place another sheet of newsprint on top. Press with an iron set at a medium temperature until the plant cuttings turn slightly paler, about 2 minutes. Attach dried cuttings to card stock or small blank cards with spray adhesive; let dry.

PROJECT: pansy and viola coasters

Save a bit of spring by floating pressed pansies and violas between squares of glass to make a collection of coasters. Because flowers fade when pressed, pansies and violas with more intense colors do best.

PROJECT SUPPLIES Basic Supplies (page 48; use pansies or violas), two 3 1/2-inch (9cm x 9cm) squares of 1/8-inch (3mm) thick glass (have a glazier cut these and sand the edges) for each coaster, self-adhesive metal tape, binder clips, 1/4-inch (6mm) scissors

HOW-TO 1. Snip flower stems close to the base (or leave them on the stems). Press the flowers as described on page 48. **2.** Arrange the pressed flowers on 1 square of glass, top with another, and join them with self-adhesive metal tape; to keep the 2 pieces of glass from sliding as you tape, hold them together with binder clips, moving from one side to the other as necessary. Remove the clips when all sides are secure.

1

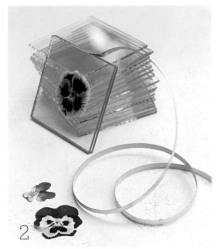

2

PROJECT: oak-leaf place cards

For a festive fall party or wedding, glue autumn leaves—in this case, from an oak tree—to place cards. Add to the ambiance by spreading colorful dried leaves across a table, and top with a sheer organza overlay.

PROJECT SUPPLIES Basic Supplies (page 48; use leaves), place cards (made of card stock), white craft glue

HOW-TO Following the instructions on page 48, place leaves between paper towels in a telephone book or in a plant press, for a week or two, depending on how thick and wet the leaves are. If you're using a telephone book, change the paper towels every few days. Once they're dry, glue one dried leaf to each place card. Write guests' names beneath the leaves.

PROJECT: leaf place mats

Encasing foliage in linen and vinyl place mats makes for a harvest-ready table decoration.

PROJECT SUPPLIES Basic Supplies (page 48; use leaves), scissors, linen or other medium-weight fabric, iron-on clear vinyl, iron

HOW-TO Press leaves, as described on page 48. Cut a 12-by-15-inch (30.5cm x 38cm) rectangle of fabric. Cut 2 pieces of the vinyl, slightly larger all around than the fabric. Arrange the leaves on the fabric. (Avoid leaves with thick stems; they can poke through.) Peel the backing from 1 vinyl sheet. Place it sticky-side down over the leaves, and smooth with your hand. Place protective paper shiny-side down on vinyl; iron according to the manufacturer's instructions. Turn it over, and iron for 4 seconds. Repeat the vinyl process with the other side. Trim the edges.

PRESSED SEAWEED

BASIC SUPPLIES

seaweed

seawater

shallow tray

blotting paper

100 percent cotton rag
paper

toothpicks, paintbrushes,
or tweezers

nail clippers (optional)

nylon netting

corrugated cardboard

plant press

weights (such as bricks or
heavy books)

electric fan

paintbrush

white craft glue or
polyvinyl acetate glue

field guide to seaweed

During the mid-nineteenth century, the shorelines of England were rife with collectors, who waded deep into the tide to collect seaweed—valued for its splendid forms and surprising range of colors—for examination and display. Much of the seaweed the Victorians preserved remains intact and can be viewed in natural-history museums, private research collections, and, in a very few cases, specialty antiques galleries. Gathering and pressing seaweed still holds a certain allure. The most natural way to learn about these plants is to visit the shore. Once you remove the seaweed from the water and examine it, you will see the same recognizable elements of beauty you find in flowers and leaves, including enticing colors and varied, intricate textures. Frame your dried collection to adorn walls or attach the specimens to card stock to create unique gift cards for the naturalists in your life. But be forewarned: Collecting seaweed can be highly habit-forming, and finding perfect candidates for pressing can provide a wonderful excuse to spend a day at the beach.

harvesting seaweed

Seaweed can be collected freely along much of the U.S. coastline, but in some areas a permit is required—check with both local and state authorities before setting out. Generally you'll find green seaweed in shallow water and brown varieties on rocky shores. Red seaweed is diverse and can be found almost anywhere. Collect only fresh seaweed, which will smell clean and should not be slimy. Use a pocketknife to gently scrape seaweed off any surface it is attached to, then immediately submerge it in a bucket of cold seawater. Keep the seaweed fresh by adding ice packs to the water and storing the bucket out of direct sunlight. Before leaving the shore, fill another bucket with clean seawater to use later. At home, sort and rinse the seaweed, trimming away any attached rocks or shells. Store seaweed in the clean seawater, and press within a day.

HOW TO PRESS SEAWEED

Some types of pressed seaweed are as translucent as watercolor, while others will remain opaque. Seaweed pressed into cotton rag paper (as in the examples on page 57) makes charming stationery.

1. Sort and clean seaweed.

2. Pour ¼ inch (6mm) cold, clean seawater into tray; place a sheet of blotting paper alongside.

3. Slide a sheet of cotton paper into water, tipping the tray so paper is submerged. Turn the paper over to thoroughly soak, and push it underwater.

4. Place the seaweed on paper; arrange with a toothpick, paintbrush, or tweezers. Use nail clippers to trim the seaweed, if necessary.

5. Carefully lift the paper at an angle so the water drips off, keeping the seaweed in place.

6. Lay it on blotting paper. Using toothpick, paintbrush, or tweezers, quickly adjust seaweed arrangement; remove any debris. Move paper and the arrangement to fresh blotting paper; cover with nylon netting. Top with another sheet of blotting paper; press gently. Replace wet blotters with clean ones.

7. Place the layers between 2 sheets of corrugated cardboard; place this "sandwich" in the plant press. (You can load several at a time.)

8. Weight the plant press down; tighten the straps. Direct a fan, placed 1 to 3 feet (30.5–91cm) away, at cardboard's open edges. Check the press initially every few hours (daily thereafter), replacing the damp blotters. When the seaweed is dry (delicate examples will dry overnight; thicker ones may take a few days), unload the press and remove the nylon netting. Seaweed will adhere to cotton rag paper naturally, but some pieces may come loose. Carefully affix these using a paintbrush and a thin layer of white craft glue. Label as desired.

A grouping of seaweed pressings makes a dramatic wall display. These simple frames are attached to large plate hangers for easy presentation.

TIP If you want to identify your seaweed, use a field guide to do so before pressing. Once dried, seaweed takes on a different appearance than when it is fresh from the sea. After the seaweed dries, you can write any information—such as the variety, location, date, person it was collected and identified by, and the field guide referenced—directly on the paper used to make the pressing.

PROJECT: framed pressed seaweed

PROJECT SUPPLIES Basic Supplies (page 54), UV-blocking acrylic or glass, cardboard, plate hangers

HOW-TO It's important to use UV-blocking acrylic or glass, because it will reduce fading. Have the glass or acrylic professionally cut to size. After pressing seaweed into paper following the instructions on pages 54-55, sandwich the work between the glass and stiff cardboard; secure with a plate hanger.

PROJECT: seaweed cards

You can create distinctive cards with small examples of pressed seaweed. Be sure to use heavy, lined envelopes if you intend to mail the cards.

PROJECT SUPPLIES Basic Supplies (page 54)

HOW-TO Before pressing, cut the cotton rag paper to twice the size you'd like your card to be. Fold the paper in half, and then unfold so that you have a guide for where to place the seaweed. Position the seaweed on one half of the paper, then follow the directions on page 55 for pressing and drying.

BOTANICAL PRINTING

Few things in nature are more effortlessly beautiful than the details of a fallen magnolia leaf, the regal outline of Queen Anne's lace, or the wispy image of a willow branch. These triumphs of design and engineering have long served as perfect patterns for prints and rubbings. Hundreds of years ago, taking a "picture" of wildlife was important for scholars cataloging their discoveries. Around 1500, Leonardo da Vinci documented how to make a print of a sage leaf; he suggested covering it with soot and oil and pressing it to paper. These days, using paint, crayons, colored pencils, and even light-sensitive paper, you can create your own picture-perfect images on fabric and paper. Begin by taking a good look at the leaves in your backyard or the flowers in your garden, or purchasing interesting examples from a plant store or nursery. (Don't pluck leaves or flowers from trees or land that isn't your own.) Then, customize bags, tablecloths, pillows, or any number of textiles by printing leaves on them, or place botanicals on light-sensitive paper or fabric to capture their skeletal images for cards and upholstery material. Or, similar to da Vinci, you can duplicate the shadow of your favorite plants by rubbing their outlines on delicate paper, but with a pencil rather than soot and oil.

ABOUT THE MATERIALS

FABRIC PAINTS Fabric paints are available in a variety of colors and can be found in most crafts stores. Because these paints tend to produce opaque colors, they are good for printing on dark fabrics.

SCREENING INKS These fabric inks are usually used for silkscreening, and tend to be thinner and produce more translucent colors than fabric paints. They can be found at art-supply stores.

OPPOSITE **When printing leaves or other plants, don't worry about maintaining botanical accuracy; the charm is in the abundance of leaves and the surprising softness of their shapes and textures. The pattern of printed lemon leaves on this tablecloth contrasts beautifully against a tea set with a complementary woodland pattern.**

RUBBER BRAYER This small, rubber roller with a handle can be used in multiple crafts. For botanical printing, it's used to press leaves against fabric.

FABRIC When printing on fabric, choose natural, untreated materials. Make sure there are no stain-resistant coatings on the fabric or other treatments that could prevent paint from adhering. Synthetic fabrics—such as rayon or polyester—aren't suitable for this technique because they can't be ironed at a high enough temperature for the fabric paint or screening ink to set without damaging the material.

LIGHT-SENSITIVE PAPER AND FABRIC FOR SUN PRINTS Both light-sensitive fabric and paper react to light, turning blue wherever you have not placed an object. The fabric is often sold as blueprint fabric and the paper is sold as sun-print paper. The paper and fabric usually come in separate kits with instructions.

PAPER FOR PLANT RUBBINGS Choose thin papers, such as Japanese rice paper, waxed tissue, and tissue paper for plant rubbing. Thicker papers, such as computer printer paper, will also work, but won't produce the same detailed rendering or ethereal, gauzy texture that thinner papers do when rubbed.

PENCIL STICKS FOR PLANT RUBBINGS Basically pencils without their wood casing, these colored sticks are harder than crayons, so they can produce crisper lines when creating plant rubbings.

LEAF PRINTS

BASIC SUPPLIES

sponge brush

fabric paints

flattened leaf

fabric

paper towels

rubber brayer

tweezers

iron

Astonishingly, there are only ten basic leaf shapes on the planet, but that small number encompasses thousands of subtly distinctive forms worthy of being elevated from object to emblem. Using little more than fabric paint and a rubber brayer, you can reproduce arboreal patterns on a variety of textiles. The best prints are achieved by using leaves that are green and pliant, especially leathery leaves, like those of the magnolia tree. Use untreated fabrics, such as linen and cotton; they are naturally absorbent and take paint well. The printing process itself is easy, but the results can be stylish and sophisticated. Cover a large canvas, such as a tablecloth, with a bunch of printed oversize leaves or a haphazard design of lemon tree branches, or isolate one small, perfect shape to embellish a book cover.

HOW TO MAKE LEAF PRINTS

When starting out, experiment with patterns and color schemes on remnants before you commit images to the fabric for your project. Try mixing leaf shapes and different colors for various effects. Stems tend to shift during this step, so print leaves and stems separately. Cut the stem from the leaf and print the leaf first.

1. Using a sponge brush and working on a protected surface, paint the underside of a flattened leaf, so the veins will be visible. Don't coat the leaf too thickly; aim for the thinnest thorough coat possible to produce a detailed image. Turn the leaf over, and place it on the fabric.

2. Cover the leaf completely with a paper towel, and roll over it several times with a rubber brayer.

3. Lift the leaf gently from the pointed tip, pulling straight up. After the leaf dries, print the stem, handling it delicately with tweezers. If you want to overlap prints of leaves, let the paint of the first leaf dry before printing the second leaf—otherwise, the first print will bleed into the second impression. When you are finished printing, heat-set all paints with an iron, following the paint manufacturer's instructions.

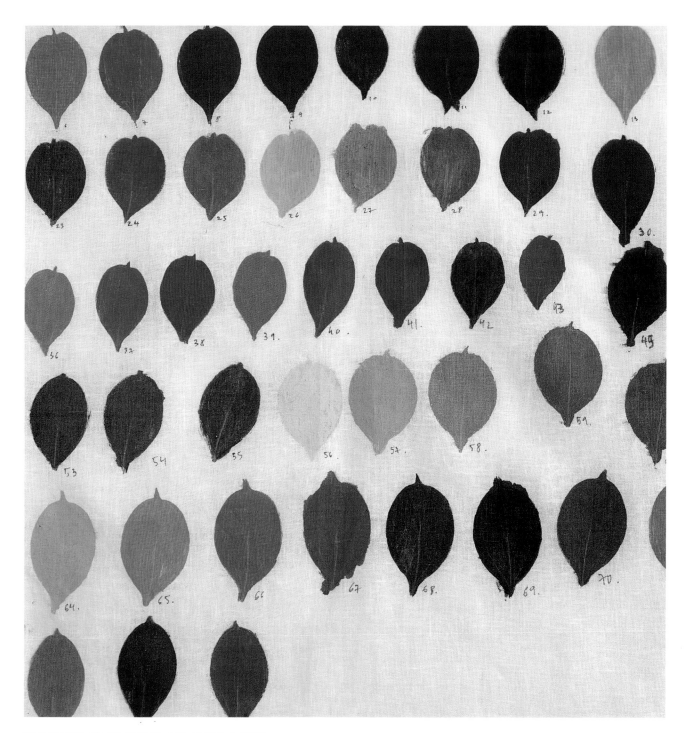

PAINT COLORS GLOSSARY

The beauty of creating your own prints is that you can use any color palette that suits your fancy. Commercial fabric paints and textile screening inks come in a relatively narrow range of colors, but mixing them together allows you to create a variety of subtle—or bold—shades. Leaves of the ruscus plant were used here to compose a wide palette. Only a few of these shades approximate the real colors of the leaves you find in nature; printing with an unusual color lets the shape of the leaf take precedence. If you make your own colors, be sure to mix enough paint to complete your project. Fabric paints are more opaque than screening inks; use them when printing lighter colors onto darker fabrics, such as white onto dark blue.

OPPOSITE A plain white tablecloth can serve as a canvas for botanical prints. Here, huge monstera leaves are printed on white linen. First, remove leaves from the branch, and print the branch first. Then print the leaves, so they look like they're coming off the branches. Try printing both sides of the leaves for variety—the underside will show the veins more clearly.

ABOVE For these sunporch pillows, mustard-yellow linen was printed with three different-size anthurium leaves in shades of red, orange, and white.

PROJECT: **printed blank books**

As these journal covers show, leaves are printing tools built for both graceful and playful designs.

PROJECT SUPPLIES Basic Supplies (page 60), fabric-covered blank books

HOW-TO Place the book on a flat surface and follow the instructions on page 60 for leaf printing. Choose leaves that complement the size and shape of your journal. Experiment with printing them in different patterns, such as on the journals pictured above. **1.** Partial print of an evergreen anthurium. **2.** Cedar eucalyptus leaves, "scattered." **3.** California bay leaves at attention. **4.** Silver-dollar eucalyptus leaves. **5.** Crossed palm fronds. **6.** Ruscus in a windblown pattern. **7.** A small branch of lemon leaves. **8.** A magnolia leaf "X-ray."

PROJECT: geometric leaf print bag

You're not restricted to random or purely natural forms when printing botanicals. In fact, leaves can be traced to produce templates for geometric patterns. Although a canvas bag is shown here, the same printing technique can be applied to all manner of fabric items.

PROJECT SUPPLIES Basic Supplies (page 60); paper or card stock; thin, oblong leaves (such as California bay leaves); canvas tote bag; pencil

HOW-TO Make paper templates of your leaf. Lay out the bag (or whatever other fabric you're printing on) and use the templates to mark with a pencil where the points of the leaves meet on your fabric. Mark out the entire pattern, and take a good look at it before printing—the best way to avoid the mid-project realization that your design is crooked. Print on the fabric—using the leaf, not the paper templates—following the instructions on page 60.

SUN PRINTS

BASIC SUPPLIES

light-sensitive cloth or fabric

delicate flowers, ferns, or other botanicals

water

Creating intricate silhouettes of ferns, flowers, and other delicate plants is easy when you use light-sensitive paper or fabric. After a few minutes in the sun, flowers and natural forms leave their shadows on the cloth or paper. The images, which bring to mind old-fashioned cyanotypes, can be easily integrated into a variety of crafts projects.

HOW TO MAKE PAPER SUN PRINTS

For this wedding reception idea, fern silhouettes, captured on light-sensitive paper, help guests find their places. Guests' names are calligraphed in white gouache beneath each image (see page 74 for more on calligraphy). The prints, paired with blue card stock inscribed with corresponding table numbers, are pinned to linen-wrapped boards. Guests can keep cards as a memento of the day.

PAPER SUN-PRINT SUPPLIES Basic Supplies (above; use 11-by-17-inch [27.5cm x 42.5cm] paper and dried ferns [see page 48 for drying instructions, under "How to Press Flowers and Leaves"]), tweezers, scissors, water, paper towels, card stock, calligraphy pen, one or more ½-inch (13mm) thick 20-by-30-inch (51cm x 76cm) foamboards, white linen, stapler, 1 ¾-inch (4.5cm) ribbon, small removable adhesive hook or pushpin, adhesive putty or removable interlocking fasteners, double-sided tape

 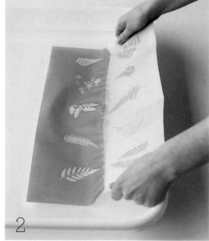 

1. Read the directions on your light-sensitive paper for specific instructions before starting. Remove paper from its protective bag. Using tweezers and touching the paper as little as possible, arrange ferns on the sheet. Leave space around each one for writing and trimming into ten 2 ½-by-4 ¾-inch (6.5cm x 12cm) cards with a fern imprint at the top center. Place the sheet outdoors or in a sunny window for 1 to 5 minutes, until it has faded almost to white. Remove the ferns with tweezers.

2. Plunge the sheet into a tray of tepid water; it will turn blue, with white images where the ferns were placed.

3. Remove the sheet, and blot the paper with towels for consistent color. Let the paper air-dry; the blue will become dark.

When it's dry, cut the sheet into cards. Cut card stock (in this case, light blue) into 3-by-5-inch (7.5cm x 12.5cm) pieces. Calligraph the name of each guest in white gouache beneath the fern; with blue ink, write the guest's table number on the card stock. Cover the foamboard in white linen; staple the linen on the back to secure it. Pin the card pairs to the boards in alphabetical order. Staple a length of ribbon (in this case, dark blue) to the back of each board; hang on a small removable adhesive hook or pushpin. Place piece of adhesive putty or removable interlocking fasteners on each corner. Make bows, then affix them to the front of the hooks using double-sided tape.

HOW TO MAKE FABRIC SUN PRINTS

Create your own distinctively designed botanical-print fabric with light-sensitive fabric. As with light-sensitive paper, you can arrange objects on the fabric to create white silhouettes of plants (or other objects). This material is wonderful for upholstering a set of white painted chairs.

FABRIC SUN-PRINT SUPPLIES Basic Supplies (page 66), scissors, straight pins, cardboard, Plexiglas® or non-UV glass (optional), water, iron, 2 muslin or natural cotton pressing cloths, 1-inch (2.5cm) thick foam, batting, staple gun, upholstery fabric

  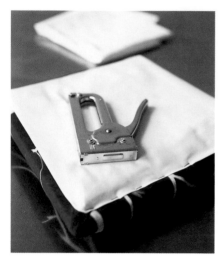

1. Working indoors, out of direct sunlight, remove light-sensitive fabric from bag and cut fabric 4 inches (10cm) larger all around than seat. Pin the fabric, slightly taut, to a piece of cardboard. Arrange objects on the fabric as desired, pinning each one securely (you can also cover the fabric with a piece of Plexiglas or non-UV glass). Place the fabric in direct sunlight. Without moving it, let it sit for the amount of time specified in the fabric's directions. Take the fabric indoors immediately, and unpin the objects (there will be only a faint image of the objects at this point). Rinse the fabric under running water, gently agitating, until the water runs clear. Lay the fabric flat in a dark room to dry. With the iron on the coolest setting, iron the back of the fabric, sandwiched between 2 pressing cloths.

2. Trace the seat board onto the foam; add ⅛ inch (3mm) all around, and cut it out. Cut cotton batting fabric 4 inches (10cm) larger all around than the seat. Lay the batting flat; center the foam and the seat board on top. Wrap one side of the batting over the seat, pull taut, and staple 1 ½ inches (3.8cm) from the edge. Wrap the opposite side over, and staple. Repeat for remaining sides. Lay the sun-print fabric facedown; place the seat on the fabric, cushion-side down, and use the same method to attach.

3. To finish, cut the upholstery fabric 1 inch (2.5cm) smaller on all sides than the seat; fold and press the edges. Place on the underside of the seat, so that the edges of the upholstery fabric cover the edges of the sun-printed fabric. Secure with staples at 2-inch (5cm) intervals. Place seats in chair frames. Keep the chairs out of direct sunlight to prevent fading.

gift tags

These custom sun-print gift tags will brighten anyone's day. Create images of your favorite flowers or other plants on light-sensitive paper (following the instructions on page 66). The images can be easily trimmed into cards and tags. Cut the paper into cards and write messages with a gel pen, or a fine-tipped paint pen in white. Punch a hole at the end of each tag, and thread a ribbon through the hole to attach the tag to a gift.

TIP To make the crispest images possible on light-sensitive paper or fabric, try laying a piece of Plexiglas over the botanicals; this flattens the objects and keeps them from moving. (Often a sheet of Plexiglas will come with a sun-print kit.)

BOTANICAL RUBBINGS

BASIC SUPPLIES

plain thin paper, such
as Japanese rice paper
or tissue paper

paperweight

crayons or colored
pencil sticks

pressed leaf or flower
(see page 48 for drying
instructions, under "How to
Press Flowers and
Leaves")

Think of botanical rubbings as flawlessly rendered still lifes of plants and flowers. The added beauty of these prints is that making them is nearly effortless; each detail of a leaf or flower is captured with just a few strokes of a crayon or colored pencil. Using this technique, similar to one traditionally implemented by botanists, you can create art to give as a present or to decorate your own home. Thicker leaves, such as those from magnolias or geraniums, work best; many flowers are too delicate, but hydrangeas and Queen Anne's lace are sturdy enough.

HOW TO MAKE BOTANICAL RUBBINGS

With this technique, you can make framed prints, a calendar, an album, or wrapping paper. When choosing a plant to rub, flatten your selections in a phone book or between sheets of newsprint under a heavy object. Leave the plants for a few days to dry out; they'll be easier to rub.

Place the pressed, dried botanical on a flat surface, and overlay it with your paper. Rub one section at a time with a crayon or a pencil stick, holding the paper with your free hand. (For large elements, such as leaves, hold the utensil on its side; for small parts, such as stems, use its tip.) Fill in details, such as small flowers, by hand-drawing with crayons or pencils.

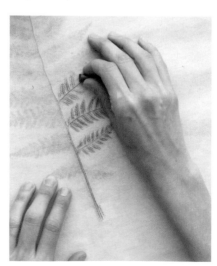

Framed botanical rubbings allow the loveliest things from outside to take root inside. Hang multiples in one area for dramatic effect. Try printing mirror images of the same branch and displaying them next to each other to bring symmetry to the display, as shown in the pair on the top shelf.

PROJECT: **botanical calendar**

To make an illustrated calendar, pick plants that are seasonally appropriate for each month—for example, pine needles in January and sugar-maple leaves in September. Try collecting plants throughout the year, when they're in season, or order them online. These rubbings were done on 13-by-19-inch (33cm x 48.5cm) Japanese rice paper, available at art-supply stores.

PROJECT SUPPLIES Basic Supplies (page 70), calendar template (page 370)

HOW-TO Sketch in the calendar dates using the template, then complete the plant rubbings above the dates. A stem of lily of the valley was used for May (see above). For the February winterberry, only a branch was used—berries were drawn in with a crayon. The leaves and stems of a geranium were rubbed in a fan shape for June. A single hydrangea bloom was repeated for August. For November, Japanese maple leaves were scattered to look as if they were falling from a tree. To assemble, punch 2 holes 5 inches apart (12.5cm) and 1 inch (2.5cm) from the top of each page. Tie with ribbon, and hang.

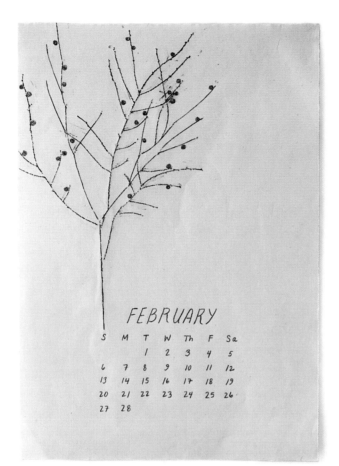

FEBRUARY

S	M	T	W	Th	F	Sa
				1	2	3	4	5
6	7	8	9	10	11	12
13	14	15	16	17	18	19
20	21	22	23	24	25	26
27	28

JUNE

S	M	T	W	Th	F	Sa
				1	2	3	4
5	6	7	8	9	10	11
12	13	14	15	16	17	18
19	20	21	22	23	24	25
26	27	28	29	30

AUGUST

S	M	T	W	Th	F	Sa
	1	2	3	4	5	6
7	8	9	10	11	12	13
14	15	16	17	18	19	20
21	22	23	24	25	26	27
28	29	30	31

NOVEMBER

S	M	T	W	Th	F	Sa
		1	2	3	4	5
6	7	8	9	10	11	12
13	14	15	16	17	18	19
20	21	22	23	24	25	26
27	28	29	30

HOW TO CALLIGRAPH

LOWERCASE LETTERS Nine pen strokes (top) combine to make most of the lowercase letters. Keep the following in mind as you write: Adding pressure to the tip of the nib will result in thick strokes; lessening the pressure will make thin strokes. It's easiest to create thick strokes using a downward motion and thin strokes while the pen is moving upward. To make a dot, as for the letter *i*, press the nib into the paper, allowing the ink to pool. Always lift your pen after each stroke; don't keep pen to paper as you do when writing cursive. Once you are comfortable with the strokes, combine them to create letters: The letter *p*, for example, is made up of 3 strokes: 2 short (the seventh and the fourth shown at the top of the chart below) and one tall (the first). Take a break every few strokes to sit back and check spacing and form.

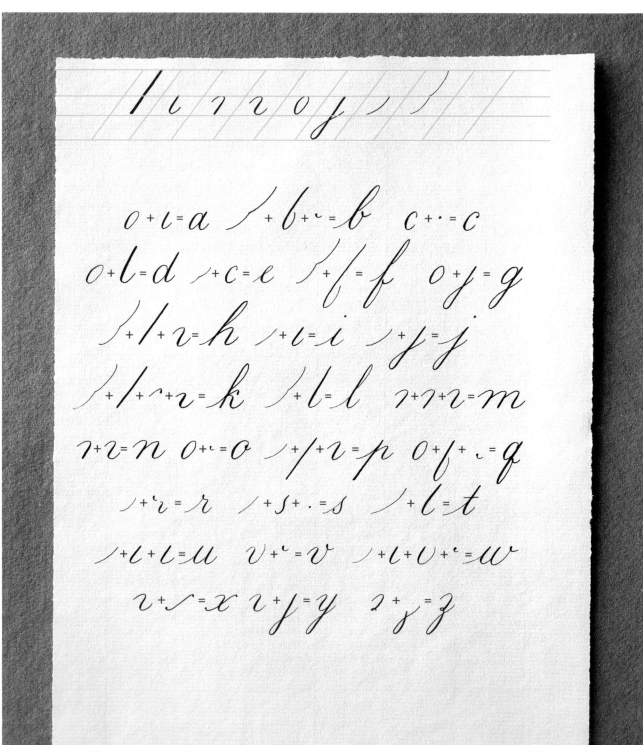

CAPITAL LETTERS AND NUMERALS More free-form and less rule-bound than the lowercase alphabet, uppercase lettering allows you to give your script a personal flourish. The seven pen strokes at the top of the chart above are used in many of the uppercase letters. Experiment with additional touches of your own (but avoid embellishments that interfere with legibility, such as loops on the letter's right side). Many of these uppercase letters cannot be connected to the letters that follow, which adds to their noble appearance. It's important to practice numerals, too, for envelopes or the family tree on page 81. Use the ones above as models, breaking each numeral down into individual strokes, as with the lowercase letters.

calligraphy pointers

Dip the pen into the ink pot so the hole in the nib is just covered. Gently tap the nib on the rim of the pot to remove excess ink. Make a few strokes on a scrap of paper to get the ink to flow. There should be enough ink to make solid lines without blotches or drips.

To write, position your paper at an angle, so that the pen's tip is aligned with a diagonal rule on the guidesheet.

At first, the technique may require some getting used to. Unlike in cursive hand-writing, you must lift your pen from the paper once, twice, or three times during the course of making a single letter. This is because each letter or number is made up of a series of different strokes.

When the nib starts to feel scratchy, redip your pen.

PROJECT: labeled storage boxes

The graceful movement of pen and ink may conjure up Victorian times, but calligraphy has all kinds of modern applications. For aesthetic organizing, add hand-lettered labels to brightly colored store-bought storage boxes.

PROJECT SUPPLIES Basic Supplies (page 75), storage boxes, card stock, round corner punch, scissors, lay-flat paste (such as Yes! paste), pencil, ruler, eraser

HOW-TO Cut labels out of card stock; finish edges with a round corner punch. Calligraph the categories. Black ink on cream paper is shown, but you can use any colors that suit your décor. Before you begin writing, use a ruler and pencil to mark guide lines on the paper; erase the lines after the ink dries. Affix labels to boxes with bookbinding paste.

PROJECT: cards and invitations

Calligraphy is perfectly suited to invitations, place cards, valentines, and other holiday cards. It also imparts an old-fashioned feel when used to inscribe messages and quotations on plain note cards.

PROJECT SUPPLIES Basic Supplies (page 75), blank cards, paper, stickers, envelopes, scissors, hole punch and/or decorative craft punch (optional), rubber stamps and ink pads (optional)

HOW-TO For sophisticated, personalized cards, use calligraphy for messages and quotations, and further decorate the paper with hole-punch dots, rubber stamps, and creative cut-outs. To write in a color, mix gouache with water for an opaque finish.

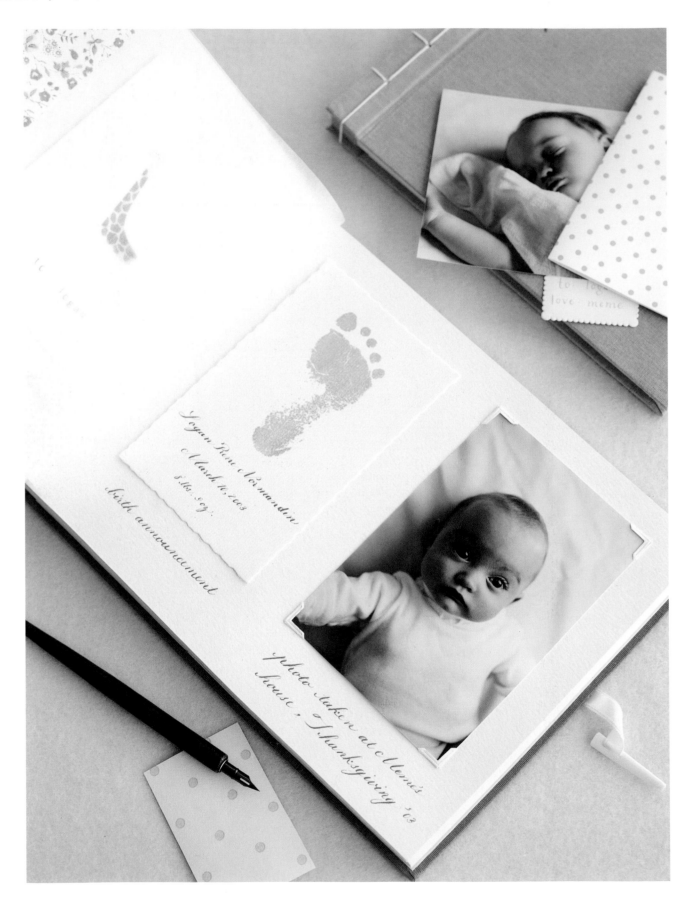

PROJECT: **baby book**

Carefully calligraphed labels and details strike a perfect note with the nostalgic feel of a handcrafted scrapbook.

PROJECT SUPPLIES Basic Supplies (page 75), blank archival-quality scrapbook, photo adhesive tape and photo corners (for assembly), photographs and other memorabilia

HOW-TO Fill an archival-quality scrapbook with photos, documents, and other keepsakes (see Albums, Scrapbooks, and Memory Boxes, page 14, for instructions), and label each item with calligraphed script. If the book has removable pages, remove each page and lay it flat before calligraphing so it will be easier to write on.

PROJECT: **family tree**

A family tree inscribed with names and dates to celebrate your ancestry makes a treasured gift.

PROJECT SUPPLIES Basic Supplies (page 75), paper, family tree template (page 375), marker, pencil, ruler, colored paper and frame (optional)

HOW-TO Copy the template onto 11-by-17-inch (27.5cm x 42.5cm) paper at 175 percent. For a 16-by-24-inch (40cm x 60cm) chart, copy each half of the 11-by-17-inch chart at 125 percent; tape enlarged halves together. Go over the template's lines with a marker, then trace them with pencil onto a sheet of thin to medium-weight paper. (To see the template more clearly, tape it to a window, center the paper on top, and trace with a pencil and ruler.) Begin by calligraphing your name and birth date at the bottom, as indicated on the template; then proceed outward to your parents, grand-parents, and so on. Frame the finished product with colored paper behind it (see Matting and Framing, page 176).

Don't worry if you make a small mistake; if you want to undo any calligraphy, gently scratch it away using a craft knife or a razor blade. Be careful not to cut through the paper.

Many candlemakers believe that simple shapes display the hues and textures of wax most beautifully. Improvise with colorants to make a collection of candles in a pretty palette such as this one.

CANDLEMAKING
POURED CANDLES, ROLLED AND CUTOUT CANDLES

With the advent of mass-produced candles in the nineteenth century, not to mention electric lights, candlemaking disappeared from the list of regular, ongoing household chores. But machine-made candles just don't have the lovely shapes or the lush colors of homemade candles. And even learning the basics of the craft provides rich rewards. The tools and methods of home candlemaking are almost as simple today as they were five thousand years ago. Candles were probably invented soon after the wheel; candlesticks excavated in Egypt and Crete date as far back as 3000 B.C. In the Middle Ages, tallow (rendered animal fat) was used to make candles in European homes. Early American colonists continued to use tallow and also formed candles from beeswax and vegetable waxes, such as bayberry (or candleberry, as it was known). In recent years, candlemaking has become both popular craft and high art, and all the supplies to make extraordinary examples are readily available. On these pages, you'll learn how to make poured candles, using melted wax, as well as rolled and cutout candles, using sheets of wax. The results are not just beautiful, they're useful, and they make excellent presents.

ABOUT THE SUPPLIES

WAX AND ADDITIVES Good-quality wax will burn cleanly and slowly. All-natural beeswax has a gorgeous pale golden color and a faint honey scent. Soy wax, made from soybeans, is another natural option. Petroleum-based paraffin wax is less expensive and sold in bead pellets. Wax is sold in blocks, for poured candles (page 84), and in sheets, for rolled and cut candles (page 102); sheets are usually beeswax. For poured candles, you can save money by mixing beeswax with a paraffin that has a similar melting point (it will be marked on the package), but use a majority of beeswax to retain its characteristic pale shade. Additives—stearic acid is a common one—are often used to make paraffin wax harder, the colors more opaque, and the candles slower to burn. You can buy wax that already includes additives, and formulations specifically for votive candles,

pillars, or other shapes, but a general-purpose wax should suit most projects.

MOLDS The number of molds available today is impressive and inspiring. Simple shapes like rounds, ovals, squares, and stars are often made of metal. More intricate molds may be made of plastic or flexible rubber.

COLORANT Dyes used to tint melted wax come in several forms, including blocks, cakes, chips, flakes, and liquids. For many of the projects here, blocks were used; shave off small bits to add to the melted wax gradually until the desired color is reached.

WICKS Your candle mold should come with instructions as to which type of wick to use. Use thinner wicks for small candles and thicker wicks for larger candles. (If a wick is too thin, the flame will be small and may be snuffed out while burning. If a wick is too thick, the flame will melt the wax too quickly.) Check to see that the wick will work with your wax type; flat-

braided cotton is a good general-purpose wick. Square-braided cotton wicks are sturdier and good for larger candles. Cored wicks, usually with a zinc core, are stiffer. Use this type for votive and container candles, and make sure to use wicks with metal tabs on one end (you can buy wicks with tabs, or purchase the tabs separately and put them on yourself) to help the wicks stand up.

WAX-MELTING SUPPLIES To melt wax, use a double boiler—a pot set into a larger pot of simmering water (wash the smaller pot thoroughly before using it for food). Wax must never be heated in a pot set directly over a heat source (see page 86). You can also use a candle-pouring pot; it has a spout and handle, making it easier to work with. You can use a candle-making thermometer (available at crafts stores) to monitor the temperature of the wax, but a candy thermometer works just as well.

POURED CANDLES

BASIC SUPPLIES

beeswax or paraffin bricks
or old candles

candle molds or containers

wicking, sized for your
molds

wicking needle or tapestry
needle

mold-release spray or
nonstick cooking-oil spray

candle-making or candy
thermometer

wax colorants

natural essential oils or
fragrance oils (optional)

parchment or waxed
paper

craft sticks

wooden skewer

double boiler or two pots

scissors

Creating your own poured candles is part science and part art. As you melt the wax according to specific guidelines, you may feel like a chemist in a lab. But once you start mixing in colors and choosing molds, you're an artist. It's surprisingly easy to play both roles and turn out beautiful, one-of-a-kind candles using the varied techniques shown on the following pages.

PREPARING WAX

1. Place beeswax and/or paraffin bricks in a double boiler. When the wax has reached its melting point according to a candle-making or candy thermometer, lower the heat and add a hardening agent such as stearic acid (if desired), using three tablespoons (45ml) of stearic acid per pound (.5kg) of wax. (Or incorporate any other additives according to package instructions.)

2. To tint the melting wax, stir in bits of colorant using a wooden spoon. Test the color by dabbing wax with a wooden craft stick on waxed paper or parchment paper. Remove from heat; if using fragrance, add it at this point.

scented candles

Adding fragrance to handmade candles is not necessary—in fact, it's almost a shame to cover up the subtle honey scent of pure beeswax. If you wish to make scented candles, however, use natural essential oils or fragrance oils intended for candlemaking, as some oils are flammable. Natural essential oils, the more costly of the two, are extracted from the bark, berries, roots, or seeds of a plant. Their names reflect the plants they're derived from—peppermint oil and lavender oil are two popular essential oils. Fragrance oils, which are usually mixed with synthetic oils or substances, can be made to mimic the scents of essential oils, so you'll also find peppermint and lavender fragrance oils. Oils with whimsical names—"Fresh Laundry" or "Christmas Morning"—are fragrance oils. People can be sensitive to both essential oils and fragrance oils, so use them very carefully and extremely sparingly, according to package instructions. Pregnant women in particular should consult their physicians before handling essential oils.

TINTED WAX COLOR GLOSSARY

Create candles in any shade by mixing custom colors. These pinecones show off some of the hues of the candles on the following pages. The numbers denote the amount of wax shavings used to tint one pound (.5kg) of bleached beeswax. However, the process isn't an exact one—the results depend both on the size of shavings and the brand of colorant used. Experiment to find colors you love—and keep your own notes about how much colorant you use so you can re-create the results if you like.

BLEACHED BEESWAX

NATURAL BEESWAX

10 SUNSHINE YELLOW, 5 RUST BROWN, 2 BROWN

3 PINK, 3 SUNSHINE YELLOW, 3 WHITE

2 PINK, 1 WHITE

6 SUNSHINE YELLOW, 4 BROWN, 4 RUST BROWN

3 VIOLET, 1 TRUE BLACK

3 WEDGWOOD BLUE

4 ARCTIC BLUE

10 BROWN, 10 RUST BROWN, 3 TRUE BLACK

5 ARCTIC BLUE, 4 SUNSHINE YELLOW

2 OLIVE, 1 TURQUOISE, 1 SUNSHINE YELLOW, ½ RUST BROWN

POURED CANDLE SUPPLIES

Molds come in varied shapes and sizes, but you don't need to invest in a large collection to get started. Multiple candles in the same shape but varying hues would make a striking display.

WICKING

MOLDS

METAL TABS

WICK PUTTY

safety tips

Different waxes have different melting points (commonly in the range of 120 to 160 degrees Fahrenheit [48–71°C]) and different flash points, the temperature at which wax catches fire (typically over 300 degrees Fahrenheit [149°C]). When you buy wax, the packaging should note both temperatures. Wax does not boil—it gets hotter and hotter until it starts smoking and can then burst into flames. Never let it even approach the flash point. Here are some essential precautions to take when working with wax:

USE A DOUBLE BOILER to melt the wax; never place the wax in a pot that will be directly over the heat source. Use a thermometer to monitor the temperature constantly. If possible, heat the wax over an electric heat source rather than a gas flame.

NEVER LEAVE WAX UNATTENDED as it melts—do not even leave the room.

IF A FIRE DOES OCCUR, do not attempt to put it out with water. As with a grease fire, water will spread a wax fire. A pot lid can be used to smother a very small fire. But it is essential that you have a dry chemical fire extinguisher easily accessible, just in case.

IF HOT WAX SPLASHES on your skin, do not rub the area. Instead, run it under cold water immediately and then remove the hardened wax.

NEVER POUR MELTED WAX—even a little bit—down the drain, where it will harden. Save excess wax for future use, or discard small amounts once they've hardened.

TIP Priming the wick, or coating it with wax, allows it to burn steadily. To do this, simply dip the wick into the melted wax, and then let the wax harden and dry.

THERMOMETER, COLORANT,
UNBLEACHED WAX, BLEACHED WAX

HOW TO MAKE BASIC POURED CANDLES

These steps illustrate the procedure for making candles using molds in relatively simple shapes. Molds may come with specific instructions, in which case you should modify the steps below accordingly.

BASIC POURED CANDLE SUPPLIES Basic Supplies (page 84), pencil, pot holders, bucket of cold water (optional)

1. To prepare the mold, coat the interior with mold-release spray or nonstick cooking spray. Fix a length of wicking to the mold according to its instructions (here wick putty is used to keep the wax from leaking out; strong tape also works).

2. Turn the mold over. Place a pencil, skewer, or stick across the opening of the mold. Pull the wick up the center of the mold and tie it to the stick, so that it will remain taut once the wax has been poured. Melt wax as described opposite.

3. Pour the melted wax into the prepared mold until it is about 1 ½ inches (3.8cm) below the rim. Using pot holders, place the filled mold in a cold-water bath—a bucket works fine. (This will cool the wax more quickly, but it is an optional step.) Let the mold sit for about 30 minutes. As air bubbles rise to the top, a small well will form around the wick. Insert a long, thin instrument, such as a wooden skewer, into the well to allow air bubbles to escape, then fill the well ¾ full with more melted wax. Repeat the process again after 45 minutes, then remove the mold from the water bath. Allow the mold to cool and harden completely, up to 24 hours.

4. Remove the putty from the bottom to release the wick. Working from the other end, gently pull the candle from the mold. The end that was at the base of the mold will be the top of the candle. Trim that wick to ¼ inch (6mm), and the wick at the other end (which was attached to the pencil) flush with the candle.

HOW TO MAKE FIGURAL POURED CANDLES

Molds for intricate candle designs are often made from flexible rubber. They are available online, and allow you to make candles that look like realistic pinecones or whimsical holiday figures such as turkeys, Santas, or bunnies.

These handsome turkeys were made using wax tinted autumnal colors and poured into a variety of molds. They sit atop a cake stand lined with wax-coated fall leaves.

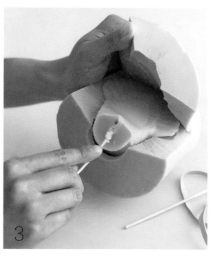

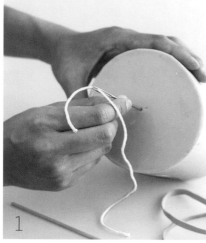

FIGURAL POURED CANDLE SUPPLIES Basic Supplies (page 84), small pliers (optional), masking tape, rubber bands, or nylon stocking

1. Coat the mold with mold-release spray or nonstick cooking-oil spray. Thread the wick onto a wicking needle or a large tapestry needle. Push the needle through the closed end of the mold (you may need to use small pliers). Place a wooden skewer across the opening of the mold, and tie the wick to it. Pull the wick taut, and secure the loose end with masking tape. Keep the mold together with rubber bands or masking tape.

2. Melt and tint wax according to instructions on page 84. Pour the wax into the mold. Wax may shrink as it cools, leaving a gap. Reheat the wax, and add more to fill in if necessary.

3. Small molds will set in a few hours; larger molds need about 24 hours. To remove the candle, take the rubber bands off, cut off the bottom wick, remove the masking tape, and trim. Gently loosen the mold—one side at a time—then carefully pull the candle out. Rub it with the nylon stocking to remove any flakes and smooth out the edges. Trim the top wick to ¼ inch (6mm).

PROJECT: **pear candles**

Candles made to resemble Forelle pears look as though they were plucked straight from a tree; for this centerpiece, they're "garnished" with Scabiosa stellata buds and seeded eucalyptus.

PROJECT SUPPLIES Figural Poured Candle Supplies (opposite), soft craft paintbrush, petal dust

HOW-TO Make the candles in a pear-shaped mold as described opposite, using wax tinted green. To give the pears their realistic blush, use a soft craft paintbrush to lightly apply petal dust, a powdered tint made for embellishing foods, to the curve of the pears; the petal dust will come off if rubbed, so don't allow the blushed sides to touch each other when the candles are displayed.

HOW TO MAKE RUBBER CANDLE MOLDS

You can fashion your own reusable rubber molds to create one-of-a-kind candles, like the realistic birch logs shown here. This same procedure can be used for molds of other objects. For those, just attach the strip of wood to the bottom of the object.

RUBBER CANDLE MOLD SUPPLIES Basic Supplies (page 84), item to cast (such as a birch log or pumpkin), 2-inch (5cm) screw, screwdriver, 1-by-$\frac{1}{4}$-inch-thick (2.5cm-by-6mm) strip of wood, container (such as a mailing tube, bucket, or any plastic container that can be cut with a craft knife), butcher's wax, rubber-mold compound, acrylic paint, candle-painting medium, small paintbrush, nylon stocking, craft knife, heavy can (optional)

1. For a birch-log candle mold, use the screw to secure a strip of wood to the top of a small log. The wood strip should be long enough to lie flat across the container, which itself is a few inches wider than the log on all sides. Cover the log with 2 coats of butcher's wax (available at hardware stores) to prevent the bark from peeling off and sticking to the mold. Then coat the log and the inside of the mailing tube with mold-release spray, and let it dry. In a clean plastic container, mix the rubber-mold compound according to the manufacturer's instructions. Center the log inside the mailing tube. Slowly pour the compound into the tube around the log, until

it's even with (but doesn't cover) the top of the log. If your log starts to float, weigh it down with a heavy can. Let the compound cure overnight.

2. To remove the mold, cut away the container with a craft knife. Then gently make 2 cuts (through to the log) along opposite sides of the rubber mold, down to about an inch (2.5cm) from the bottom. As you carefully pull apart the 2 sides, you may need to cut more deeply. Remove the object from the mold, and run hot water through the mold to rinse out any loose pieces of bark. To make the candle, follow the instructions for basic poured candles on page 87, using brown tinted wax.

3. To paint the candle, mix ivory-colored acrylic paint with candle-painting medium according to the manufacturer's instructions. Using the paintbrush, coat the candle and let it dry. With a stocking, gently rub the surface to remove paint in spots to create a barklike texture.

Birch log and pinecone candles (the pine-cones were made in store-bought flexible molds) sit atop plates covered with faux snow, creating a cozy winter scene.

The pale hues of vintage glass bottles inspired the colors of these candles. They also evoke the ocean, appropriately enough for candles cast in sand.

HOW TO MAKE SAND CANDLES

As every seaside castle builder knows, a little water is all it takes to convert sand into a moldable material with limitless possibilities. Sand candles turn that process inside out—sand becomes the mold, not the medium. Here, glass bottles and other objects are used to make impressions in a bucket of sand.

SAND-CANDLE SUPPLIES Basic Supplies (page 84), fine-grained sand (available at crafts stores), glass bottle (or other object to shape candle), large container (such as a plastic bin or pail), pencil, paintbrush

1. Melt and tint beeswax according to the instructions on page 84. Combine sand with water by mixing with your hands until it packs firmly enough to hold an imprint.

2. Set the glass bottle into the sand, packing sand tightly around it; be sure there are several inches (7.5-10cm) of sand underneath the bottle, too, and that it stays upright. Grip the bottle firmly, and carefully ease it straight up and out of the sand. If the sand walls crumble, mix in a little more water and start over.

3. Cut a wick several inches (7.5-10cm) longer than the candle will be, and dip it in melted wax to stiffen it; let the wax dry. Use a pencil to make a hole at the bottom of the container. Place one end of the dry wick in the hole, and bury it using the pencil.

4. Making sure the wick stays upright and centered, pour the wax in a slow, steady stream (the wax will make a dent in the sand if it's poured too fast). Wax cools quickly, so if you're making more than 1 candle, return the wax to the heat between pours.

5. Let the candle set until it's completely cool (overnight is best) before removing it.

6. Dust off excess sand with a paintbrush (you can leave some clumps for effect), and use scissors to cut off the nub of excess wick and wax at the base. Trim the wick at the top to 1/4 inch (6mm).

If it weren't for the wicks, this collection of candles could be mistaken for a sand castle. They were shaped using sand buckets, and would make an excellent hostess gift for a visit to a beach house.

Be creative—try small flowerpots, shells, and sand-castle buckets for molds. Insert tapered objects into the sand with their narrow ends pointing down, so the impression remains intact when you remove the object.

The wax for these little candles was tinted seashell shades and poured into depressions in sand made by real shells. Either side of these candles can be used as the top, but sand inhibits burning. So if you place the molded side up, be sure to scrape away the sand from the wick.

Mini flowerpots with ribbed rims make impressions in sand that can turn out charming candles just bigger than votives. They would be perfect dotted along a table set for a garden party.

HOW TO MAKE FLOATING CANDLES

Floating candles add instant atmosphere to almost any setting—there's just something magical about fire dancing on water. Even better, there's no trick to making them. Like little boats, the candles float because of the way they're made. They're flat on the bottom and not too thick, so they won't tip or sink. You can buy molds for making them, but chances are, you've got the perfect tool in your kitchen already: Muffin tins, cookie cutters, and tartlet molds all have just the right shapes. Use the basic technique, shown here with muffin tins, for the other molds on the following pages.

FLOATING-CANDLE SUPPLIES Basic Supplies (page 84; use wicks with tabs); muffin tins, cookie cutters, and tartlet tins for molds; nylon stocking

1. Coat molds with mold-release spray or nonstick cooking-oil spray. Melt and tint wax according to the instructions on page 84 (using wax bricks or old candles), and pour into the molds.

2. Carefully lower in the wicks. After candles harden (which takes about 1 to 2 hours), lift them out by the wicks. If they resist, put the molds in the freezer until they pop out easily. Wipe off any haze with the stocking. Trim wicks, if necessary, to ¼ inch (6mm) before floating and lighting.

Float muffin tin candles in a shallow bowl with orchid blossoms. For uniform results when making candles in a variety of muffin tins and other small baking molds, pour the wax to a depth of no more than one inch (2.5cm). The large candles will burn for about three hours, the mini ones for one hour.

PROJECT: cookie-cutter floating candles

With a set of graduated star-shaped cookie cutters, you can make a constel-
lation to supply your dinner table with a galaxy of gentle light. Float some in
little bowls, and set others in shallow dishes of water. To use a cookie cutter
as a candle mold, choose one in a simple, broad shape with straight (rather
than curved) lines.

PROJECT SUPPLIES Floating-Candle Supplies (see opposite), masking tape, aluminum foil

HOW-TO Prepare cookie cutters as molds: Run masking tape along the edge of the
cutter, snipping tape at the corners so you can fold the tape up; place the cutter
on aluminum foil, pressing tape down to secure it. Melt and tint (if desired) the
wax, as described on page 84, and make the candles as described opposite. Beeswax works best for this project; it has a lower melting point and more viscous consistency when melted, which prevents it from leaking out of the makeshift mold.

HOW TO MAKE CONTAINER CANDLES

As the name implies, the wax for these candles is poured not into a mold, but into a decorative container. Use small pretty cups, glasses, or jelly jars, or get creative and use unexpected containers, such as eggshells and lemons, shown here. Just choose vessels that will hold wax and won't present a fire hazard (even so, never leave lit candles unattended). As you'll see from the following four projects, the technique for making them is similar but varies slightly depending on the container you choose.

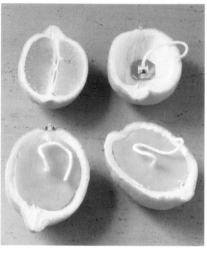

PROJECT: lemon candles

These candles add bright charm to a set table. Make them the day you'll use them—as the rinds dry out, they pull away from the wax. It's best to set them into a dish once they're lit, in case of spills.

PROJECT SUPPLIES Basic Supplies (page 84; use wicks with tabs), lemons, waxed paper

HOW-TO Cut wicking into 3- to 4-inch (7.5-10cm) lengths; fit with wick tabs. Melt and tint (if desired) the wax according to the instructions on page 84. Cut the lemons in half lengthwise, and carefully remove the pulp. Place the halved rinds on waxed paper, and press the prongs of the wick tab firmly into the lemon rind. Hold the wicks taut with one hand and pour wax in with the other. Hold 2 to 3 minutes until skin forms on surface of candle, then release and continue to let harden. Cut wick to $1/4$ inch (6mm) before burning.

using old candles

If you're making small candles, instead of starting with new wax, you can melt down old candles, combining several in different colors. As you melt the wax, remove the wicks with tongs. Pieces of crayons can be added to tint the wax in desired shades.

PROJECT: teacup candles

Mismatched vintage teacups that have lost their saucers make charming receptacles for candles. You'll find them for next to nothing at thrift stores and yard sales. Give them as gifts, or collect an assortment of cups in patterns and colors that complement each other, and display them together.

PROJECT SUPPLIES Basic Supplies (page 84; use wicks with tabs), teacups

HOW-TO Melt and tint the wax according to instructions on page 84. Cut the wicking to the cup's height plus 2 inches (5cm). Fit 1 end with a wick tab; tie the other end around a skewer. Dip the wicking and the tab into melted wax to coat them. Remove and stick the tab to the cup's bottom. Pour in the wax, stopping about ½ inch (13mm) below the cup's rim. Allow the wax to set, about 1 hour. If a well develops in the wax while it's hardening, use another skewer to prick a circle of holes about 1/16 inch (1.6mm) deep around the wick. Pour in the melted wax until the surface is about ¼ inch (6mm) below the rim. Let it harden completely, at least 1 to 2 hours. Cut the wick to ¼ inch (6mm) before burning.

PROJECT: seashell candles

Recall walks on the beach with an assortment of candles fashioned from seashells. Deep shells, like clams and qua-hogs, work best and burn the longest.

PROJECT SUPPLIES Basic Supplies (page 84), bleach, seashells

HOW-TO Clean the shells in a weak solution of bleach and water; let them dry. Melt and tint (if desired) the wax according to the instructions on page 84; pale shades of pink are lovely with shells. If a shell has a tendency to wobble, stabilize it by resting it on top of a cup. Cut the wick to 2 to 3 inches (5-7.5cm), and attach it to a metal wick tab. Pour the melted wax into the shell, then place the wick and the tab in the bottom of the shell, being careful not to burn your fingers. If the wick droops, trim it slightly. Let it cool until hardened, at least 1 to 2 hours. Trim the wick to ¼ inch (6mm) before burning. And be careful: The top layer of the wax hardens first, but the melted wax underneath will spill out if the candle is moved before it has a chance to cool.

PROJECT: eggshell candles

What could be more fitting for a spring table than a dozen brightly colored eggs doubling as candles?

PROJECT SUPPLIES Basic Supplies (page 84; use wire-core wicking), straight pin, eggs, vinegar (optional), food coloring, egg carton, funnel, eggcups

HOW-TO Use a pin to make a hole in the top of each egg, and then enlarge the holes. Pour out the eggs, and reserve them for another use. Remove the shells to one-third of the way down and clean them well (you can use vinegar), then dye them (if desired) with food coloring according to package instructions. Place the shells in an egg carton. Melt and tint wax according to instructions on page 84. Cut wire-core wicking to 4-inch (10cm) lengths, flatten one end, and fasten to the bottom of the shells with bits of warm wax. Use a funnel to fill the shells with wax. Let the wax harden, at least 1 to 2 hours. Trim the wicks to ¼ inch (6mm), and place the candles in ceramic eggcups before lighting.

ROLLED AND CUTOUT CANDLES

BASIC SUPPLIES

beeswax sheets

baking sheet

hair dryer

cotton wicking

craft knife

ruler

cutting mat with a grid

These creations start with sheets of beeswax—not melted wax—so they're a breeze to make. The sheets (usually 8 ½ by 16 ¾ inches [21.5cm x 42.5cm]) are sold in multiple colors and smooth or textured finishes. They're wonderfully malleable: Roll them up around a length of wicking to make a taper or a pillar candle (pillars are wider), or sandwich the wicking between fun shapes formed with a cookie cutter. Add wooden picks to the shaped ones to create custom birthday candles.

HOW TO MAKE ROLLED CANDLES

Both taper candles and pillar candles are made by rolling sheets of beeswax around a wick. It is important that the edges on the sheets of wax be perfectly straight and the corners square. Trim them on a cutting mat with a grid, and remove any bits of wax or buildup. For wider candles, it helps to roll against a ruler.

ROLLED CANDLE SUPPLIES Basic Supplies (see above)

With a ruler and craft knife, cut a sheet of wax that's the width you want the height of your candle to be. Cut the wicking ½ inch (13mm) longer than this measurement. Lay the wicking near the edge of the sheet, allowing a ½-inch (13mm) overhang. Fold the wax edge over the wicking, and roll tightly until the candle is the desired thickness. Trim excess wax, and smooth the edge. If you need to add another wax sheet to reach the desired thickness, add it flush with the first sheet, and keep rolling. Continue adding sheets as necessary.

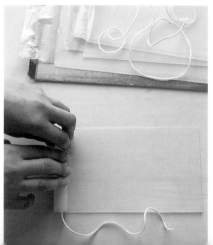

After rolling a candle, try adding one more layer of wax around the outside in a different color for a pleasing contrast.

Handmade rolled candles, whether thin tapers or substantial pillars, make a welcome gift. To package them as shown here, cut a band of pretty paper to fit around the center of the candles, and secure it with double-sided tape. Also cut paper to wrap around a matchbox, and secure with double-sided tape. Use ribbon to bind the matchbox to the candle (using a small piece of double-sided tape to prevent the box from slipping).

HOW TO MAKE CUTOUT CANDLES

With a selection of cookie cutters and several beeswax sheets, you can create candles to suit any occasion.

CUTOUT-CANDLE SUPPLIES Basic Supplies (page 102), metal cookie cutters, cocktail picks or flat toothpicks

1. Place a wax sheet on a baking sheet; apply low heat from a hair dryer. Cut 4 or 6 shapes (depending on the thickness you want) with a cookie cutter. You'll layer the shapes to create a more substantial figure (the more layers you use, the more opaque the candle will be and the longer it will burn).

2. Align a length of wick down the center of one of your shapes, leaving a little space at the bottom, and allowing ½ inch (13mm) to extend over the top. If you'll be placing the candle on top of a dessert, align a pick (a cocktail pick for larger shapes and flat toothpicks for smaller ones), at the bottom, leaving a bit of space between the wick and the pick. Lay another shape on top, and press them together with your fingertips, beginning at the center and working outward. Repeat to join the remaining layers, adding equal numbers on both sides of the wick. Apply low heat from a hair dryer; press again so the layers adhere to each other.

Flowers in four shapes and sizes, combined with leaves, make for a garden of sweet treats. To add a monogram, use small alphabet cutters or a sharp knife to cut a letter freehand. Apply leaves, letters, and any other details the same way as the leaves—with a little pressure from your fingertips and gentle heat from the hair dryer.

If you're making multiple candles, run the cutters under hot water every so often to remove buildup and ensure a clean silhouette.

PROJECT: **tapers with toppers**

This project combines two techniques—making rolled candles and making cutout candles. The results have both elegance and whimsy, and can be adapted to suit any holiday or other motif.

PROJECT SUPPLIES Basic Supplies (page 102), metal cookie cutters

HOW-TO Following the instructions on the opposite page, cut 4 or 6 of the same shape from beeswax sheets. Following instructions on page 102, make a taper, but use a wick that is ½-inch (13mm) longer than the combined height of the taper and the shape you're attaching. With a craft knife, cut a ½-inch (13mm) deep notch in the top of the taper, carefully maneuvering around the wick; remove any excess wax with the knife. Pull the wick taut, and fit an equal number of cutouts in grooves on both sides of the wick. If necessary, soften excess wax with a hair dryer, and use it to secure the cutouts. Press the cutout layers to adhere.

CLAY

Although it generally starts out as an ordinary block, clay can become most anything in a crafter's hands: Careful pulling and pressing might yield a delicate gardenia; a series of neat trims could turn out a tiny star-shaped button. While true clay comes from the earth, the clays used on the following pages are manufactured. Polymer clay was developed around the 1930s, along with other plastics, but wasn't sold as a modeling compound until a few decades later. It and other man-made clays can be rolled into a perfect sphere or a long snake, or sculpted into a variety of shapes. They can be stretched and squeezed. Two colors can be smooshed together to create a new shade. If you're not satisfied with a clay creation, squish it into a ball and start over. The clays used on the following pages don't need to be baked in a kiln; the oven in your kitchen— or air alone—is enough to set your finished works of art.

ABOUT THE MATERIALS

CLAY Both polymer clay, which is set by baking, and lightweight air-dry clay—the two clays used for the following projects—are sold in plastic-wrapped cubes and come in a wide array of colors. If you can't find the exact shade you're looking for, you can mix existing colors to achieve the perfect hue. You can also knead in acrylic paint to tint it (see page 109 for instructions). Lightweight air-dry clay holds its shape nicely, can be spread thin, and is more malleable, and hence preferable for sculpting lifelike flower petals. Because it's lightweight, it's also ideal for crafting pieces that are meant to be worn. To store unused clay, tightly wrap it in plastic and tuck it into an airtight container.

OPPOSITE Dainty clay gardenias make a present extra-special, no matter what's inside the box. The same flowers can be wired to bobby pins (right) or headbands (page 108) to make pretty hair accessories.

CLAY-SCULPTING TOOLS You can purchase tools for cutting, decorating, shaping, and smoothing clay. Several of the projects that follow instruct you to use the rounded end of a clay sculpting tool; feel free to improvise.

CLAY SCISSORS You'll find specialty clay scissors in many crafts stores, but a plastic knife or any pair of small, inexpensive scissors will work just as well. Wash scissors you use for paper or fabric after working with clay.

PROJECT: gift-box topper

(OPPOSITE) A gardenia, which is a relatively flat flower, works well as a gift topper when made from clay. You can also use a lightweight air-dry clay flower to make a napkin ring or multiple flowers to make a garland. Simply follow the instructions below, then string to desired length.

PROJECT SUPPLIES Basic Supplies (page 108), tapestry needle, thin ribbon or seam binding

HOW-TO Make and dry a clay gardenia, following the instructions on page 110. Thread a tapestry needle with a length of thread. Draw the tapestry needle through the base of the flower. Use the thread to cinch the wide ribbon, as shown opposite.

AIR-DRY CLAY FLOWERS

BASIC SUPPLIES
lightweight air-dry clay
clay-sculpting tools
clay scissors
acrylic paint (optional)
rolling pin (optional)
toothpick (optional)

Nothing breathes life into a room or brightens a friend's day quite like a bunch of flowers. With lightweight air-dry clay, you can create blooms—which will never wilt or need water—with the most natural-looking petals. Use them to adorn headbands, gifts, and more. The flowers on these pages were made in life-size dimensions; once you've mastered those, try casting some in miniature to make dainty earrings or charms.

PROJECT: clay-flower headband

A crown of faux blooms is a lovely accent for a flower girl or a Halloween fairy. You can also wire lightweight air-dry clay flowers to individual barrettes.

PROJECT SUPPLIES Basic Supplies (see above), headband or barrettes, seam binding or ribbon, bonding cement, tapestry needle, white cloth-covered wire

HOW-TO Wrap a headband or the top half of a barrette with seam binding or ribbon and use bonding cement to secure the ends. Following the instructions beginning on page 109, make flowers, as desired. (The number will vary based on the size of the flowers and the size of the headband; there are 11 various flowers on the headband pictured.) Once the flowers have dried, push a tapestry needle through the base of each. Cut a 15-inch (38cm) length of very thin white cloth-covered wire; a thick wire will be harder to wrap tightly, and will keep the headband from lying flat. Thread 1 end of the wire through the base of the center flower. Holding the flower tightly against the headband or barrette, wrap the wire twice on each side of the flower to secure. Continue attaching flowers on either side. When all the flowers are attached, trim any excess wire and tuck the ends underneath the flowers.

Be sure all the flowers are completely dry before using them in a project.

ROSE   DAISY   RANUNCULUS

clay each time and working in circles from the center outward. Curl the petals outward, opening them more and more with each rotation away from the center.

daisy

The daisy's long fringed petals are made from a strip of clay wrapped around the familiar bright-yellow center.

PROJECT SUPPLIES Basic Supplies (opposite)

HOW-TO Mix a marble-size ball of clay to the desired center color. Use a rolling pin to flatten a ball of white clay about 2 inches (5cm) wide and 7 inches (18cm) long, taking care not to allow the clay to become too thin to remove from your work surface. Using clay scissors, cut thin strips on one side without cutting all the way to the other side. Attach the uncut edge of the strip to the centerpiece, pinching it at the bottom to secure the strip. Wrap the strip of petals around the center, pinching it at the base as you go. Shape the petals outward and away from the center. Finish the daisy with a toothpick, making small pricks in the center to add texture.

ranunculus

The ranunculus is a dense flower with thin petals. Work carefully to avoid tearing the clay.

PROJECT SUPPLIES Basic Supplies (opposite)

HOW-TO Create a distinctive center with a pea-size ball of black clay. Make small green inner petals, then attach them to the center, pressing the petals along its bottom. Mix the desired petal color; ranunculus comes in yellow, orange, pink, and white. Sculpt the petals as you would rose petals (see above), but keep each one the same size. Wrap the petals as you would rose petals, but don't curl or fold them. Instead, thin the petals' tips by pinching each one.

tip

To tint white clay, knead in a few drops of acrylic paint until the desired color is reached. Wear rubber gloves to avoid staining your skin.

rose

A rose's petals are generally not all the exact same color. For the most natural-looking results, try using two or three slightly different shades of clay on the same flower.

PROJECT SUPPLIES Basic Supplies (opposite)

HOW-TO Mix very small batches of clay to the desired colors; each petal will require a ball of clay about the size of a pea. Work one petal at a time, gently flattening the clay in your hand, taking care not to press it too thin. Unevenly shaped petals will make the finished flower appear realistic. Slightly curl the first petal around itself to form the rose's center. Make the second petal. Wrap the second petal around the first, then attach the two by gently pressing them together at the base. Continue in this way, using a slightly larger ball of

PEONY   GARDENIA   MARIGOLD   LEAF

crafting petals one at a time and an-choring them to the center petal. Keep in mind that a gardenia's petals are narrower than a rose's and square at the ends. Try using clay scissors to shape the petals' ends. Gently press the round end of a clay-sculpting tool inside the petals to give them a curved, realistic appearance. Once you have a full, tight, upward-facing center, sculpt the surrounding petals out and down to capture the gardenia's shape.

marigold

Marigolds are thick and tightly packed with petals.

PROJECT SUPPLIES Basic Supplies (page 108)

HOW-TO Mix batches of clay in shades of orange, yellow, or red. Each petal will require a ball of clay about half the size of a pea. Make petals 1 at a time. Form the petals by flattening them in your hand, making each roughly the same size. Attach them together at their bases. To achieve a dense bloom, first fill the flower with four rotations of petals. Then attach the petals under-neath until you've created four rows of petals. (Try using a different color for the last two rows of petals on the bot-tom.) Finish the marigold by wrapping the base in green clay, creating the flower's receptacle. Gently press it into an oblong shape, and add lines to it using the pointed end of a clay-sculpting tool.

peony

A peony's spindly center pieces are easily mimicked with extra-thin ropes of clay.

PROJECT SUPPLIES Basic Supplies (page 108)

HOW-TO Form the peony's center with a pea-size ball of dark red clay. Make a long, narrow snake of yellow clay; cut it into 1-inch (2.5cm) pieces. Attach the 1-inch (2.5cm) pieces to the center and trim them to a uniform length with clay scissors. Blend white and red clay to create petals, leaving the clay streaky rather than completely mixed. Make

the petals one at a time. Pinch each petal's tip to thin it, and pull it into a ragged, wavy edge. Encircle the center with one row of petals, curling each one upward. Repeat, securing rows of larger petals under the first, stretching them out and away from the inner petals.

gardenia

A first-time clay-flower sculptor might start by crafting a gardenia, which has the fewest petals.

PROJECT SUPPLIES Basic Supplies (page 108)

HOW-TO Using white clay, form the gar-denia as you would a rose (page 109),

leaf

Leaves are easier to craft than flowers; the more you make as "filler," the more space you can have between blooms.

PROJECT SUPPLIES Basic Supplies (page 108)

HOW-TO Sculpt a leaf as you would a petal, using clay scissors to trim it into shape or make its edges serrated. Use the pointed end of a clay-sculpting tool to make a crease down its center and add veins; add a short, narrow snake of clay for a stem.

POLYMER-CLAY TRINKETS

BASIC SUPPLIES

polymer clay

butter or plastic knife

toothpick

rolling pin (optional)

Handcrafted objects needn't be grand in scale or complicated in design to be impressive. The diminutive polymer clay trinkets that follow—beads and buttons—are easy enough for a child to mold. An adult's hands might produce more refined stripes and dots, but children's pieces, with less-than-perfect squiggles and crinkles—have an appeal all their own. Grown-ups, of course, have to help when it's time to bake the clay.

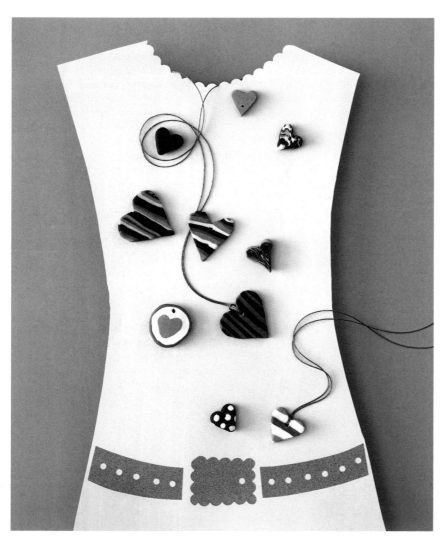

PROJECT: necklaces

These pendants make heartfelt adornments. Make the beads, then string them onto silk cord knotted into a loop large enough to go over the recipient's head.

PROJECT SUPPLIES Basic Supplies (above), small cookie cutters, silk cord

HOW-TO Make pendants: The bigger hearts were made by cutting striped clay (page 112) with small cookie cutters. The small hearts were shaped by hand. To make marbleized clay, mash 2 colors of clay together in your palms until the colors are incorporated in a single ball but not smoothly blended. To make a polka-dotted heart, roll the first color of clay (the color for the dots) into a thin strand. Cut the strand into pieces, then roll the pieces into tiny balls. Roll the second color of clay into a ball; arrange the tiny balls atop it. Roll to smooth the dots, then shape the polka-dotted ball into a heart with your fingertips. The round pendant was created by pressing a flat, handcrafted heart into a bead, made using the Bull's-Eye technique (page 112). Poke a hole with a toothpick, for hanging, before baking according to package instructions.

three techniques

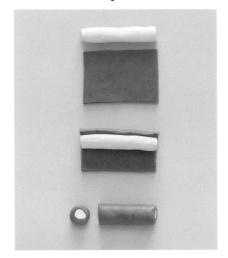
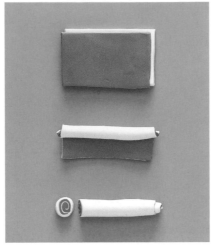

BULL'S EYE Roll a piece of clay into a log between your palms. Use a rolling pin to flatten a piece of different-colored clay into a sheet; trim to form a rectangular sheet (the length should match that of the log). Put the log on the rectangular sheet, then roll the two together so the sheet wraps around the log. Roll it again between your palms. Cut slices to desired thickness with a sharp knife. Poke a hole, for hanging, with a toothpick or paper clip. Bake as directed on package instructions.

SWIRLS Use a rolling pin to flatten two pieces of different-colored clay into sheets. (If you like, you could use three pieces.) Stack the sheets, and trim the sides of the stack to form a rectangle. Roll them into a log. Roll them again between your palms to the desired width (this will also help the sheets of clay stick together better). Cut slices to desired thickness with a sharp knife. Poke a hole, for hanging, with a tooth-pick or paper clip. Bake as directed on package instructions.

STRIPES Use a rolling pin to flatten several pieces of different-colored clay into sheets. Stack the sheets; trim the sides of the stack to form a rectangle. With a plastic knife, cut the rectangle into slices. Lay the slices on their sides so they touch (stripes facing up). Flatten with a rolling pin to the desired thickness. Cut out shapes with a small cookie cutter. Poke a hole, for hanging, with a toothpick or paper clip. Bake as directed on package instructions.

clay pointers

Whatever you're shaping, you'll need to work with clay that's soft and pliable. A fresh piece of clay may feel hard or crumbly when you first unwrap it— just knead and roll it in your hands to improve the texture.

If the clay becomes too stiff, wrap it in an old damp washcloth (some of the pigment will leach out) to revive it.

To keep flowers from flattening as they dry, bunch paper towels into mounds and place the flowers on top; the mounds will support the flowers from the bottom.

Experiment with clay-sculpting tools to add texture to petals and leaves. Your fingerprints naturally lend texture to the clay; mimic a plant's veins or a flower's petals by pressing into it.

Wash your hands thoroughly after handling clay to avoid ingesting any of the chemicals it contains.

When baking polymer clay, pay atten-tion—if it burns, your crafts are ruined.

When you're working on a project with multiple flowers of the same type, vary their size and colors to make their appearance more realistic.

If you're working with several colors of clay, make sure your hands are clean when you switch colors so the shade doesn't transfer.

PROJECT: colorful clay buttons

These buttons were tailor-made for kids. Use them to replace the buttons on a plain shirt to make it more fun to wear.

PROJECT SUPPLIES Basic Supplies (page 111)

HOW-TO Make disks, following the instructions opposite, or flatten a ball for a solid button. To make a polka-dotted disk, roll the first color of clay (the color for the dots) into a thin strand. Cut the strand into pieces, then roll the pieces into tiny balls. Roll the second color of clay into a ball; arrange the tiny balls on top of it. Roll to smooth the dots, then flat ten the polka-dotted ball. Flower-topped disks are made in a similar fashion, but the dots (and a thin rope of clay, for the stem) are arranged in a flower pattern. To craft shapes (such as hearts, stars, or flowers), trim the disks with a plastic knife, or cut out from flattened clay using a small cookie cutter. Poke 2 or 4 holes in the shapes with a toothpick to make buttons. Bake the buttons according to package instructions. Stitch them onto clothes.

DECOUPAGE

Decoupage is artistic sleight of hand. What appears to be a painted design is actually paper glued in place. What looks like lacquer is just a few coats of clear varnish. And what begins as an unremarkable piece of furniture becomes a distinctive design statement. The word *decoupage* derives from the French *découper,* meaning "to cut." The craft owes much to the exquisite Asian lacquerwork so widely admired in seventeenth-century Europe. Imports from Asia were in high demand, so artisans, particularly in Venice, mimicked them by cutting out prints and engravings, gluing them to furniture, and covering them with varnish. The technique was called *lacca povera,* or "poor man's lacquer." A similar process, using flowers and other motifs, was popularized in England, and by the nineteenth century, decorative images were made specifically for this purpose. The Victorians used them on furniture as well as lamps and screens. As in the past, modern decoupage is used on a variety of objects, but is most popular on furniture. Yet today's decoupage tends to be a bit more whimsical. You can choose nearly any paper to work with, including pages from damaged old books, wallpaper, maps, and scraps of colorful paper. Try mingling oversize shapes with smaller ones to emphasize scale. As you work, the pattern itself will draw your eye, and the furniture will fade dutifully into the background. It won't disappear, but it will seem to—almost like magic.

ABOUT THE MATERIALS

FURNITURE Start from scratch with an unfinished piece. You can also revamp a piece you already have, or a flea-market find. If the furniture is painted, sand it and paint it another color, if you like. Because intricate curves make the paper application difficult, it's best to use furniture with simple lines.

OPPOSITE **Traditional decoupage motifs are small in scale, but incorporating larger, bolder patterns gives this craft a modern sensibility. Here, large leaves from one wallpaper form the basic pattern; flowers from another fill in the spaces. To unify the design, larger leaves were interspersed with slender fronds.**

DECOUPAGE ARTWORK Thin paper is best for decoupage because it will create minimal texture on the surface of the furniture. Wallpaper and inexpensive prints—such as those from damaged books—provide ready-made designs. Cut out the images carefully with scissors or a craft knife. Origami paper and other paper can also be used. Construction paper is not a good choice, because it tends to fade.

WATER-BASED SEALANT GLUE This acts as both an adhesive and a sealant: It can be applied to affix the paper designs to the furniture, or as a topcoat to seal the design. The sealant can also be applied to the top of the paper design to strengthen it before applying to the furniture. Keep a box of baby wipes handy while working with the sealant to keep hands clean.

BRAYER Use this handled roller to press trapped bubbles from under the paper. It will help keep your decoupaged images flat against the surface and prevent creases from forming.

BASIC SUPPLIES

decoupage artwork

scissors

low-tack masking tape

water-based sealant glue (such as Mod Podge)

pencil

ruler

craft knife

brayer

paper towels

water-based satin varnish

HOW TO DECOUPAGE FURNITURE

If the furniture you begin with is unfinished, you'll need about a week to let the paint cure. Although the paint may dry in a day, it will continue to harden over the course of the week. You'll also need to allow time for the varnish to dry between coats. Look for botanical wallpapers—new or vintage—at wallpaper stores, antiques shops, or online auctions.

DECOUPAGE SUPPLIES Basic Supplies (page 115), unfinished piece of furniture, fine sandpaper, damp cloth or tack cloth, latex paint, paintbrushes, baby wipes (optional), kraft paper

1. If using unfinished furniture, lightly sand the item with fine sandpaper; wipe with damp cloth to remove dust. Paint with latex wall paint, and let cure for 1 week; lightly sand surface with the sandpaper before proceeding. Tape kraft paper to a flat work surface. Tape a section of wallpaper on top. Brush wallpaper with sealant glue to strengthen. Let sealant dry according to the manufacturer's instructions.

2. Using a craft knife, carefully cut out the motifs. Stick small loops of masking tape onto the back of the motifs and arrange them on the piece of furniture until you are pleased with the design. To wrap a cutout around a corner, fold the paper over the corner and pinch it with your fingers to crease. To glue paper over the seam where two doors meet, use masking tape to position a motif so it crosses over the doors.

3. To cut the paper at the seam, mark the seam with a pencil and ruler. Remove the taped image, then carefully cut along the line with a craft knife. (Do this anywhere the paper runs across a seam, such as at the edge of a door when wrapping a motif around a corner.)

4. Remove 1 taped motif at a time, lightly marking the spot on the furniture with a pencil (under the image). Pull off the tape; brush the back of the paper with sealant glue, and quickly apply the image in the correct spot. Take care to match up images at the seams. Smooth with clean fingers (remove sealant from hands with baby wipes, if necessary).

5. Run a brayer over the image you've just glued to remove any air bubbles. Excess glue may squeeze out along the edges; quickly wipe it away with a paper towel.

6. Using a very thin paintbrush, apply additional glue to edges that curl, or places where there wasn't enough glue. Smooth the image with the brayer again; remove excess glue. Let the glue sealant dry overnight. Then apply water-based satin varnish. Brush the entire piece; work quickly, as varnish dries fast and can turn cloudy if you go back over already-covered areas. Apply at least 3 coats to protect the surface, or more for a smoother finish; allow it to dry overnight between each coat.

PROJECT: **botanical-print dresser**

Choose a dresser—either unfinished or finished—with no curves or moldings on the drawers so the prints can be smoothly applied. This project simply uses the pages of old broken books, making it distinct from other decoupage that requires cutting intricate designs. Books with botanical prints like the ones shown here can be purchased inexpensively at flea markets, online auction sites, and tag sales. The yellow background of this dresser brings out the same shade in the artwork.

PROJECT SUPPLIES Basic Supplies (page 115), dresser, fine sandpaper, latex paint, paintbrushes, kraft paper, flashlight, awl or pushpin, square ruler, drill (optional), decorative knobs (optional), appropriate hardware (optional)

1. Remove hardware from the dresser, then sand, paint, and cure as described on page 116. Tape kraft paper to a flat work surface. Secure botanical prints to the sheet of kraft paper with masking tape. To strengthen the prints, brush each one with glue sealant. Let it dry according to manufacturer's instructions.

2. Using a pencil and ruler, create a kraft paper template of a drawer. This will allow you to determine how many prints you'll need and what each print's dimensions should be. Cut off one section of the drawer template to use as a guide for sizing the prints. Cut just outside the pencil line, adding about 1/16 inch (1.6mm) extra on one side, so prints will overlap slightly. Lay template on top of a print, and mark the corners, as shown. Cut prints to size, using a craft knife and ruler.

3. Using masking tape on the back of the images, lay out your design on the furniture, stepping back occasionally to see how it looks. For balance, this design alternates airier grass prints with images of denser foliage. When you finish your design, remove drawers from the dresser before applying glue.

4. Remove tape and brush the back of a print with glue sealant. Quickly apply it to the end of a drawer; smooth with a brayer to remove air bubbles. Repeat at other end, then at the center, overlapping if necessary. Let dry overnight. Apply at least 2 coats of varnish to protect the surface; work quickly, as varnish may turn cloudy if brushed over already-covered areas. Allow each coat to dry overnight.

5. Once the varnish is completely dry, you can replace the original drawer pulls easily by shining a flashlight on the inside of the drawers and looking for where the light shows through the small hole in the front of each drawer. Use a small awl or pushpin to puncture the paper over each hole, and then attach drawer pulls. If you are adding new pulls, measure out their placement with a pencil and a square ruler.

6. This dresser originally had 1 knob per drawer, but installing 2 per drawer gives it a more elegant appearance. Drill new holes (right through the paper), then attach the knobs and hardware.

PROJECT: **three bears clothes hangers**

Goldilocks's three bear friends can live right in the bedroom closet with these cute and useful kid-sized hangers. A set of three makes a nice baby shower gift, and they're easy to make: Each bear's face is constructed of just nine circles glued together.

PROJECT SUPPLIES Basic Supplies (page 115; use origami or craft paper in 3 contrasting colors), bear template (page 376), 3 wooden hangers

HOW-TO Trace the 9 circles of the template onto your various papers and cut out. Remember to choose a basic color for the bear's head and ears, and contrasting colors for its mouth, the inside of ears, the nose, and the eyes. Make sure the surface of the hangers is clean and dry. Mark with a pencil where the head should be placed. Follow the instructions for decoupaging on page 117, gluing down the head first, then layering the ears, mouth, eyes, and nose over the head. You can omit the extra step of varnishing, if desired.

PROJECT: **bird dresser decals**

Positioning paper birds along the bottom of a drawer makes them look as if they're perched on a wire. These bluebirds are cut out of different patterns and shades. You can achieve a similar effect using reds (for cardinals), yellows (for canaries), or pinks (for any bird at all).

PROJECT SUPPLIES Basic Supplies (page 115; use origami or other patterned paper, wallpaper, or card stock), bird template (page 376), painted dresser or other furniture

HOW-TO Enlarge the template to desired size. Trace the template onto your paper, and cut out as many as you want, making sure to cut out a contrasting color or pattern for the wing. Make sure the dresser's surface is clean and dry, then mark where you want to place the birds. Decoupage the birds onto the dresser, using the basic instructions on page 117. You can omit the extra step of varnishing, if desired.

PROJECT: **whale step stool**

Any kid will have a whale of a time sitting or stepping on this little stool. Even though shades of blue work for this aquatic animal, you could use a child's favorite colors instead.

PROJECT SUPPLIES Basic Supplies (page 115; use origami or other patterned paper—choose a darker solid blue for the eye and underwater section, and a different pattern for both of the whale's other parts), whale template (page 376), unpainted stool, light and dark-blue acrylic paint

HOW-TO Enlarge the whale template and place it on an unpainted stool. With a pencil, extend the waterline that runs through the whale's body to the edges and down the sides of the stool. Remove the template. Paint the sky and the legs of the stool light blue, and the ocean a darker shade. Let the paint dry and cure for about a week, then decoupage the whale onto the stool: Cut out the whale template in 2 colors (1 for above the sea, and 1 for below). Mark where the whale's body will go on the surface, and then follow the basic instructions for decoupage on page 117. If desired, finish with a coat of water-based satin varnish once the glue is completely dry (apply according to the manufacturer's instructions). This will protect the stool from moisture in the bathroom.

PROJECT: **dog and cat chair backs**

What suits a friendly Scottie better than plaid? Or a kitten better than calico? If you aren't able to find the perfect pattern in a decorative paper, simply photocopy a favorite fabric to make a paper version.

PROJECT SUPPLIES Basic Supplies (page 115; use calico or plaid paper), cat or dog template (page 376), painted child's chair

HOW-TO Enlarge the cat or dog template, trace it onto your paper, and cut it out. Add details, such as eyes, nose, whiskers, and collar. Clean the surface of the chair, and let it dry. Make a mark with a pencil to indicate where the cat or dog's body will go. Follow the basic decoupaging instructions on page 117. You can omit the extra step of varnishing, if desired.

HOW TO ETCH GLASS

An elegant mirror with regal monogram and laurel motif, surrounded by a gilt frame, adds polish to an entryway. The instructions below are specific to the mirror, but the technique can be adapted for any glass surface.

ETCHING SUPPLIES Basic Supplies (page 123), mirror, template (page 377), low-tack spray adhesive, pencil, ruler

1. Clean and dry the glass surface thoroughly before starting the etching process. Photocopy the template or another design; for a monogram, print a letter from a computer or enlarge one on a photocopier. Center a piece of self-adhesive shelf liner on the mirror, carefully smoothing it to remove all bubbles and creases. With a pencil and ruler, draw a border around the inside edge of shelf liner; use this as a guide to center the template. Coat the template back with spray adhesive; line the template up with the border, and smooth it out over the shelf liner. With a craft knife, carefully cut out the monogram and design on the template, cutting through the shelf liner as well. As you work, peel up the cutout shelf liner and template to reveal the mirror. Press down the edges of the remaining shelf liner.

2. Wearing rubber gloves, use a paintbrush to fill in the stencil with a thick, even coat of etching cream, following the manufacturer's instructions. Leave it on for the recommended time.

3. If the cream is reusable (check the label for manufacturer's instructions), scoop it into the container; rinse mirror with a sponge or paper towels and warm water (do not reuse the sponge for other purposes). Peel back the stencil to remove.

Be sure to apply a smooth, thick layer of etching cream; a thin, uneven coat will result in an inconsistent finish.

Practice on a jar until
you're comfortable
with the process.

PROJECT: etched glasses and kitchen canisters

Etched accents transform plain drinkware and kitchen canisters into functional decorative items.

PROJECT SUPPLIES Basic Supplies (page 123), blue painter's or masking tape, transfer paper, adhesive hole reinforcers, alphabet and other decorative stickers or templates (pages 377–378).

HOW-TO Choose a design. For stripes, apply lines of painter's or masking tape cut to desired width; use adhesive hole reinforcers (for loose-leaf paper) to make polka dots. For leaf designs, photocopy templates; to make monogrammed glassware, print letters from a computer. Make stencils: Place the templates or letters on a piece of shelf liner with a piece of transfer paper in between. Trace the outline of each shape, then remove template and transfer paper, and cut out forms with a craft knife. Press the design onto the glass. For the leaf glasses at left and the kitchen canisters on page 122, use stickers as "reverse stencils." For canisters: Mark a border using masking tape; use the border as a guide to keep letters level. Spell words using stickers (use store-bought stickers or make your own using the templates on page 378), and place a cutout patterned sticker underneath the lettering. With a paintbrush, apply a thick layer of etching cream to the glass. Leave the cream on for the recommended time, then rinse with warm water. Remove stencils.

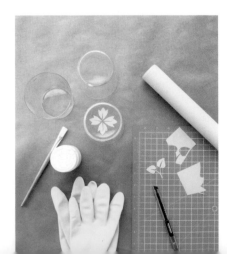

PROJECT: polka-dotted windowpane

An etched window, which lets light through but provides privacy, is the perfect solution for a bathroom that offers no view or faces a neighbor's window. The apothecary jars are etched with the same pattern, only in reverse.

PROJECT SUPPLIES Basic Supplies (page 123; use clear, self-adhesive shelf liner), paper, circle template, marker, tape, squeegee, pencil

HOW-TO Create your own meandering dot pattern on paper with a circle template (shown at left) and a marker. Carefully position paper on the outside of the glass, with the design facing in; tape it in place. Cover the inside of the glass with self-adhesive shelf liner. Smooth with a squeegee to eliminate bubbles. Line up the template circles with those on the paper and trace them with a pencil. Using a craft knife, cut around the circles. Peel off the self-adhesive shelf liner, leaving dots on the glass. Use a paintbrush to apply a thick coat of etching cream to the entire surface of the glass; even out with a squeegee. After the recommended time, remove the cream with the squeegee. Remove the remaining cream with a damp sponge. Peel off the dots.

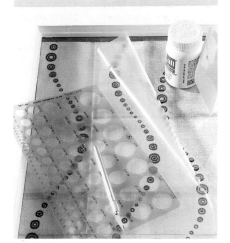

FABRIC FLOWERS

Play Mother Nature by creating gifts that feature lifelike blooms made from lightweight fabrics. The dainty flowers on the following pages may look ethereal, but they'll hold their shape well over time thanks to a store-bought stiffener, which makes even sheer material sturdy enough to cut with flower-, leaf-, and petal-shaped craft punches. Punched-out blooms can stand in place of real flowers in arrangements, or be used as embellishments for jewelry or hair accessories. Experiment with different fabrics and punches, and try mixing and matching different flowers in a single project. The creations are, some might say, as fresh as a daisy—so much so, you may want to keep one for yourself.

ABOUT THE MATERIALS

FABRIC Select very thin, lightweight fabrics, such as voile, thin shirting, or Indian cotton.

LIQUID FABRIC STIFFENER Apply this to fabric according to the manufacturer's instructions. The treated fabric will be rigid enough to be punched; the stiffener also keeps the punched flowers from fraying.

CRAFT PUNCHES You'll find flower punches in many shapes and sizes. Some resemble real flowers; others are more abstract. You'll also find punches in the shape of leaves and individual petals. The latter are more suitable for projects that involve

OPPOSITE **For a realistic presentation, punch flowers in several sizes and shades. When affixed to branches, they'll appear even more natural.**

petals being affixed to a flat surface (joining individual petals into three-dimensional flower shapes would be very difficult).

FLORAL PIPS These small wires with colored tips are used to make the stamens of silk flowers.

FLORAL WIRE Floral wire comes in several gauges; the higher the gauge, the thinner and more flexible the wire will be. The bouquets that follow were made using 24-gauge floral wire.

FLORAL TAPE Green floral tape is used to join the petals and stamen of each flower to its stem. When wrapped around the length of a stem, floral tape has a matte appearance. When a roll is unwrapped, the inner surface is smooth. Stretching the tape activates the wax on the inner surface and allows the tape to stick to itself.

BASIC SUPPLIES

fabric
shallow tray
medium paintbrush
liquid fabric stiffener
craft punches

PROJECT: blooming branches

Dozens of tiny cotton flowers (opposite) cling to branches gathered from the backyard.

PROJECT SUPPLIES Basic Supplies (see left), branches, hot glue

HOW-TO Punch fabric flowers (see "How to Punch Fabric Flowers," page 130). To achieve a naturally variegated look, punch the blooms from three shades of pink fabric and with punches in slightly varied sizes. Attach blooms to branches with hot glue; let dry before placing in a vase for display.

HOW TO PUNCH FABRIC FLOWERS

For some of the projects that follow, such as the pansies shown opposite, different-colored petals were layered to make a single bloom.

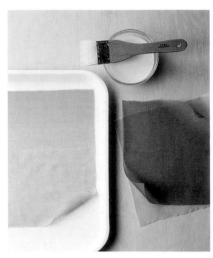

1. Lay a piece of fabric in a shallow tray. With a medium paintbrush, apply enough fabric stiffener to saturate, but not soak, the fabric. Let it dry, about 1 hour. Repeat with any remaining fabric.

2. Punch out petals and leaves as close together on the fabric as possible.

PROJECT: everlasting bouquets

A trio of vintage-style keepsake bouquets includes (clockwise from left) pink violets, blue hydrangeas, and purple-and-gold pansies.

PROJECT SUPPLIES Basic Supplies (page 129), micro hole punch, floral pips, contact cement, floral wire, floral tape

HOW-TO Punch fabric flowers (see "How to Punch Fabric Flowers," above). Using a micro hole punch, make a hole in the center of each bloom. Slip a pip through each hole, and secure it with a dab of contact cement. To make a stem, cut a length of floral wire, and wrap it around each pip with green floral tape. For leaves, glue floral wire to each one to create veins and stems. Wrap stems with floral tape. Gather blooms and leaves into a bouquet, and either tuck them in a vase or wrap the stems in more floral tape to join them.

PROJECT: punched-flower hair accessories

These clips are easy enough to create in multiples. They would make sweet gifts for a bridal party, or favors for a spring shower.

PROJECT SUPPLIES Basic Supplies (page 129), micro hole punch, floral pips, needle, thread, contact cement, bobby pins or hair combs, green paper (optional), leaf punch (optional)

HOW-TO Punch fabric flowers, following the instructions above. Using a micro hole punch, make a hole in the center of each bloom. Cut stem from a pip close to end. Slip a pip through each hole, and secure it with a dab of contact cement. With a needle and thread, hand-stitch blooms to bobby pins or combs; secure the back side of the stitches with contact cement. For a gift, insert the hairpins through holes made in a large leaf cut from green paper, and inscribe the recipient's name on the card.

PROJECT: **floral-pattern fabric boxes and books**

Bold patterns make a lasting impression on fabric-covered boxes and journals. Experiment with patterns and designs: The green diamond design here is made from the same petal craft punch used to create the brown flowers.

PROJECT SUPPLIES Basic Supplies (page 129), fabric-covered boxes or journals, grid ruler, glue stick

HOW-TO Punch fabric flowers and petals (see "How to Punch Fabric Flowers," page 130). Lay out your design. For linear patterns, use a grid ruler as a guide to keep them running straight. Apply petals or flowers with a glue stick; make sure to cover the back of each shape completely with the adhesive to prevent curling.

PROJECT: **fabric-flower card**

An array of petals and leaves appears to sprout from this greeting card.
Surprise the recipient with a card depicting her favorite flowers.

PROJECT SUPPLIES Basic Supplies (page 129), cards, pen, envelope, white craft glue,
pen, ribbon, double-sided glue dot

HOW-TO Punch fabric flowers and leaves (see "How to Punch Fabric Flowers,"
page 130). Glue just the centers of leaves and flowers to a card, so their tips curl
upward a little. Use different colors of fabric and different-shaped flowers to make
a vibrant bouquet. Layer leaves first, and place smallest flowers last, gluing the
flowers in place as you work. Draw stems and write a message by hand. With a
double-sided glue dot, affix a knotted ribbon on top of the stems as a bow.

Gilding lends a silvery luster to the interior of an ordinary display cupboard; it is also an accent on the doors. The pale-green base color matches the walls for a built-in effect. Polished-nickel knobs complete the look.

GILDING

You've likely seen an antique gilt picture frame or opulent gold fireplace mantel in a museum, or even in someone's home. These objects are coated in tissue-thin leaves of metal that are carefully glued to the surface in a process known as gilding. The technique dates back as far as 1500 B.C., when Egyptian craftsmen coated wooden furniture and sarcophagi in gold foil; many of these precious objects have been found in the tombs of the pharaohs. Examples of gilding appear in artwork from many traditions—among the most renowned are Orthodox Byzantine iconography, Italian Renaissance paintings, and aristocratic furniture from the sixteenth century. Traditionally, gilding is done in gold leaf, but you can also use other types of metal leaf. There are multiple methods for gilding, some quite complicated and labor-intensive. Yet, for the purposes of the home crafter, all you'll need are a few supplies, an object to gild, and several hours. The real beauty of this craft is that in relatively little time you can turn the humblest object—a flea-market chest, or even a hollow egg—into something truly luxurious.

ABOUT THE MATERIALS

GILDING LEAF This is essentially metal pounded into a very thin layer. Gold leaf comes in a variety of colors, including pink, yellow, and white. White gold is actually half gold, half silver. Because pure silver leaf can tarnish, most silver gilding is actually done with metal leaves made from nontarnishing alloys. Metal leaf is the catchall term used for imitation gold (also called composition leaf), aluminum, copper, and other gilding leaf that is not genuine gold or silver. Beginners should practice with metal leaf. Gilding leaves usually come separated by tissue paper in a booklet. Some gilding leaf comes attached to tissue paper; the leaf is transferred once its surface is pressed onto an object. Gilding leaf is very thin and delicate; you will need to handle each sheet very gently to prevent it from tearing. Close windows and turn off fans when working with the leaf; the smallest movements in air—even your breath—can make it more difficult to work with.

SIZE Size is what is used to apply gilding leaf to wood or other surfaces. Like paint, size can be oil- or water-based; oil-based size is often used for outdoor applications and will give the leaf a shinier, more luminescent appearance. Yet oil-based size also tends to be more toxic, and takes longer to dry. Water-based size is used for the projects in this book. The size is white and can be used for all colors of leaf. Let the size set and become tacky, per manufacturer's instructions, before applying the gilding leaf.

GILDER'S TIP This boxy brush is used to apply the gilding leaf to the object. To use, first create static on the brush by rubbing it against your hair or a sweater. Lightly touch the brush against the leaf; it will rise up off the stack and stick to the brush, at which point you can transfer the leaf to the item you're gilding. Touching the delicate leaf directly with your hands can cause it to rip, or even disintegrate. Brushes come in a variety of widths; smaller ones are better for working with small or intricate objects.

MASK Wear a dust mask while working to keep your breath from disturbing the delicate metal paper.

GLOVES Wearing white cotton gloves will keep the oils on your hands from staining or tarnishing the leaf, and will also keep the leaf from sticking and tearing.

BASIC SUPPLIES

gilding leaf

water-based size

gilder's tip

soft, natural-fiber paintbrush

dust mask

cotton gloves

HOW TO GILD

This technique can be used for any gilding project; in this case, a cabinet. Any ordinary, windowed cabinet can become the focal point of a room when a silvery finish is added to the interior. The color of the cabinet underneath could compromise the result, so paint the interior silver before applying the size and leaf. Remove the back of your cabinet and paint it silver, too, so any cracks in leafing won't show. Let the paint cure for a week before applying the size and gilding leaf. If the paint hasn't cured, solvents in the size may cause the paint to bubble. If using gilding leaf other than gold or silver, you can paint the cabinet white; this will make the color appear brighter.

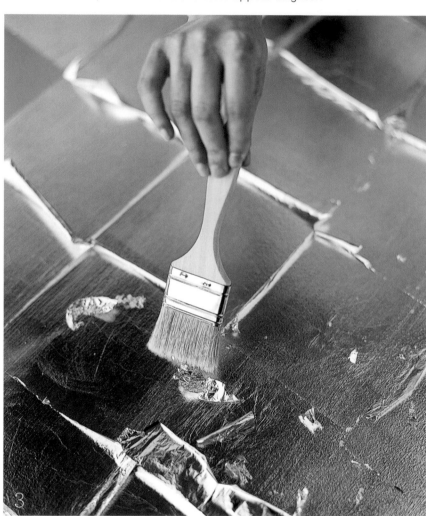

GILDING SUPPLIES Basic Supplies (page 135; use aluminum leaf), cabinet or other furniture with windows, silver paint, 4-inch (10cm) paint roller

1. Apply size to the cabinet with a paint roller, and let it set until tacky, following manufacturer's instructions (about 20 minutes). Generate static on the gilder's tip brush by brushing it against your hair or a sweater. Holding the booklet or stack of leaf at a slightly downward angle, touch bristles of brush to the edge of an exposed aluminum leaf sheet; slide the sheet about ½ inch (13mm) over the booklet edge. Bring the leaf to the surface of the cabinet. Hold the sheet near the surface—it will adhere to the size when the gilder's tip gets close.

2. Tap the sheet into place with the soft, natural-fiber paintbrush (make sure that it is dry). Continue, overlapping squares by ¼ to ½ inch (6–13mm).

3. Smooth the edges of the leaf with the dry brush.

 When handling gilding leaf, always work in a draft-free room, and wear a dust mask to keep your breath from disturbing the paper.

PROJECT: **gilded mirror**

This softly reflective surface, backed with silver leaf, is reminiscent of the deep patina on antique mirrors. In fact, the project is a form of *eglomise*, the classic French technique of painting or applying metal foil to the back of glass. Gelatin sheets dissolved in water are used as an adhesive in this project, because the mixture dries clearer than white size, which would be visible through the glass.

PROJECT SUPPLIES Basic Supplies (page 135; use silver-leaf booklet), gelatin sheets, 1 cup (200ml) distilled water, small metal pot, two 1-inch (2.5cm) brushes, glass from a picture frame (or have a piece cut to fit), lint-free cloth (optional), small paintbrush (such as #12), cotton balls, acrylic clear coat

HOW-TO Place one gelatin sheet and 1 cup (200ml) distilled water into a small metal pot. Slowly heat the solution; stir with 1-inch (2.5cm) brush until gelatin dissolves, forming size solution (this will make silver leaf adhere to glass and enhance the leaf's reflective properties); keep the pot over low heat. **1.** Clean and dry the piece of glass. Starting at one corner, and using the same 1-inch (2.5cm) brush, apply gelatin mixture to 3 1/2-inch (9cm) area of the glass. Generate static on the gilder's tip brush by brushing it against your hair or a sweater. Holding the booklet at a slightly downward angle, touch bristles of the brush to the edge of an exposed silver-leaf sheet; slide the sheet about 1/2 inch (13mm) over the booklet edge. **2.** Touch the edge of the sheet to the edge of the wet glass. Quickly move your hand away from the edge; the sheet should slide off the booklet onto the glass. Tilt the glass to help wrinkles "fall out." (To redo, wipe off the silver leaf with a lint-free cloth.) Repeat the process to cover the entire glass, laying the silver leaf in rows, overlapping squares about 1/8 inch (3mm). After adding the last square, let dry 15 minutes. Fill in any missed spots with gelatin mixture and the #12 brush, wetting only the exposed glass; cover it with small pieces of silver leaf. Let it dry for 30 minutes. Wipe off any excess gelatin mixture with a cotton ball. **3.** Use a dry 1-inch (2.5cm) brush to apply acrylic clear coat to the back of silver to seal the mirror. Let it dry several hours before placing it inside the frame, with the glass side facing outward.

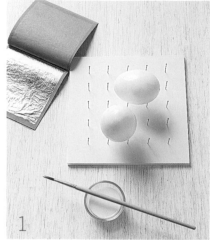

PROJECT: gilded eggs

This is the sort of Easter basket you can display year-round. Blown eggs covered in yellow-, pink-, and white-gold leaf make an elegant centerpiece, particularly when set atop a bed of spray-painted hay in a sponge-painted basket, with a vintage metallic ribbon bow on each side. You will need 3 or 4 sheets of metal leaf for each egg.

PROJECT SUPPLIES Basic Supplies (page 135; use gold leaf in various shades), foamboard, flat-head pins, blown-out eggs, basket, hay, gold spray paint, gold acrylic paint, sponge, vintage metallic wide ribbon

HOW-TO 1. Stick flat-head pins into a piece of foamboard to create a drying rack for the eggs that won't rub off the gilding leaf. Coat the eggs with size and set them gently onto the pins; let set until size is tacky, following manufacturer's instructions (about 20 minutes). Set your gold leaf sheets and paintbrush nearby so that they are easily accessible as you work. **2.** Put on gloves and mask. Rub a thin gilder's tip brush on your hair or a sweater to create static, and lift one gold sheet from the packet. Drape it over the egg and smooth it with your fingers. Repeat until the egg is covered. Go over the egg with a soft, clean, natural paintbrush to even out the texture and brush off any extra flakes, and then set it on the pins. Repeat the process with the remaining eggs. While the eggs are drying, or before you even start gilding, sponge paint the basket and spray paint the hay. To present the eggs, set them atop a bed of hay in the basket. Tie ribbon bows to each side of the basket.

PROJECT: gilded bowls

To make application easy, this project calls for paper-backed sheets of gold leaf. These sheets are less delicate and can be lifted by hand, without a gilder's brush. Just rub against the paper side, and the gold leaf will transfer onto the bowls.

PROJECT SUPPLIES Basic Supplies (page 135; use paper-backed gold leaf), clean shallow wooden or ceramic bowls

HOW-TO Brush a thin coat of size on the bowl. Let set until tacky, 15 minutes. Carefully take a sheet of paper-backed gold leaf, place it metal-side down in the center of the bowl, then rub the paper gently with your fingers until the metal has been transferred to the bowl; discard the backing. Repeat laying and rubbing sheets, overlapping them and then working from the center out to make a T shape, then outward until the bowl is completely covered. Little bits of metal leaf will be left on the paper backing; use these to fill in holes or cracks. When the surface is completely covered, brush with the gilding brush; this step will press down the leaf and break off any loose flakes, giving the bowl a finished look.

GLITTERING

Glitter is often associated with the shimmering fairy dust of childhood art projects. Yet this lustrous powder was once used in very refined crafts. Traditionally, glitter was made of glass, which creates a much more beautiful sparkle than the plastic varieties you may have used in grade school. As with many decorative arts, the Victorians embraced glitter, embellishing holiday cards and handblown ornaments with the fine, luminescent confetti. Holiday crafts are still wonderful applications for glitter, but this material can also be used for all sorts of projects, casting a sheen over iconic items (candles and candleholders) and unexpected ones (such as decorative birds) year-round. Today, you can find both glass and plastic glitter in crafts stores and online, and you'll likely find a use for each, depending on the craft. Additionally, various sizes of glitter can be layered to create different textures, make an item more brilliant, or create a subtler glow. One of the greatest advantages of glitter is its ability to turn an ordinary object into something magnificent. Once you've collected a few varieties of glitter and begun to experiment with them, you may find yourself with a new favorite pastime—one that is childlike in its simplicity, yet at the same time very grown-up.

ABOUT THE MATERIALS

GLITTER Glass glitter comes in a range of consistencies. Ultrafine glitter is like powdery sand and will stick to your fingertips, while fine glitter has slightly larger pieces. Coarse glass glitter tends to look like granulated sugar. Shard glitter is the largest variety of glass glitter, and resembles broken pieces of glass. Some glitter is uniform in size, while other glitter—such as shard—has varying shapes that refract light more brilliantly. Powder glitter, which is made of plastic, is so fine that it will coat an object uniformly. It is perfect for coating lightweight objects, such as silk flowers, because it won't weigh them down. Powder glitter is sometimes used as a base coat on objects, with larger glitter—such as shard glitter—layered on top. Standard plastic glitters—the type you find at crafts stores—also come in many colors, sizes, and shapes. Plastic glitter is less expensive than glass glitter, and is particularly well-suited for children's crafts projects.

OPPOSITE **Humble blown eggs take a dramatic turn when coated in fine glitter. A variety of different-size eggs, such as those of quail, chicken, and goose, will add dimension to the display.**

BASIC SUPPLIES

glitter (the type will depend on the project)

kraft paper

white craft glue

small bowls (one for each color of glitter)

spoon

paintbrush (the size will depend on the project)

GLITTER GLOSSARY

SHARD GLASS GLITTER

COARSE GLASS GLITTER

FINE GLASS GLITTER

CRYSTAL CLEAR GLITTER

COARSE PLASTIC GLITTER

POWDER GLITTER

PROJECT: glittered eggs

In addition to chicken eggs, those from quail and goose were used in this project to create an interesting range of sizes. You can find these eggs at some specialty stores and farmer's markets. You can also purchase all varieties of blown eggs online.

PROJECT SUPPLIES Basic Supplies (page 143; use powdered glitter in various colors), foamboard (optional), flat pushpins (optional), waxed paper (optional), eggs

HOW-TO Start by making an egg drying rack with foamboard and pushpins as described for the gilded eggs on page 140. (Alternatively, you can dry the eggs on a sheet of waxed paper.) Blow out each egg. Rinse the inside of each egg thoroughly; let dry. Set out your bowls of glitter and other supplies on a clean work surface. Pour a small amount of white craft glue into a bowl. Using a small paintbrush, cover an egg with white craft glue. Gently set the egg in a bowl of glitter. Spoon the glitter over the egg, covering the entire surface. Remove the egg carefully from the bowl; set on the egg drying rack or waxed paper to dry for 1 hour before displaying.

PROJECT: **glittered candles**

Thanks to a dusting of fine glitter, ordinary pillar and taper candles get a high dose of glamour. Set in an assortment of tall glass candleholders and shallow glass dishes, this arrangement is well-suited for a holiday dinner or other festive event.

PROJECT SUPPLIES Basic Supplies (page 143; use fine glitter), dust mask, light-colored pillar or taper candles, large cardboard box, masking tape, spray adhesive

HOW-TO Lay kraft paper over your work surface. Fill a few bowls with fine glitter. Place a few taper candles or one pillar candle in a large box. (Cover the wicks with masking tape before spraying.) Wearing a dust mask, spray the adhesive outside or in a well-ventilated area. Spoon glitter over the candles to coat; let dry overnight on the kraft paper. Remove tape from wicks.

PROJECT: **glittered candleholders**

These vintage-style candleholders are made of brioche pans hot-glued together, then covered in red and silver glass glitter. For maximum shine, mix in a little gold or silver glitter. You can also vary the size of the brioche pans for smaller or larger candles.

PROJECT SUPPLIES Basic Supplies (page 143; use fine glass glitter in silver, red, and gold), hot-glue gun and glue stick, brioche pans (2 for each candleholder), white acrylic paint

HOW-TO Lay kraft paper over your work surface. Hot-glue 2 brioche pans to one another at the bottoms. Cover the pans completely with 2 coats of white acrylic paint, letting them dry completely between coats. (The paint will keep the glue from rusting the tin and the light color will make the glitter appear brighter.) With a small paintbrush, apply white craft glue to the interior of 1 tin, and then spoon the glass glitter over the surface. Once the glue has dried, shake off any excess glitter. Repeat on the inside of the other tin and on both exteriors. Apply glue generously to the center seam, and apply an additional coat of glitter to hide it.

PROJECT: **glittered gift tags**

Covering strips of double-stick tape with glitter is a quick way to add shine to simple store-bought tags. Double-stick tape comes in a variety of widths; buy several to create different patterns on the tags.

PROJECT SUPPLIES Basic Supplies (page 143; use fine glitter), double-stick tape, tags

HOW-TO Cover your work surface with kraft paper. Cut a piece of tape a little longer than the length or width of your tag. Lay the tape down where desired, then cut the ends flush with the tag's sides. Spoon glitter over the tape, and shake off excess. Create multicolored stripes by applying 1 strip of tape, coating it in glitter, then applying another strip and coating it in another color. To create a woven effect, apply 1 strip of tape to the tag, then apply glitter. Apply another strip of tape, perpendicular to the first strip; apply another color of glitter to this strip. Finish by applying another thin strip of tape, parallel to the first strip, along the long edge of the tag, and coat that in glitter of a different color. Hand-write or stamp names and greetings on the tags to finish.

PROJECT: glittered stencil cards

Making bold glitter letters and numbers is a snap when you use a simple paint stencil. Plastic stencils work best, but you can also use cardboard stencils.

PROJECT SUPPLIES Basic Supplies (page 143; use fine plastic glitter in variety of colors), stencils, cards, stiff stencil brush, craft knife

HOW-TO Cover your work surface with kraft paper. Fill small bowls with glitter. Lay a stencil of your choice over the front of a card, positioning it in the center. Holding the stencil firmly with one hand, apply dots of white craft glue onto the card, inside the stencil, and onto the stencil just around the opening. Using the stiff stencil brush, smear the glue from the surface of the stencil and inside the stencil inward, so that it does not push the glue beyond the borders of the stencil. Remove the stencil and spoon glitter over the glue. If the edges of the shape look smeared, use a craft knife to scrape away any excess glue or glitter.

PROJECT: crystal-glitter-coated cards

Covering paper cards with coarse clear or "crystal" plastic glitter allows the designs to show through, while giving the cards an icy shimmer. You can embellish store-bought cards, or make your own from papers with interesting patterns.

PROJECT SUPPLIES Basic Supplies (page 143; use coarse clear plastic glitter), cards or papers, waxed paper (optional)

HOW-TO Cover your work surface with kraft paper. If you're making a card, cut the paper to size and fold it in half. Use a small paintbrush to coat the front of the card with a thin layer of white craft glue. Sprinkle clear plastic glitter over the card and shake off any excess; let it dry. If the card is buckled or warped, sandwich it in waxed paper and press it between the pages of a heavy book to flatten (a phone book would work well), leaving for a few hours.

JASMINE TULIP

Amiability and Love.

Thy heart is like a jasmine-bell;
It yields its wealth of feeling,
Like perfume from the blossom's cell,
On every zephyr stealing.

I've twined with it a tulip, to
Within the heart of
Thou'lt find a deep, warm passion, which
Can never change or

JEWELRY MAKING
BEADED JEWELRY, CHAINS, AND CHARMS

Making your own jewelry is a revelation. When you admire pieces through a glass case in a shop, it's hard to imagine that you could actually create dazzling earrings, sweet charm bracelets, and elegant necklaces with gleaming stone pendants yourself. But most anyone can learn jewelry making. The meditative process of stringing beads, tying knots, and twisting wire does call for patience and practice. And, along with a few fundamental techniques, you'll also need some specific supplies. They are readily available at the bead stores that are proliferating thanks to the popularity of this craft (if there's no store in your area, you can find everything you need online). When you're just starting out, it's wise to experiment using inexpensive materials—buy wire made of a base metal and some glass or plastic beads, for example, rather than fourteen-karat gold and semiprecious stones. Play around with the tools and techniques, trying the ideas on the following pages. As you master the basics, you can turn your attention to the design of your creations—and that's the really enjoyable part. Do you like bold pieces, or more subtle ones? Is your sensibility classic, modern, or perhaps a little edgy? Whatever your style, people are sure to notice a piece you lovingly created by hand. And what a pleasure to say, "I made it myself."

ABOUT THE MATERIALS

BEADS Glass, wood, plastic, metal, or semiprecious stones—beads come in almost every material imaginable, as well as a vast variety of shapes and sizes (not to mention prices). Browsing at a specialty bead store is a great way to familiarize yourself with what's available, and to get inspired. To keep beads from rolling around, plan your design by laying out the beads on a towel, felt, or a bead design board.

OPPOSITE Beads made from semiprecious stones, like these peridots, can produce lovely jewelry. To package a pair of earrings as a gift, hang them from tiny holes punched into a piece of card stock (the one shown is a vintage calling card). Wrap with tissue and ribbon in a color that complements the jewels.

CHAIN, CLASPS, AND WIRE

Chains, of course, are the starting point for many necklaces and bracelets (and even belts). The links may be delicate and dainty or big and chunky. You can invest in 14- or 18-karat gold or sterling silver, which will stand the test of time. Or pay less for gold- or silver-tone chain, or chain made of metals, such as brass, copper, or steel, or even plastic, all of which can make beautiful pieces. Chain is usually sold by the foot (30.5cm) (or the inch [2.5cm], for more expensive versions), which means you need to add the clasp yourself. There are several styles, most of which attach to a jump ring, a simple loop used as a connector. (Or you can buy a chain necklace or bracelet with a clasp already in place.) Use lengths of wire to turn a bead into a pendant, or to join beads to one another. Choose fasteners, jump rings, and wire in the same metal and finish as your chains.

SILK CORD Use this strong cord for stringing beads for necklaces and bracelets. It comes in different colors and thicknesses and can be part of the design of a piece of jewelry (as when the beads are spaced along the cord and separated by knots); or it can be purely functional (as when the beads are flush against one another).

PLIERS AND CUTTERS In order to manipulate the thin wires and small links, you'll need both chain-nose pliers and round-nose pliers, as well as wire cutters.

BEADED JEWELRY

BASIC SUPPLIES

beads

tweezers

chain, silk cord,
or thin ribbon

chain-nose pliers
and round-nose pliers

wire cutters

clasps, jump rings,
and bead tips

wire

ball pins, head pins,
eye pins

bonding cement

Your first experience with making beaded jewelry may have been lacing colorful plastic and wooden baubles onto a length of yarn or string. Indeed, you can still employ that basic technique to make some stunning pieces. But working with beads can mean much more. In addition to stringing pieces together, use wire to transform them into pendants or link them together, and in turn you will have infinite options for earrings, bracelets, and necklaces. Many of the pieces shown on the following pages are made with semiprecious stones for heirloom-worthy accessories, but the techniques can be used with any beads.

The standard length for bracelets is 7 inches (18cm). A necklace might be as short as 14 inches (35.5cm) for a choker or as long as 45 inches (114cm) for a lariat. Lengths from 16 to 20 inches (40.5–51cm) are common.

MATERIALS GLOSSARY

1. TWEEZERS Use pointed tweezers for grasping the silk cord when tying knots and for selecting small beads.

2. CHAIN Chain comes in many different metals and styles. Be sure to match the scale of your chain and bead.

3. PLIERS AND CUTTERS Chain-nose pliers have a tapered tip; the pincers are round on the outside but flat, with ribbing for grip, on the sides that touch. Use this versatile tool for opening jump rings and crimping bead tips. Round-nose pliers are also tapered, but the tips are completely rounded. Use them for making loops and wrapping wires. Use cutters for snipping wire. Choose good-quality tools that feel comfortable in your hands.

4. BALL PINS Thread stones onto these wires, then twist the wires to make a pendant.

5. BEAD TIPS When you're stringing beads, you'll use these to hide the knot at each end; then you attach the clasp or jump ring to the bead tip.

6. SILK CORD This is for stringing beads. It comes in many colors and different thicknesses. Use the thickest cord the bead can take.

7. EAR WIRES These are the foundation for pendant-style earrings. Ear wires come in various styles and different metals.

8. JUMP RINGS These little circles of metal are connectors, frequently used for joining pendants or clasps to chains. Many of the projects that follow use open, or split, jump rings; with these, the metal ends meet but are not joined. Closed jump rings are continuous circles of metal.

9. CLASPS You can find these in different styles. Use them for necklaces and bracelets.

10. EYE PINS These have a loop on one end and are used to join beads to chain or another link.

11. WIRE Use wire to turn beads into pendants that can be joined together or attached to chain. It's worth using good-quality wire, such as 14- or 18-karat gold or sterling silver. However, you should practice new techniques on inexpensive wire. Look for 22- to 26-gauge wire (a higher number indicates that the wire is thicker).

12. HEAD PINS These wires are the same as ball pins but flat on one end. They are also used to make pendants.

13. BONDING CEMENT Use dabs of this glue to secure knots when stringing beads.

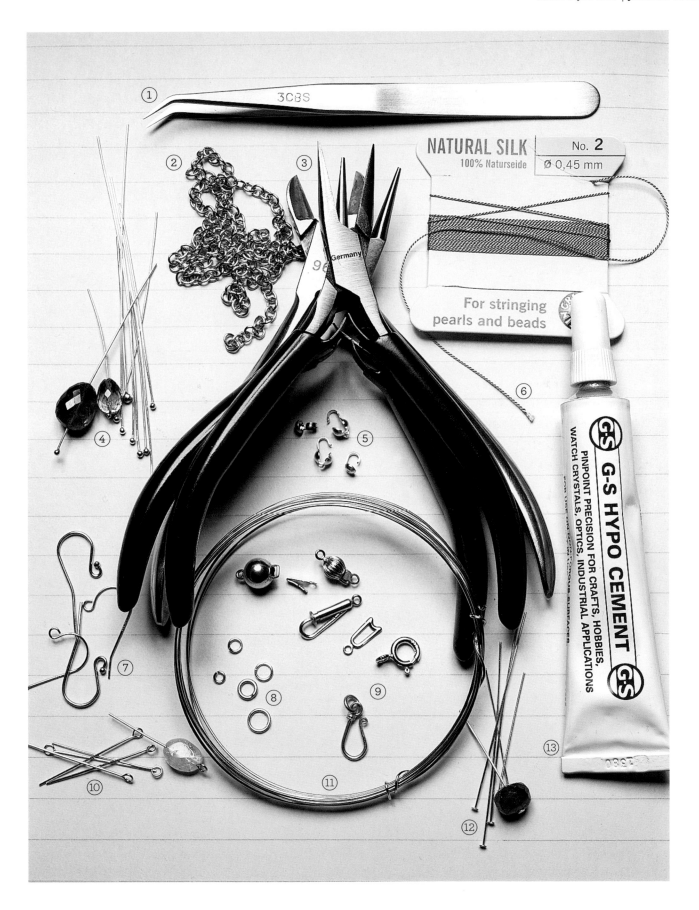

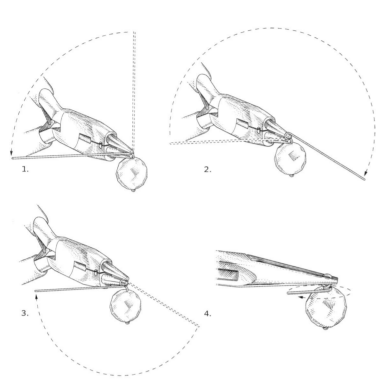

1.

2.

3.

4.

HOW TO MAKE A CENTER-DRILLED PENDANT

To make many of the jewelry pieces shown on these pages, you'll start by turning a bead into a pendant, which means adding a wire loop to the bead. The loop can then be used to link the bead to a chain for a necklace or bracelet or to ear wires for earrings (such as the ones on page 152). Follow the steps here and below, depending on how the hole is drilled through the bead.

1. Insert a head pin (or ball pin or eye pin) into a center-drilled bead. With round-nose pliers (the pincers should be horizontal), grasp the wire just above the bead, or higher if you want a longer shank on the pendant. Turn the pliers so that pincers are stacked vertically, as shown, bending the wire 90 degrees.

2. With your hands, wrap wire over the pliers in the other direction, to form half a loop.

3. Take out the pliers and fit the loop around the bottom pincer. Then bring the wire around to complete the loop. (Take off the loop with the pliers so you can open it. Attach the pendant to a chain or a closed jump ring. Hold one end of the loop with one pair of pliers; use another pair to gently twist the other end toward you—don't widen the circle to form a U shape. Attach the pendant, then close the loop again.)

4. To finish the loop, hold it firmly between chain-nose pliers, and wrap the wire around the shank until you meet the bead. Clip with wire cutters; tuck in the wire end with chain-nose pliers.

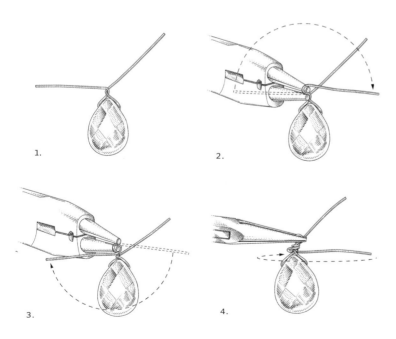

1.

2.

3.

4.

HOW TO MAKE A TOP-DRILLED PENDANT

For this technique, you use a length of wire instead of a head pin.

1. With wire cutters, clip a 3-inch (7.5cm) piece of wire; thread it through the bead. Bend it on either side with the tip of the round-nose pliers, getting as close to the bead as possible. Then twist once with your hands at the top of the bead to secure, as shown.

2. With round-nose pliers (the pincers should be vertical), grasp the horizontal wire just above the twist. With your hands, wrap the wire over the pliers in the other direction to form half a loop.

3. Take out the pliers and fit the loop around the bottom pincer, then bring the wire around to complete the loop. (Take off the loop with the pliers so you can open it. Attach the pendant to a chain or a closed jump ring. Hold one end of the loop with one pair of pliers; use another pair to gently twist the other end toward you—don't widen the circle to form a U shape. Slide the pendant or chain, then close the loop again with the pliers. This keeps the shape of the ring in a neat circle.)

4. While firmly holding the loop between chain-nose pliers, wrap the wire around the shank until you meet the bead. Clip both ends with wire cutters; tuck in the ends with chain-nose pliers.

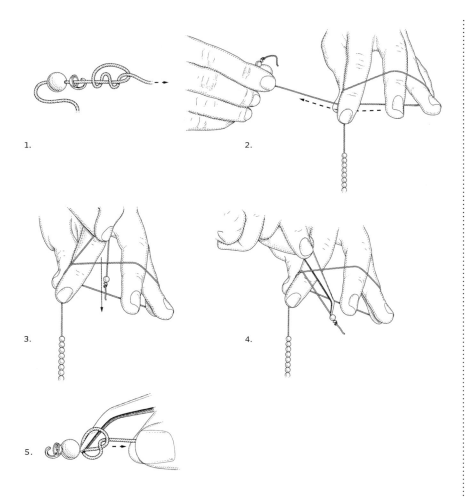

HOW TO LINK BEADS

You can link beads together with wire to create bracelets and necklaces without using chain or cord. Cut 1 foot (30.5cm) of wire for a bracelet; 2 to 3 feet (61–91cm) for a necklace.

Create a wrapped loop as described in "How to Make a Center-Drilled Pendant" (opposite), but without a bead (wrap underneath the loop at least twice). Slide a bead onto the wire. Create a wrapped loop on the other side, perpendicular to the first one; trim the wire. At this point you have a bead with a wire loop on each end. Repeat the process: Make a wrapped loop and slide a second bead onto the wire. But before you wrap the loop on the second end, open it like a jump ring. Hold 1 end of the loop with 1 pair of pliers; use another pair to gently twist the other end toward you (don't widen the circle to form a U shape). Attach it to the first bead, close the wire, and wrap. Continue adding beads to the desired length.

HOW TO STRING BEADS

Making knots between beads keeps them secure if the string breaks, but is optional. It also requires fewer beads, since the beads are spaced along the string. Start by unwinding silk cord (use the thickest cord appropriate for your beads); it may come with a beading needle on one end, or you can add a twisted wire needle yourself. Double-knot the other end. Dab bonding cement on the knot, then slide on a bead tip, covering the knot. String beads in your planned pattern, finishing with a second bead tip. (If you're not making knots between beads, skip to the end of step 4.)

1. To make a knot after the first bead, pull the first bead flush to the bead tip covering the end knot.

2. Wrap the cord around one hand as shown; let other strung beads rest on your work surface so they don't come unstrung.

3. Drop the end with the first bead through the loop.

4. Insert tweezers into the loop; pinch the cord at the bead.

5. Keep the cord pinched with the tweezers as you let the looped cord come off your hand; gently pull the cord to form a knot, guiding the knot right above the bead. (To leave spaces between beads, grasp the cord with tweezers where you want the knot, not against a bead.) Continue; tie the last knot just before the second bead tip. Dab that knot with cement glue and close bead tips with round-nose pliers. Attach clasps with jump rings.

GEM GLOSSARY

Inspiration comes in many colors—these are some of the stones available as beads. They are cut into shapes that highlight their beauty, such as squares or teardrops. Some are faceted, so light can bounce off their angles and surfaces. Others are smooth and lustrous.

AQUAMARINE

EMERALD

IOLITE

OPAL

TURQUOISE

APATITE

CHALCEDONY

TOPAZ

PERIDOT

TANZANITE

SAPPHIRE

PERUVIAN OPAL

AVENTURINE

AMETHYST

TOURMALI

ZIRCON

JADEITE

GARNET

RUBY

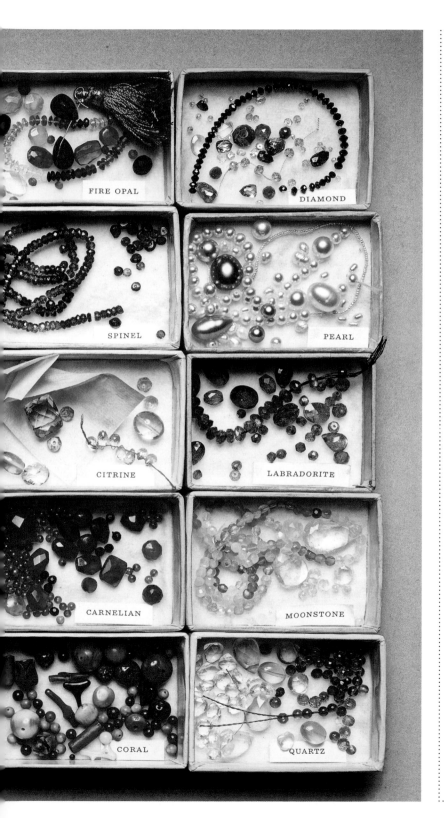

FIRE OPAL

DIAMOND

SPINEL

PEARL

CITRINE

LABRADORITE

CARNELIAN

MOONSTONE

CORAL

QUARTZ

about semiprecious-stone beads

Whatever your favorite stones, whether the familiar turquoise or emerald or the lesser-known labradorite or chalcedony, it's likely that you can purchase a strand of beads made from them. The beads will have made quite a journey to get to you: There are opal mines in Australia, rocks containing citrine in Brazil, and deposits of peridot in the southwestern United States.

Most stones crystallize as a result of the natural agitation of the planet, be it the flow of volcanic magma, the endless shifting of water currents, or the commotion of gases.

Many of the finest stones—those with the best color and the fewest flaws—are turned into jewelry with settings. Stones that will become strung beads tend to have more impurities, known as inclusions, but that can be part of their charm—you can really see the natural beauty of the stone in them. Keep in mind that some stones are dyed to enhance their hue; the dye can rub off on clothes and will mask the stones' intrinsic loveliness—ask whether the stones are natural before you purchase them.

Stones are sometimes sold singly, but more often in strands. Prices, which range from a few dollars to hundreds of dollars per strand, depend on several factors: the number of beads per strand; their size, which ranges from two to twenty-five millimeters in diameter; as well as the quality, determined by color and number of inclusions. You'll also choose according to shape, such as round, oval, square, or teardrop, and the stones' cut, which is dictated by its facets.

Before making your final decision, it's a good idea to hold the gems near your face or against your wrist—depending on how you intend to use them—to see what color suits you best.

PROJECT: beaded necklaces

Opposite, from top: Tiny garnet, medium aquamarine, and large tanzanite beads are strung on silk cord. Pale, round citrine and small and large green apatite beads are spaced along a knotted cord. A rainbow of sapphires (although they're thought of as blue, they can be pink, yellow, or colorless) are linked with wire loops.

PROJECT SUPPLIES Basic Supplies (page 154)

HOW-TO For the garnet, aquamarine, and tanzanite necklace, follow instructions for stringing beads on page 157, without making knots between the beads. For the citrine and apatite necklace, follow those same instructions, alternating the small citrine and apatite beads between the large apatite beads and making knots to hold them all in place. For the sapphire necklace, use top-drilled stones, and follow the instructions for linking beads, also on page 157.

PROJECT: beaded bracelets

Unlike the necklaces on the opposite page, these bracelets were all made using the same technique—attaching stones pendant-style to a simple, delicate chain. The varying effects show how much the choice of stone dictates the overall look of the piece. These stones are, left to right: amethysts arranged in gradational colors; fire opals, which are orange, also gradated; coral beads; a mix of oval stones, including citrine, tourmaline, and aquamarine; and rubies, sapphires, and emeralds.

PROJECT SUPPLIES Basic Supplies (page 154)

HOW-TO For all the bracelets, make center-drilled pendants and attach them to a chain (page 156) using ball pins; for the ruby, sapphire, and emerald bracelet, give them longer shanks, coiling the wire at least four times.

In just one afternoon, you could create multiple jewelry pieces for holiday gifts (some of these even incorporate jingle bells along with the glass beads).

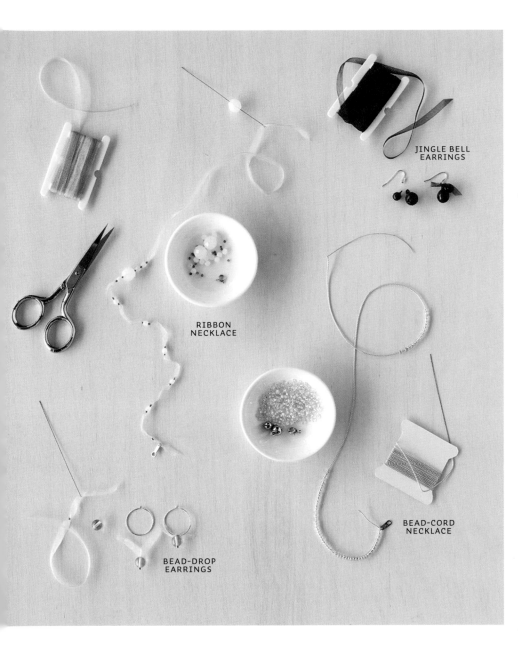

JINGLE BELL
EARRINGS

RIBBON
NECKLACE

BEAD-CORD
NECKLACE

BEAD-DROP
EARRINGS

PROJECT: basic beaded jewelry

The necklaces and earrings shown here were made by using slightly different (and easier) techniques than the ones described on the previous pages.

PROJECT SUPPLIES beads, beading needle, 5mm-wide ribbon, earring findings, clasps, connectors, and earring hoops, silk beading cord, liquid seam sealant

HOW-TO Ribbon necklace: To create a necklace with spaces between beads, use a beading needle and 20 inches (51cm) of 5mm-wide ribbon (or vary the length). String on larger beads, using seed beads (very small beads) to secure them. Tie on clasps and connectors at ribbon ends using a simple knot. Bead cord necklace: For a necklace that's a continuous strand of beads, use 20 inches (51cm) of silk beading cord (or vary the length); tie a connector to each end of the cord. Thread beads onto the cord at opposite end; if you wish, add 2 jingle bells (embellished with a small ribbon knot) at the midpoint. Affix a clasp to the other end with a knot. Jingle-bell earrings: Hook or slide jingle bells onto earring findings and adorn with a ribbon knot. Bead-drop earrings: To make the bead drop on the hoop earrings, use a beading needle and 5 inches (12.5cm) of 5mm-wide ribbon. String on a seed bead, then a larger bead; switch your needle to the other end of the ribbon, and pass it through a large bead from the bottom to lock the beads in place. Tie the beads onto the earring hoop, and secure them with a knot; trim ends as necessary.

For the ribbon projects, apply liquid seam sealant to ribbon ends immediately after cutting so they don't fray.

CHAINS AND CHARMS

BASIC SUPPLIES
chains
charms
chain-nose pliers
wire cutters
jump rings
clasps (optional)
ribbon (optional)

Sometimes a length of chain alone can make a striking and surprising piece of jewelry—even better, you can combine several, mixing styles, metals, and colors. Big links make a bold statement, and thinner ones are more understated. Charms, while familiar and always lovely on a classic bracelet, can also feel fresh and modern when worn in new ways.

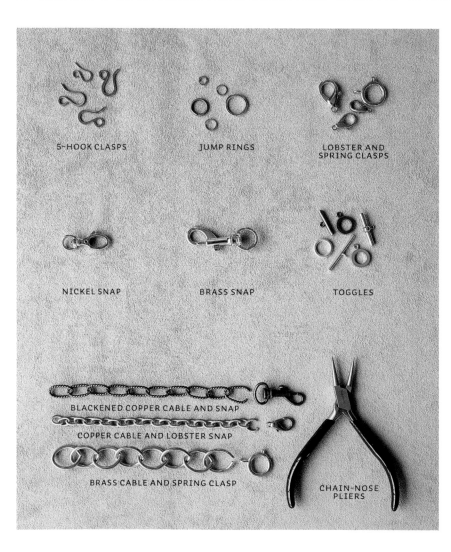

5-HOOK CLASPS

JUMP RINGS

LOBSTER AND SPRING CLASPS

NICKEL SNAP

BRASS SNAP

TOGGLES

BLACKENED COPPER CABLE AND SNAP

COPPER CABLE AND LOBSTER SNAP

BRASS CABLE AND SPRING CLASP

CHAIN-NOSE PLIERS

ABOUT CHAINS AND CHARMS

Despite the varied effects you can create, there's essentially one technique you need to know when working with chains and charms: how to open and close links (and jump rings, which are small round connectors that are used as links). To open a chain link or a jump ring, it's best to hold one end of the loop with one pair of pliers; use another pair to gently twist the other end toward you (don't widen the circle to form a U shape). Here are a few more useful techniques:

TRIMMING CHAIN TO LENGTH Decide how long you want your chain to be. Thin chains can be cut with wire cutters. For chains with thicker links, use two pair of pliers to open a single link so you can take off part of the chain.

ADDING A CLASP They come in several styles, some of which are shown here. The one you choose is largely a matter of aesthetics; a simple spring clasp is discrete and purely utilitarian, while a toggle clasp or a large snap can be part of the design of your piece. You can add a clasp directly to the chain, or link the two pieces with a jump ring. For either, use pliers to open the links for the jump ring as described, and then close the links or jump rings.

JOINING LENGTHS OF CHAIN Open a jump ring as described above, slip two chain links onto it, and close the jump ring.

ADDING A CHARM Attach charms to chains using a jump ring, as described above.

PROJECT: chain bracelets

A chunky chain and a clasp or snippet of ribbon is all it takes to make these stylish accessories.

PROJECT SUPPLIES Basic Supplies (opposite)

HOW-TO Start with a length of chain to fit your wrist; 7 inches (18cm) is usually about right. Add a clasp in a matching metal tone. Or, for ribbon bracelets: For the brown ribbon, cut grosgrain ribbon ends on the diagonal (so they don't fray), and thread the ends through the end links of the chain. Put the bracelet on, and pull the ribbon ends to make the bracelet the right size. Tie the ribbon ends. For the purple ribbon, cut ribbon ends on the diagonal, and thread through the 2 end links of a piece of 3- to 4-inch (7.5–10cm) chain. Wrap the ribbon around your wrist, and tie the ends.

PROJECT: chain necklaces and belts

You might want to mix and match several different chain necklaces, as shown here. The belts, of course, are meant to be worn one at a time.

PROJECT SUPPLIES Basic Supplies (opposite)

HOW-TO For the necklaces, trim chain to the desired length, and add a clasp. For the belts, from top: **1.** Trim the chain to fit around your waist, and add a clasp. Thread ribbon through the chain links so the bow will hide the clasp. Buy a few different ribbons so you can customize this belt. **2.** Link 3 lengths of chain to a wide belt clasp. **3.** Cut the chain so it wraps around your lower waist twice. Attach an S-hook clasp to one end. Holding the other end at your left hip, wrap the chain around your body, and mark the spot where it meets the end at your hip; attach a jump ring to the chain at that spot (do not join the 2 pieces of chain). Mark a spot at your right hip; make a swag with the chain and attach it with a jump ring to that spot. Drape the remaining chain back to the left side, and loop the S-hook through the jump ring and a link in the chain to secure the belt. **4.** Cut a thick chain to fit around your hips; add a clasp. Cut shorter lengths of thinner chain to swag across the front. Attach with jump rings.

Before laying paper in the marbleizing solution, you can move the paint, which will then create different patterns. When the paint is speckled it creates a stone pattern (front row, center); it can also be raked (front row, right) or swirled (back row, right).

M MARBLEIZING

Don't let the intricacy and kaleidoscopic beauty of a marbleized design fool you. Those ripples of color may look hand-painted or machine-printed, but they're actually created by liquid. Take a closer look, and you'll detect the telltale signs of motion: tiny waves, graceful swirls, and dappling reminiscent of raindrops falling on a pond. In fact, all marbleized patterns begin as paint floating on water. Marbleizing dates to the twelfth century, when it was practiced in China and Japan. Called *suminagashi* ("ink floating") in Japanese, the technique involved using absorbent papers to pick up ink from a water bath. Over the following centuries in Europe, the process of marbleizing was veiled in secrecy by close-lipped guild members practicing the art and selling their wares; by not sharing their formulas and methods, they made sure that the goods they produced were rare, and hence more valuable. In the mid-nineteenth century, however, their trade secrets were published by an English master marbler, Charles Woolnough, and marbleizing emerged as a popular pastime. Today, you can follow in this tradition to make your own rich designs. Marbleize paper to use as stationery or add distinctive swirls of color to simple wooden boxes or bins. In doing so, you'll be clued in to an age-old secret: Although it appears elaborate, marbleizing is actually quite easy.

ABOUT THE MATERIALS

ALUM Alum is a mordant, a chemical that makes paint adhere to paper.

PAINTBRUSHES, KNITTING NEEDLE, RAKE These tools are used to manipulate floating paint and create patterns.

PAPER It's important to use uncoated paper products, so the alum can bond properly. For gift wrap, use oversize pieces of paper so one sheet will cover a box. Use card stock or other heavy paper to make cards.

CLOTHESLINE, CLOTHESPINS, IRON To minimize warping, clip alum-coated paper to a clothesline to dry (this will take about 1 hour). Once it is dry, iron the paper on a medium setting to flatten it.

ABSORBENT GROUND GESSO

Wooden objects are brushed with gesso, an art supply used for priming canvases and other surfaces, before being marbleized. If you're marbleizing a painted wooden object, combine the gesso with acrylic paint (follow package instructions), then apply the mixture to the area you'll be marbleizing.

LIQUID ACRYLIC PAINTS Speckle paints onto the surface of the marbleizing solution—they're what add color to your paper or objects.

METHYL CELLULOSE When mixed with water, methyl cellulose, a thickening agent, forms a syrupy liquid on which the paint floats.

PANS AND TRAYS Use shallow pans, which will allow you more control. For most projects, baking pans will work. If you're marbleizing larger sheets of paper, use photo-developing trays.

BASIC SUPPLIES

alum

pencil

uncoated (nonglossy) medium-weight paper, or wooden objects, such as boxes

paintbrushes

clothesline and clothespins

iron

absorbent ground gesso (for wood projects)

methyl cellulose

whisk

shallow baking pans or trays

liquid acrylic paints

knitting needle or skewer

rake (see "Making a Rake," page 171)

plain newsprint

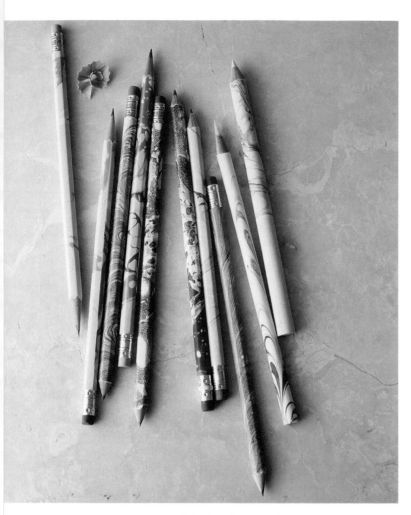

PROJECT: marbleized pencils

Take poetic license with a box of ordinary pencils, and dress them up in shades of pink, orange, and red.

PROJECT SUPPLIES Basic Supplies (page 169), ruler, scissors, white craft glue, small paintbrush, plain wooden pencils

HOW-TO Begin by marbleizing paper following instructions on page 170, then cut dried paper into strips (about 1 by 6 3/4 inches [2.5cm x 17cm]). Brush the back of a strip of marbleized paper with white craft glue; affix one long edge of paper to the pencil, then roll it against a hard surface to wrap the pencil and remove air bubbles. Sharpen the pencils once the glue has dried.

PROJECT: marbleized cards and gift wrap

The dreamy curves of marbleizing lend themselves to a number of decorative paper crafts, for Valentine's Day or any time of year.

PROJECT SUPPLIES Basic Supplies (page 169), paper or card stock, decorative paper punches, grommet, twine, alphabet rubber stamps, ink pads

HOW-TO Marbleize the paper or card stock, following instructions on page 170. To make a card with a cutout (such as this heart-shaped one), use a craft knife. You can also use a paper punch to make a gift tag. Fit the tag with a grommet and a length of twine to hang it from a package. Rubber stamps are perfect for writing greetings; both tag and card are stamped with a valentine message.

PROJECT: **marbleized picture mats**

Create handcrafted mats to enhance botanical prints or other illustrations.

PROJECT SUPPLIES Basic Supplies (page 169), store-bought photo mats, adhesive spray, craft knife

HOW-TO To complement the colors of botanical prints, this project features marbleized white papers in subtle green stone and swirl patterns. Marbleize paper, following instructions on page 170; let dry. Coat a store-bought mat with adhesive spray, and affix it to the back of marbleized paper. With marbleized paper facing down, use a craft knife to cut around the inside and outside edges of the mat, and remove the paper "window." (For more on matting and framing, see page 176.)

PROJECT: **embellished-edge notepads**

Marbleized paper may look like it came from a Venetian stationery shop, but it's easy to make at home. Dipped (on the three unbound sides) in a bath of color, these notepads make wonderful gifts.

PROJECT SUPPLIES Basic Supplies (page 169), plain notepads, paper towels, heavy book (or other weight)

HOW-TO Begin by brushing the alum mixture on the notepad's edges, keeping the pages tightly closed as you work; let them dry. Marbleize the edges (page 170), then rinse, and wrap the pad loosely in paper towels. Weight each notepad with a heavy book while it dries.

PROJECT: magazine holders

Beautiful objects can also be useful. These marbleized wooden organizers do their job with panache.

PROJECT SUPPLIES Basic Supplies (page 169), plain wooden magazine holders

HOW-TO Paint magazine holders with absorbent gesso mixed with acrylic paint, as desired (these are pale green); let dry about 1 hour. Marbleize one side, following the instructions on page 170, using the same color of paint with just a little bit of contrasting colors and the stone pattern technique.

PROJECT: desk catchall

A custom desk organizer upgrades your workspace, and is the perfect place to stow handmade marbleized stationery. If you accidentally get the marbleizing solution on one of the other sides, you can touch up your piece with paint afterward.

PROJECT SUPPLIES Basic Supplies (page 169), wooden desk caddy

HOW-TO Paint a wooden caddy with absorbent gesso mixed with acrylic paint, as desired; let dry about 1 hour. Marbleize the front surface, following instructions on page 170. Touch up the sides as needed.

Black-and-white photography looks particularly refined when mounted and framed in a gray or white French mat.

MATTING AND FRAMING

Matting and framing are the best ways to protect and present illustrations and photographs, but you don't need to rely on a professional framer. In this chapter, you'll learn techniques that the experts use for mounting pictures onto mats, sealing frames, and applying a dust cover to the back of a frame. It's less expensive—and often quite fun—to do the work yourself, particularly when you embellish the mat to suit your particular tastes or the character of whatever you're framing. For example, covering a store-bought mat in fabric or textured paper will give it a distinctive surface that can contrast against your walls; simply adding a border of paint or ribbon to a mat can enhance a vintage photo's classic appeal. Ultimately, a mat is the visual bridge between an image and a frame, the space that allows these two elements to balance and complement each other. Decorating the mat can affect how you see an image and the frame; the busier the design on the mat, the less noticeable the frame may become. Subtle changes in a mat's dimensions, color, thickness, and texture will play a part in the overall look of your framed photographs and artwork. Framing your mat and artwork or pictures will give them a refined look, and ensure that they'll be preserved for many years to come.

ABOUT THE MATERIALS

MAT BOARD The mat serves as a protective barrier between the image and the glass. Every mat consists of at least two boards: the window mat, which contains the opening that displays the image, and the mounting mat (or back board) on which the image is affixed. Mat boards can be made from a variety of materials, including wood pulp and cotton. If you want your artwork to look good for many years to come, it's worth investing in an acid-free mat board. Works of art, especially those on paper, disintegrate over time and are vulnerable to damage from vapors released by the work itself and from external forces, such as humidity, pollutants, light, and insects. Photographs are especially susceptible because of the chemicals used in processing and their sensitivity to light. To avoid discoloration of your artwork, use acid-free mat board. Although an acid-free mat won't necessarily protect against deterioration, it won't contribute to it. Also, look for mat boards that are lignin-free; lignin is a by-product of wood pulp that can darken when exposed to light. One-hundred-percent rag mat board, which is made of cotton, is best for framing valuable pieces of art because it is pH balanced (close to 7 on the pH scale). You can also use an acid-free and lignin-free mat board made of a combination of rag and purified wood pulp. These are often called *conservation, museum-quality,* or *archival* boards, and they are only marginally more expensive than non–acid-free boards. Mat boards also come in a variety of thicknesses, ranging from two- to eight-ply. The thickness affects the depth and thus the look of the window. Conservators recommend that you use at least four-ply board for adequate depth.

LINEN HINGING TAPE This tape is used to affix artwork to a mat, or to connect the mounting mat with its window board. The adhesive is pH balanced, so the tape will not discolor the artwork.

FRAME Frames are made from a variety of materials, and nearly any store-bought variety will work for the projects in this section. If yours comes with a backing made of cheap cardboard, replace it with foamboard to better preserve the artwork.

HANGING WIRE This is used to hang frames. Threaded hanging wire that is coated with rubber will be easier to work with and less likely to hurt your hands.

EMBELLISHING MATS

There are multiple ways to embellish a regular store-bought mat board; the possibilities are limited only by your imagination. Covering a mat in fabric—such as velvet or twill—will add distinctive texture, while covering it in paper—such as wallpaper or a map—can highlight specific visual aspects of whatever you're matting. Adding a border or transferring an image to a mat is an elegant, stylish touch.

PROJECT: French mat

The French mat is a venerable framing technique, long used to accent drawings and etchings. The mat is decorated with a band or bands of color and is usually highlighted with a border of gold or black ink. The traditional method requires an incredibly steady hand to paint the perfectly straight lines, but you can create an excellent facsimile quickly using tape as a stencil to guide your brush.

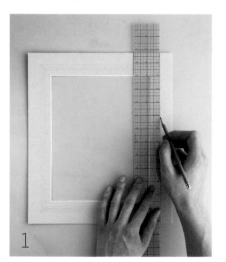

PROJECT SUPPLIES pencil, quilter's ruler, or straightedge; museum-quality mat board; low-tack masking tape; gouache (an opaque watercolor) in desired color; small paintbrush; India ink (optional); colored pencils (optional)

HOW-TO 1. With a pencil and quilter's ruler, lightly draw lines about $\frac{1}{2}$ inch (13mm) around the window of the mat. For added detail, you can draw additional sets of lines outside the first outline; these will serve as guides for additional embellishment after painting. Use the lines on the quilter's ruler to help make these additional outlines perfectly perpendicular to the first. Here, two sets of lines were drawn around the first. **2.** Apply strips of low-tack masking tape along the drawn lines closest to the window of the mat. To ensure crisp results, lightly smooth the tape along the edges where the paint will be applied. Using gouache, paint the area of the mat between the tape and the window. Let the paint dry, then carefully remove the tape. Let the mat dry completely overnight. **3.** Lines of India ink, black, white, or colored pencil can be added over the remaining guides. Repeated tracings over the same guides will produce varied intensities. To create thicker lines, fill in between the lightly drawn lines with evenly applied pencil strokes. To ensure the cleanest lines, keep pencil points sharp and ink nibs clean as you work.

You can use the French matting technique on any color of mat board. Here gray mats are used to frame black-and-white photos. Bands of yellow gouache and regular pencil adorn the light gray mat. On the dark gray mat, white-colored pencil was used to make the thin band around the black band.

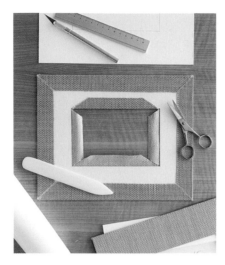

PROJECT: cloth-covered mats

Give pictures a pleasing sense of dimension by framing them with two mats: one that perfectly fits the picture, and an oversized version covered in fabric.

PROJECT SUPPLIES picture with mat, paperboard, pencil, ruler or straightedge, craft knife, scissors, fabric, positionable mounting adhesive or spray adhesive, bone folder, craft knife, frame that is 2 inches (5cm) larger than the original mat

HOW-TO For this project, you can purchase a larger mat with a bigger window, or make your own paperboard mat. Use thin 2-ply mat or paperboard to keep the outer-covered mat from becoming too thick. Lay the picture's mat on top of your paperboard and use a pencil to trace the outside border and window of the mat. With a ruler, mark an outline ¼ inch (6mm) around the lines for the mat's outside border. This will be the size of your insert. Use a craft knife and the ruler (or straightedge) to cut out the insert and its window. You may want to cut the window slightly larger, so that the underlying mat shows once framed. With scissors, cut the fabric 2 inches (5cm) longer and 2 inches (5cm) wider than the insert. Working in a well-ventilated area and following the manufacturer's instructions, apply positionable mounting adhesive or spray adhesive to the back of your fabric; this will make the fabric

tacky. Affix the fabric to the insert, centering it so that there's a 1-inch (2.5cm) border on each side. Miter the outside corners of the fabric by notching them at 45-degree angles and then folding over, as shown, then affix to the inside of the insert. Smooth with a bone folder. Using a craft knife, cut an X in the fabric in the insert's opening. Trim the excess fabric, then fold and smooth the fabric flaps and affix them to the inside of the insert. Place the finished insert against the frame, followed by the original mat, print, and backing board. You may want to tape the mats together so that the back mat and the picture do not shift in the frame.

PROJECT: **paper-covered mats**

Use outdated (but still attractive) maps and nautical charts to cover mats and frame photos from a trip.

PROJECT SUPPLIES pencil, acid-free mat, map or nautical chart, craft knife, ruler or straightedge, positional mounting adhesive or spray adhesive

HOW-TO Trace the outside edges and the window of the mat onto the back of the map. Using a craft knife and straightedge, cut along the outline of the mat you've drawn. Measure the depth of the mat's beveled edge; trim the window of the map mat to account for this depth. This will allow a clean white edge to show around the photo. Working in a well-ventilated area and following manufacturer's instructions, apply adhesive to the back of the map. Affix the map to the mat, let dry, and frame.

FRAMING

BASIC SUPPLIES

acid-free mat board	frame
scissors	flathead screwdriver
linen hinging tape	hammer
artwork	white craft glue
weighted objects (such as smooth rocks)	kraft paper
	self-healing mat
plush towel	spray bottle
glass cleaner	hair dryer
paper towel	fine sandpaper
pencil	hinged frame hangers
foamboard	plastic-coated hanging wire
framing brads	
craft knife	wire cutter
straightedge	rubber bumpers

Framing artwork and treasured family photographs will give them a professional, finished look, and protect them from moisture and fluctuations in temperature. Adding a paper dust protector on the back of the frame will prevent dirt and other particles from infiltrating. All you need to frame like a pro are a few specialty items, some household objects, and a fine attention to detail.

HOW TO FRAME A PICTURE

The following mounting and framing techniques are used in professional frame shops. Changes in temperature and humidity cause the layers of mat board and backing to expand and contract, creating a vacuum that can suck dust and other particulates into the layers. Sealing the artwork with the paper backing keeps it clean inside the frame.

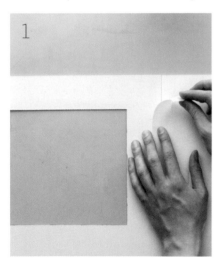 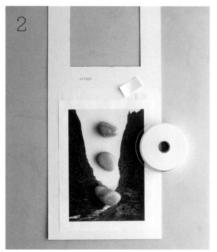 

1. Place the window mat facedown and the mounting mat faceup, with top edges touching. Cut a strip of tape and join the two sections of the mat, making a hinge between them.

2. Place the artwork on the mounting mat, centering the image where you want to affix it, and fold over the window mat. Adjust the artwork to make sure it is centered. While the window is still down, place a few weighted objects—such as clean smooth stones, a can of soup, or a stapler—onto the image to keep it from moving. Lift the window mat up again. Cut four 2-inch (5cm) pieces of hinging tape. Stick 1 piece, sticky-side up, to the back of the artwork an inch (2.5cm) from one of the top corners; leave about an inch (2.5cm) of the tape exposed at the top. Repeat on the opposite top corner. Stick the remaining pieces of tape—sticky-side down—horizontally over the exposed tape that is already stuck to the back of the mat. Take care not to tape over the front of the picture.

3. Lay a towel out on a flat surface. Remove the glass from your frame and lay it gently on the towel. Clean both sides of the glass with glass cleaner and a paper towel. Lift the glass up, with one edge resting on the towel, and look through it to make sure there are no streaks, dust, or fibers.

4. Trace the outline of the mounted artwork onto a piece of foamboard, and cut it out with a craft knife and a straight-edge. This will be the backing for the frame. You may want to cut out multiple pieces of foam to create a sturdier backing. Place the glass and mounted artwork into the frame, followed by layers of foamboard to ¼ inch (6mm) of the edge of the frame. Starting about 1 inch (2.5cm) from one corner, insert a framing brad where the foamboard and frame meet; hold the edge of the frame to keep it from slipping, and wedge the brad in by pushing it with a flathead screwdriver (and a hammer for more force). Apply brads around the corners and then move to the sides of the frame, applying brads every few inches (7–10cm).

5. To apply a paper dust protector to the back of the frame, first apply white craft glue to the back edges of the frame.

6. Lay a piece of kraft paper onto a self-healing mat, or another surface that you can cut on. Turn the picture frame, glue-side down, onto the paper. Let the glue dry. Trim the excess paper from the sides with a craft knife.

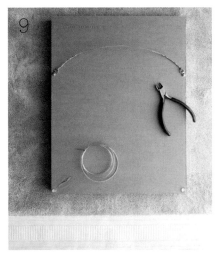

7. Flip the frame back over onto the towel, to protect the glass from breaking or scratching. With a spray bottle, liberally spritz the paper; it will ripple slightly. Use a hair dryer to dry the paper completely. Even if the paper appears dry, continue drying it until it pulls taut like a drum.

8. To give your frame a professionally finished look, rub fine sandpaper against where the frame and paper meet. This will remove any jagged pieces of paper that might otherwise show once you hang the frame.

9. To attach the hanging hardware, measure one-third of the way down from the top of the frame and make a mark on each side with a pencil. Screw in the frame hangers at the pencil marks. For the hanging wire, measure the width of your frame, and then add about 12 to 14 inches (30.5–35.5cm)—about 10 inches (25.5cm) for wrapping the ends of the wire, and 2 to 4 inches (5–10cm) for slack. For example, 29 inches (74cm) of wire was cut for this 16-inch (40.5cm) wide frame. Insert one end of the wire into one of the hangers and double knot, leaving a 5-inch (12.5cm) tail. Wrap the tail around the longer piece of wire. Repeat on the opposite side, making sure to leave enough slack in the wire to hang the picture. Add rubber bumpers to the bottom corners of the back of the frame.

HOW TO MAKE A MOSAIC

Whether you're making this elaborate mosaic tabletop or a simple serving tray, the process is the same. First, choose your materials and plan a pattern; sketching beforehand may help you visualize your design. Next, glue your tiles in place, then apply grout, let dry, and seal.

MOSAIC SUPPLIES Basic Supplies (page 187), wooden tabletop, heavy-duty craft glue, pencil, ruler

1. Make sure the tabletop is clean before you begin. Place it in a spot that has even ventilation so the grout will dry uniformly overnight; otherwise, it may crack. Draw a design, using a ruler for straight lines. The design shown has two octagons, one inside the other, following the shape of the tabletop.

2. Fit tile nippers over a section of a plate and squeeze the handles firmly until a piece snaps off. Repeat until the plate is in large pieces; then cut those into smaller ones.

3. Lay out individual pieces in a section of the design, and then use glue to attach pieces one at a time. Repeat until tabletop is covered. (To attach a sheet of tiles, spread an even layer of mortar on the surface, then place the sheet on mortar, pressing firmly.) Let the pieces dry overnight.

about broken china

Using broken china to make a mosaic is called *pique assiette,* which loosely translates to "plate stealer" or "scavenger." Incorporating pieces into a mosaic is a wonderful way to reuse damaged dishes that have sentimental value. A shard from a broken plate may also inspire an unusual pattern. But you'll need more than one dish to create a mosaic; search for similar pieces at flea markets, where vendors often have extra boxes of broken china on hand. Measure the area of the surface to be tiled and estimate how many plates you'll need. For the smoothest surface, use china pieces of similar thickness.

4. Mix grout according to package instructions; use a wooden stick to spread it evenly over the mosaic. Wearing gloves, use fingertips to press the grout into crevices.

5. Wipe off any excess grout with a damp sponge or rag, being careful not to wipe away the grout in the crevices. Switch to a dry rag for any residual grout. Let the grout dry overnight. Take the table outside, and apply the grout sealant. Wipe off any excess, and let it dry for one day in a well-ventilated spot.

Ceramic tile's durability makes it ideal for outdoor use.

PROJECT: sea-glass table

Bits of sea glass soften a geometric tile arrangement. Use sheets of tiles to cover a large surface with a repeating pattern—here, 1-by-2-inch (2.5cm x 5cm) white tiles with black accents (the black accents will be replaced with sea glass).

PROJECT SUPPLIES Basic Supplies (page 187), tabletop, craft knife, mortar, spackling knife, sea glass

HOW-TO Using a craft knife, cut sheets of tiles, slicing through the paper facing, to fit the surface of the table; cut out individual tiles to cover side edges. If tile sheets don't completely cover the surface, use a tile cutter to cut extra pieces to fit. Cut out black accent tiles to fill in with sea glass. Apply a thin layer of mortar to the tabletop and sides with a spackling knife. Lay tile sheets, paper side up, on the surface, pressing down firmly, and apply individual tiles to sides. Let dry according to mortar package instructions. Moisten paper with a damp sponge, and peel off. Using a craft stick, apply mortar to sea glass and place it in the empty spaces. Let dry overnight. Grout and seal as described opposite.

PROJECT: mosaic flowerpots

Bedecking small household objects, such as these terra-cotta planters, with china fragments adds a delightfully unexpected flourish—and requires only a few plates per pot. Here some of the pots are edged with the border patterns of china, and one (far left) wears a dainty flower design that was once part of a saucer.

PROJECT SUPPLIES Basic Supplies (page 187), terra-cotta pots

HOW-TO Use nippers to break plates into small pieces. To replicate a plate's pattern, keep the cut pieces organized in the original design as you lay out materials. Carefully glue them on the pot, leaving small crevices in between, and then fill in the remaining surface with additional pieces. Grout and seal as described on page 188.

PROJECT: mosaic mirror

The broken rims of plates are used to create the scalloped curves edging this mirror frame. An assortment of off-white and floral fragments gives the frame a variegated effect.

PROJECT SUPPLIES Basic Supplies (page 187), wooden mirror frame

HOW-TO Use tile nippers to break plates so that you have large sections of curvy plate borders and smaller pieces from the centers. Affix the large sections to the frame's perimeter with heavy-duty craft glue to make a scalloped edge. Fill in the remaining area with smaller fragments. Grout and seal as described on page 188.

sea glass

You'll find pieces of sea glass, broken fragments of bottles and other glass objects worn smooth by tumbling waves, on many beaches across the country. Green, brown, and clear are among the most common colors, owing to the vast number of bottles manufactured in these hues. Other colors are more difficult to find. Pieces found near the ocean have a frosted patina, because of heavy corrosion, whereas shards that emerge from lakes and rivers are usually more translucent. If you can't find sea glass at your local beach or you live far from water, you can still pick some up at online auction sites. Fragments that are roughly the same size are best for the projects in this chapter.

PROJECT: **sea-glass tray**

Pieces of sea glass and broken pottery shards combine with ceramic tiles to make this mosaic tray. Use a sheet of 1-inch (2.5cm) square tiles in green or blue.

PROJECT SUPPLIES Basic Supplies (page 187), craft knife, masking tape, mortar, spackling knife, sea glass, pottery shards (optional)

HOW-TO With a craft knife, cut a sheet of tiles, slicing through the paper facing, to fit inside the tray. If tiles do not completely cover the surface, use a tile cutter to cut extra pieces to fit. Cut out individual tiles at random from the sheet to fill with sea glass and pottery shards. Apply a thin layer of mortar to the tray. Lay the tile sheet, paper side up, on the surface, pressing down firmly. Let it dry. Moisten the paper with a damp sponge, and peel it off. Using a craft stick, apply mortar to the sea glass and pottery shards; place them in the empty spaces. The shards should be flush with the tiles. Let the mortar dry overnight. Tape off the inside and top edges of the tray with masking tape. Grout and seal, following instructions on page 188.

NATURE CRAFTS
ACORNS, PINECONES, AND SHELLS

The forest, the sea, and the garden are among the most inspirational places to discover new crafts materials. The natural world is full of intricate objects—one reason that so many artists have incorporated botanicals, shells, nuts, seeds, and wood objects into their work over the centuries. The soft forms of flowers and other plant life are covered in other sections of this book; here the focus is on the sturdier, hardier trio of acorns, pinecones, and seashells. As with so many crafts inspired by nature, the Victorians were particularly fond of covering all manner of objects with these finely detailed, yet strong and long-lasting items. The Victorians also arranged shells, pinecone scales, and acorn caps and nuts to mimic the forms of various flowers. Next time you're on a nature walk, look through the grassy expanses below a towering oak, peer under the boughs of a pine forest, or comb the beach at low tide or after a storm. You'll likely find items that will spark your imagination with their colors and forms, and encourage your own fanciful work. But remember that being a good neighbor means asking before you take: Always check with local authorities, or the landowner, before picking up items that are not on your property. And bear in mind that in addition to being abundant in the natural world, acorns, pinecones, and shells are also available for purchase online or at crafts stores.

ABOUT THE MATERIALS

ACORNS These little nuts are both the seed and fruit of the oak tree. They first appear when branches start to bud in early spring. If spared by migrating birds, the buds go on to become green acorns. Over the summer, they darken to a warm brown and, in turn, announce their ripeness by falling to the ground in the autumn. For the crafts here, gather healthy-looking acorns from the ground (but don't collect the nuts in areas where oak blight threatens the tree population, such as in California, where acorns should only be collected for propagation). The caps are often separated from the nuts; make sure to pick up a good amount of both so you can find tops and bottoms that fit together.

PINECONES Conifers produce both male and female cones; the male cones are smaller and more papery, and fertilize the female cones, which tend to be sturdier and last longer. Different types of trees produce different-shaped cones. Some are thin and oblong, while others are small and stubby. The curvatures of their scales are as distinctive as the trees from which they come. Eastern white pines produce cones with long, elegant scales, while Norway spruce trees feature fluttery specimens with pointy tips. If a variety of cone types isn't abundant where you live, look online or in crafts stores.

SHELLS With each trip to the shore you'll likely find a variety of shells. These former homes of mollusks and bivalves can be large (such as the conch shell) or small (such as rice shells). The best time to look for them is at low tide, particularly during a full moon, when the sea recedes farther than usual. The day after a storm is also a good time for shelling. Some states ban the collection of shells with animals living in them, so be aware of laws in your area. Many crafts stores and online vendors also sell an ample variety.

OPPOSITE **At the turn of the twentieth century, novelty pincushions were a part of many ladies' sewing kits. This tiny one, made from velvet ribbon tucked inside an acorn cap, is the color of a young nut.**

ACORN CRAFTS

A mature oak tree can drop millions of acorns in its lifetime, plenty for creatures to eat as well as for humans to collect. Generally, one growing season isn't long enough for the massive nutrient buildup a bumper crop requires, so the largest number of acorns come during "mast" years, every three to ten calendar years, depending on natural conditions. Collect acorns in autumn, after they've fallen to the ground; clean them with a damp cloth and spread them out to dry before using them. Fashion your treasures into irresistible crafts with the help of twists of wire or dabs of glue.

PROJECT: acorn pincushion

Look for soft velvet ribbon in an earthy tone to make these mini pincushions. Choose pale green to emulate a new acorn, or toasted brown for a more mature-looking nut.

PROJECT SUPPLIES acorn caps, string, paper, ruler, pencil, scissors, disappearing marker, velvet ribbon, needle, thread, sand, wood glue

HOW-TO Measure the inside circumference of the acorn cap with a string and divide by 2—this will be the length needed for the top of your pattern. To make an acorn-nut pattern, draw the top length onto a piece of paper, adding 1/4 inch (6mm) seam allowance on each side, and freehand draw an acorn-nut shape below the straight line (as shown at left). With a disappearing marker, trace the pattern twice, on the bias, onto velvet ribbon; cut out. With the right sides facing, whipstitch the edges (see below for instructions), leaving the top open. Turn the pouch right side out. Pour sand into the velvet pouch. Sew a running stitch around the top, and cinch closed (see below for instructions). Apply wood glue to the inside of the cap, and tuck in the top of the pouch so that the cap acts as a lid; let the glue dry.

how to make a whipstitch

Thread a needle and double knot the end. Pass the needle through the back of the fabric and pull the thread through. Pass the needle through the back of the fabric again, repeating, so that you have small stitch marks along the edge of the fabric. Weave the needle through the thread on back of the project for about 1 inch (2.5cm), and knot.

how to make a running stitch

Thread a needle, double-knot one end. Pass the needle from the back of the fabric to the front and make a stitch. Do not tug on the needle or the fabric will pucker. If you're stitching in a straight line, the stitches and the spaces between them should be of equal length. When you're finished, weave the needle through the thread on the back of project for about 1 inch (2.5cm), and knot.

PROJECT: acorn-topped boxes

Acorns make winsome knobs for small lidded containers. Look for wooden containers at flea markets or crafts stores. For extra shine, polish the acorns first with butcher's wax (available at hardware stores).

PROJECT SUPPLIES wooden box, stain or varnish (optional), matching acorn nuts and caps, wood glue, rotary tool, 1/16-inch (1.6mm) bit, pencil, 1/2-inch (6mm) #2 brass screw

HOW-TO If your box is unfinished, stain or varnish it as desired. Find an acorn cap and body that fit together, and join them with wood glue. Drill a 1/16-inch (1.6mm) hole in the lid of the wooden box with the rotary tool. Position the acorn at an angle on the top; with a pencil, mark the acorn through the hole in the lid. Drill through the mark, about an inch (2.5cm) deep. Align the acorn and the lid holes; join with the screw.

PROJECT: acorn garland

This wall hanging, made of acorns and pinecones, looks as though it's a carved-oak frieze magically released from an Arts and Crafts–style dining room; in fact, it was inspired by a similar vintage find. Some of the wires are connected to acorn nuts and caps, while others are only connected to the nuts to create acorn clusters.

PROJECT SUPPLIES matching acorn nuts and caps, rotary tool, 1/16-inch (1.6mm) bit, 16-inch (40.5cm) lengths of 22-gauge wire (plus more for hanging), wire cutters, brown floral tape, 24-inch (61cm) lengths of 16-gauge wire, pinecones

HOW-TO 1. To connect acorns and caps to wire, use the rotary tool to drill two 1/16-inch (1.6mm) holes through the caps. Insert one end of a length of 22-gauge wire into each of the holes; bend the wire, twisting at the top of the cap. Wrap wire with floral tape. Attach nuts to the caps with wood glue. **2.** For acorn clusters, drill 1/16-inch (1.6mm) holes through the tops of the acorns crosswise. Thread each one with a length of wire; twist, and wrap with brown floral tape, stretching the tape as you wind it around the wire to help it adhere. **3.** For pinecones, wrap wire around the bottom-most scales. Make pinecone "flowers," following the directions on page 198, and attach their bases to lengths of wire. Use floral tape to connect two 24-inch (61cm) lengths of 16-gauge wire together, and arrange the pinecones, pinecone "flowers," and acorns along it, setting the smaller items at the ends. Floral-tape the stems to the main wire, leaving 1/2- to 1-inch (13mm–2.5cm) spaces between the items facing in 1 direction. Stop at the center. Repeat on the other end, working in the opposite direction. To make loops for hanging, twist two 22-gauge wires together, wrap them with floral tape, and twist them around the back in a loop, 5 inches (12.5cm) from the center; repeat on the other side.

PROJECT: acorn napkin ring

This acorn-and-oak-leaf napkin ring has a wire stem; the leaf was preserved in a glycerin solution to make it last and prevent it from becoming brittle. You can also buy preserved leaves, or substitute ones cut from paper or felt.

PROJECT SUPPLIES oak leaves, glycerin (available at drugstores), water, rotary tool, 1/16-inch (1.6mm) drill bit, 16-inch (40.5cm) lengths of 22-gauge wire, matching acorn nuts and caps, wood glue, brown floral tape, brown seam binding

HOW-TO To preserve oak leaves, mix 1 part glycerin in 2 parts hot water, and let the leaves soak in the mixture for 3 to 4 days, then hang them to dry on a clothesline for about 10 days. To make napkin rings, start by drilling two 1/16-inch (1.6mm) holes through 2 acorn caps. Insert one end of a 16-inch (40.5cm) length of a 22-gauge wire into each one; bend the wire; and twist. Attach nuts to the caps with wood glue. Attach wire to the end of the leaves. Wrap wires with floral tape. Wrap leaf wire and 1 acorn wire together with brown floral tape, stretching the tape as you wrap it tightly; repeat with the other acorn wire, facing in the opposite direction. Wrap the wires with brown seam binding; glue at each end. Bend into a ring.

PINECONE CRAFTS

BASIC SUPPLIES

pinecones

floral cutters

small bowl

wire cutters

thread-covered
floral wire

card stock

scissors

cardboard box (at least
4 inches [10cm] square)

tacky glue

tweezers

cloves or tiny plant
parts (for centers)

gold stamp pad
(optional)

brown floral tape
(for stems, optional)

heavy floral wire
(for stems, optional)

Pick up a pinecone and admire its scales: You'll find that each one is as beautifully wrought as a flower petal. Yet blossoms made of pinecones will last much longer than ordinary flowers. It's easy to effect the transformation from cone to bloom—just snip the scales off the stem, and then glue them together in the shape of a flower. The examples on these pages take advantage of pinecones' varied looks.

HOW TO MAKE PINECONE FLOWERS

The shape of a pinecone flower will depend largely on the shape of the cone it's made from. Some cones, such as those from Norway spruce, have long scales that will be more fitting for creating larger flowers, while others, such as cones from the sabulosum tree, are more appropriate for smaller flowers.

1. With floral cutters, remove the pinecone's base. Starting at the cone's bottom, slip one blade of the cutters behind a scale; snip it off. Continue, working upward until all scales have been removed and only the stem remains.

2. Fill a small bowl with scales. Use the cardboard box as a work surface. Snip 4 inches (10cm) of thread-covered floral wire; form a small hook on one end. From card stock, cut a disk a bit larger than the desired size of the bloom's center. Secure the disk to the box top by poking a wire through both, letting the hook rest in the center so the wire won't fall through. Using tacky glue and tweezers, affix scales in a flower shape to the disk; the hook will become covered with glue. For a fuller blossom, add another layer inside the first, using smaller scales, adding up to five layers for larger blooms. Use tacky glue to attach one or more cloves or tiny plant parts in the center; let the piece dry, and remove

the bloom from the box. For an allover sheen, gently press each flower facedown into a golden stamp pad. To burnish only the tips, press the edges into the pad. To create a stem, wrap wire in brown floral tape, starting at base of the blossom; or cut off wire, if desired, for a stemless bloom.

3. To make buds and leaves for a vine (see candlesticks, page 201), affix tamarack buds and large scales to 4-inch (10cm) long wires: Wrap floral tape around the wires and bases of bud or scale, adding tacky glue where necessary. Cut a piece of heavy floral wire as long as the desired length of your vine. Alternating between small flowers (see above), buds, and leaves, lay the stems against the main wire; wrap these stems in place with brown floral tape, laying the next one against the wire, wrapping it, and so on until the vine is complete.

PINECONE GLOSSARY

1. Eastern white pinecones have long scales. Brown, natural canella berries are good centers for flat blooms.

2. The tiny cones of the sabulosum tree are ideal for delicate flowers. Use snipped cloves or the top of a poppy pod for centers.

3. Douglas fir cones result in plump blossoms. Tamarack buds can be used as centers or as buds.

4. For zinnialike florets, use blue spruce cones combined with ricegrass as centers.

5. Layer Norway spruce cones to create big flowers; dried weeping grass makes pretty tufted centers.

PROJECT: **candlesticks**

These climbers include flowers made from sabulosum cone scales, buds from the tamarack tree, and leaves, which are single Norway spruce cone scales.

PROJECT SUPPLIES Basic Supplies (page 198), tall candlesticks

HOW-TO Make pinecone flowers and vines, as described on page 198. Wrap finished vines around candlesticks.

PROJECT: **napkin rings**

Sliding a pinecone flower into a knotted ribbon and using it as a napkin ring makes for a natural table dressing. A set of them would be well suited to an autumn occasion.

PROJECT SUPPLIES Basic Supplies (page 198), thin velvet ribbon

HOW-TO Make a flower from pinecones, as described on page 198. These flowers are made from Norway spruce cones. Loosely tie a ribbon around a cloth napkin, leaving knotted section in front with about 2 inch tails cut at an angle. Slide wire stem of pinecone flower into the knot and tighten.

PROJECT: **hurricane candle shades**

Pinecone flowers and paper leaves are a natural fit for clear hurricanes. Set a trio of these embellished glass covers on a holiday mantel or table.

PROJECT SUPPLIES Basic Supplies (page 198), paper leaves (these embossed leaves were purchased online, but you can also make your own simple versions), hurricane lamps, wide colorful velvet ribbon, double-sided tape, thin gold satin ribbon, hot-glue gun and glue stick

HOW-TO Make a large pinecone flower (these are made from Norway spruce cones), as described on page 198, for each hurricane. Glue paper leaves to the back of the pinecone flowers. Wrap the top of each hurricane with wide ribbon, affixing it in the front with double-stick tape. Wrap the thinner, gold ribbon in the center of the wide ribbon, affixing the ends in the front of the hurricane, so that a small amount of the ribbon hangs down on each end. Hot-glue a pinecone flower where the gold ribbon comes together.

PROJECT: salt and pepper holder

Upturned seashells make ideal vessels for salt, pepper, and other table seasonings.

PROJECT SUPPLIES Basic Supplies (page 204; use 4 scallop or clamshells [or a pair of each]), hot-glue gun and glue stick

HOW-TO Clean the shells (see below) to remove all grit. Let the shells dry. For the base, turn 2 shells top-side up, and glue them together at the hinge. Top with the other two shells: Lay them faceup and crosswise over the base, and affix with hot glue. Let dry completely before filling with salt and pepper.

PROJECT: shell soap dish

Turn a pretty pair of clam or scallop shells into a soap dish.

PROJECT SUPPLIES Basic Supplies (page 204; use 1 large scallop or clamshell and 1 small scallop or clamshell), newspaper

HOW-TO Wash 1 big shell and 1 small shell (see below), and let them dry completely. Using bonding cement, affix the big shell to the small shell, back to back. Place the shells in a crumpled ring of news-paper, small shell down, so the paper supports the top shell. Let dry thoroughly.

washing shells

Getting all the grit out of shells by hand is a challenge; instead, rinse well in the sink, then slip them into the utensil basket of the dishwasher, and run them through a gentle cycle. They'll be clean and ready for craft projects when they come out.

PROJECT: seashell lights

Cast a dreamy glow over outdoor spaces by gluing a collection of beach treasures to a string of outdoor lights. Use only UL-approved lights, which should not overheat when lit.

PROJECT SUPPLIES Basic Supplies (page 204; use small scallop or clamshells), masking tape, miniature outdoor string lights (UL-approved), small nails, hammer

HOW-TO Tape a 2-foot (61cm) section of lights to your work surface with bulbs lying flat. Apply a thin layer of bonding cement along the hinge edge of a shell, and press it into place at the plastic base of a light. Do not let the cement touch the bulb. Repeat for each bulb. Let each one dry about 5 minutes before continuing with the next section. Hammer small nails into the underside or side of a beam or molding, and hook the lights on them.

ORIGAMI AND PAPER FOLDING

While many crafts projects benefit from a little artistic license—a few extra brushstrokes here, a bit more glitter there—you'll rarely get pleasant results if you don't follow origami and paper-folding instructions precisely. However, if you execute each step exactly, you're practically guaranteed a perfect finished piece every time.

Although the Japanese often get credit for creating folded-paper artwork—the word *origami* was derived from the Japanese words *oru*, meaning "to fold," and *kami*, meaning "paper"—the craft originated in China in the first or second century and wasn't practiced in Japan until five hundred or six hundred years later. Over the following centuries, paper-folding methods were passed down through generations and slowly spread through Europe. The first printed work on origami, *Senbazuru Orikata* (*How to Fold One Thousand Cranes*), was published in 1797. Since then, paper-folding enthusiasts have debated whether origami should mean strictly folding square paper, or if the craft might encompass other materials (fabric, sheet metal) or methods (cutting, gluing). Some of the projects that follow, such as the folded crane, embrace origami in its truest form. Others, such as miniature shopping bags, are modern interpretations. Fundamentally, though, each is made in much the same way as the very first folded-paper crafts: with paper, patience, and precision.

ABOUT THE MATERIALS

PAPER You'll find thousands of styles of paper made specifically for origami. Each sheet is a perfect square of thin, easy-to-fold paper. Some are patterned, others are solid; some are printed on both sides, others have one printed side and one plain side. You don't need to use "origami paper" for these crafts—unless the directions specify otherwise, any thin paper will do. Patterned wrapping paper will work well. But when a square of paper is called for, origami paper is particularly convenient; you can follow the same folding instructions on different-size squares of paper to make smaller and larger variations of an object.

BONE FOLDER Although optional, a bone folder—a tool traditionally used in bookbinding—will help you make the most precise folds. Simply lay a ruler where you want your fold, and run a bone folder alongside it for a crisp crease every time.

BASIC SUPPLIES

paper
bone folder (optional)

OPPOSITE **The crane is a widely recognized symbol of peace. A few dozen hung on a Christmas tree make a striking holiday presentation.**

PAINTING CHINA AND GLASS

A painted design is one of the easiest ways to breathe new life into an old set of dishes, a flea-market mirror, or even a glass-fronted cabinet. The tradition of painting on ceramics and glass has a storied past. Chinese and English artisans hand-painted intricate designs on fine china for centuries, and this dishware is still coveted by many discerning collectors. In the eighteenth century, painting on the reverse side of glass—a technique called *eglomise*—first became the rage in France, and gradually spread across the continent and the globe, showing up on American clock faces and Chinese snuff bottles. Today, you can practice these crafts in many contemporary ways by modernizing mismatched dishware and tiles, creating easy picture frames on glass, or designing fanciful patterns on the bottom of serving trays and glassware. Best of all, if you don't like your designs, it's easy to scrape away the dried paint, and begin anew.

ABOUT THE MATERIALS

GLASS AND PORCELAIN You can paint on virtually any glass, ceramic, or porcelain surface. Look for these items at flea markets, or even in the back of your cupboards or closets. If you're painting a piece that you want to use for eating, make sure that it is heatproof. Because the paint must be "fired" in your oven to help bond the paint to the surface of the dish or glass after it's been applied, heatproof porcelain, crockery, and terracotta are your best options. Large pieces of glass can be unwieldy; if you need to purchase a large piece for a project—such as for a tabletop—find a glazier who delivers.

OPPOSITE **A collection of mismatched dishes is given a harmonious look when painted with a similar dotted design. Search flea markets, online auction sites, or even your own collection for plates, bowls, and other dishware to embellish.**

CERAMIC PAINT Paints used on ceramics come in both water- and oil-based formulas. Oil-based paints generally offer a wider spectrum of colors than those that are water-based, but will take longer to dry. Many paints come packaged in tubes with penlike tips; if they don't, use an applicator bottle as described on page 222. If you're painting dishes or glassware that will come into contact with food or drink, use a water-based, food-safe paint, such as Porcelaine.

GLASS PAINT A number of different types of paint can be used on glass; which one you choose will largely depend on your desired effect. Here is a brief breakdown:

GLASS PAINT Paint labeled specifically as GLASS PAINT comes in both oil- and water-based varieties. It is more transparent than other types of paint, and it's a good choice if you want to create the look of stained glass, which allows you to see through the painting. The colors can be combined, but should not be thinned, as they may not adhere well to the glass. Drying times vary.

JAPAN PAINT This oil-based paint is often used for window signs. It is opaque, lusterless, and usually comes in a can. It is quick drying and cleans up easily with turpentine.

ENAMEL PAINT Enamel paints are usually oil-based and quite opaque, but shinier than Japan paint. They contain highly concentrated pigments, and are a good choice if you want to cover a large area. There is no mixing necessary and drying typically takes a few hours.

ARTISTS' OIL PAINT Traditionally used on canvas, these paints are superior to Japan paint and enamel varieties when you need a metallic color, such as gold. Otherwise, they can be messier and harder to work with than other paints and may take up to a week to dry. (If the paint is too runny or too thick, it will not adhere well to the glass.) Clean up or thin artists' oil paint with turpentine or mineral spirits.

DOT-PAINTING ON CHINA

BASIC SUPPLIES

scissors

red transfer paper

clear tape

ballpoint pen

food-safe ceramic or porcelain paint (such as Porcelaine)

paint applicator bottles

paper muffin cup liners

wooden coffee stirrers

straight pin

baby wipes

Painting on china or ceramics is a great way to embellish dishware. Uncomplicated designs can be drawn freehand (practice on old or broken dishware, porcelain tiles, or scrap paper until you're comfortable with the technique). You can also use templates for more precise application of the paint. Many of the projects in this section use the dot-painting technique; a dotted design template is first transferred to the dishware using transfer paper and a ballpoint pen, and these dots are then covered with porcelain or ceramic paint. Prolong the life of your work by hand-washing dishes with mild soap and a nonabrasive cloth or sponge, avoiding the painted areas.

HOW TO DOT PAINT ON PORCELAIN AND CERAMICS

Adorn an entire set of dishes in a single afternoon or create a stylish display over time. Use red transfer paper, which is easily seen on dark and light colors; the marks will disappear after the pottery is "fired" in the oven. To diversify your collection, paint all the dishes with one color but vary the motif, or create a single motif in different shades.

PAINTING SUPPLIES Basic Supplies (above), template (page 381), ceramic plate

 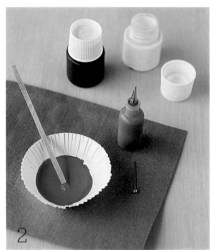 

1. Photocopy or print the template onto regular paper, enlarging or reducing it as desired; cut it out. Cut a piece of transfer paper slightly larger than the template. Place it under the template, and tape both to the plate. Firmly trace the template with a ballpoint pen. Remove the template and transfer paper; a faint design should be visible on the plate.

2. Mix paint colors (add white paint to make lighter shades, if desired), then pour into applicator bottles.

3. Squeeze the bottle gently for small dots and harder for larger ones. Apply the paint to the dish following the traced design with evenly spaced dots. Use a straight pin to unclog the bottle tip as necessary. Let the paint dry for 2 hours, then remove transfer lines with a baby wipe. Heat the plate, following paint manufacturer's instructions, to set the paint. If you have extra paint left over, insert a pin into the bottle tip before storing.

PROJECT: bordered plates

A polka-dot border (shown on the bottom plate above) is a breeze to do freehand, and complements more intricately decorated dishes (use the template on page 381 for the flower design on the blue plates above). For a gift, tie a stack of painted salad and dinner plates with a length of ribbon.

PROJECT SUPPLIES Basic Supplies (opposite), ceramic plates

HOW-TO Working clockwise around each plate, apply a dot border in one color, followed by a second row in a contrasting color. Intersperse the second row of dots between every 2 dots in the previous row. Let paint dry and heat to set, following paint manufacturer's instructions.

224

PROJECT: **embellished tea set**

A plain green teapot and cups get a decorative boost when dot-painted in a floral motif. A tile, painted in the same design, makes the perfect serving trivet.

PROJECT SUPPLIES Basic Supplies (page 222; use food-safe ceramic paint, such as Porcelaine), template (page 381), tea set, a 6-inch (15cm) square tile

HOW-TO Apply the template onto the tea set following the instructions on page 222. Apply dots of paint over the transferred design, squeezing the bottle gently for small blooms and harder for larger ones. Let paint dry and heat the ceramics to set according to the paint manufacturer's instructions. Decorate a complementary trivet from a 6-inch (15cm) square tile by trimming it with a variation of the same pattern, using blue paint.

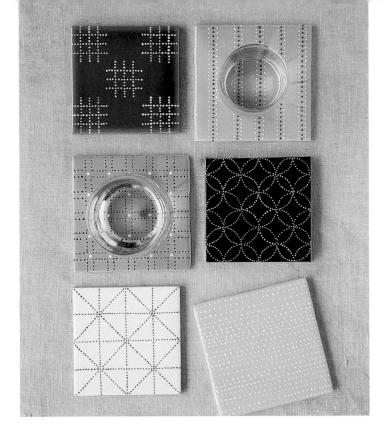

PROJECT: painted-tile coasters

Square tiles make great coasters. They cost just a few dollars at tile stores and can be adorned with any number of modern patterns.

PROJECT SUPPLIES Basic Supplies (page 222), 4-inch (10cm) ceramic square tiles, templates (page 384), clear plastic ruler, pencil, felt surface protectors.

HOW-TO Following the instructions on page 222, use the templates to create a circular design or checkerboard motif on tiles. For other designs: Draw a pattern onto each tile using a pencil and a clear plastic ruler and cover the markings with paint. Wipe any visible lines clean once the paint is dry. Add felt surface protectors to the undersides of coasters before using.

PROJECT: dot-painted bathroom accessories

For personalized bathroom storage, paint a monogram and floral prints onto oversized ceramic canisters. You can also add similar paint details to bathroom tiles and vases.

PROJECT SUPPLIES Basic Supplies (page 222), templates (pages 382–383, 386), ceramic canisters, small vase (optional)

HOW-TO Using the alphabet templates on pages 382–383 and following the instructions on page 222, dot-paint a single monogram on a large canister and a matching floral design on the smaller ones. A high-contrast paint color will show up best. To complete the look, paint a dot design, using the template on page 386, on the bathroom tiles nearby and on a bud vase in a coordinating hue.

PAINTING ON GLASS

BASIC SUPPLIES

glass surface to be painted

glass cleaner or mild dishwashing liquid

decal paper

craft knife

Japan or enamel oil paint (except for metallic colors)

artists' oil paint (in metallic colors)

paintbrushes

razor blade (optional)

Reverse painting on glass, also called *eglomise,* is a lasting decorative technique that will add charm to all manner of glass-ware, mirrors, and even picture frames. Though the result might look ornate, all the projects in this section can be easily completed with the guidance of stencils. Erase mistakes by scraping away the dried paint with a razor blade. To prolong the life of your painted designs, never put these items in the dishwasher. When washing, use warm water and try to avoid rubbing the painted area.

HOW TO PAINT ON GLASS

To embellish a glass serving tray like this one, search for images from wallpaper samples, clip-art books, textiles, or even wrapping paper. Create a stencil by copying the design onto decal paper and cutting out details with a craft knife. The most delicate designs of these flowers are painted first, so that they show up once the tray is turned right side up.

PAINTED TRAY SUPPLIES Basic Supplies (above; use a serving tray); wallpaper, textiles, or wrapping paper; clear rubber feet

1. Clean tray with glass cleaner or mild dishwashing liquid, and dry. Copy your design onto decal paper, peel off the backing, and apply it to the underside of the tray. Use a craft knife to lightly carve out and peel away the design, leaving behind the outlined areas to fill in with color. This process will essentially make a stencil.

2. For a floral design like the one shown on the tray opposite, apply the paint in layers, letting each one dry completely before adding the next. Start with the most detailed part of

the design: Use a thin brush and work freehand, or place a copy of the design on the other side of the tray and trace it. Let it dry, and then layer larger expanses of color right over those details. The design may appear messy as you work, but when viewed from the other side, the details will be visible.

3. When the entire design has dried, carefully peel away the decal paper. Attach clear rubber feet (available in hardware stores) to the 4 corners of the tray bottom to elevate the tray and keep the paint from getting scratched.

PROJECT: reverse-painted tumblers

Butterflies painted on the underside of a set of tumblers are surprisingly three-dimensional when viewed from the other side. Light passing through the glass heightens the effect.

PROJECT SUPPLIES Basic Supplies (see opposite; use flat-bottom glass tumblers), wallpaper, clip art, or other design

HOW-TO Copy your design onto decal paper, peel off the backing, and affix to the bottom of glasses. Use a craft knife to lightly carve out and peel away the design, leaving behind the outlined areas to fill in with color. Begin painting the finest details, working freehand; let them dry, and then paint in the next most detailed areas. Continue filling in colors, letting the paint dry between each layer, until the design is finished. Once the paint has dried completely, remove the decals from the glasses.

PROJECT: painted picture-frame border

Daguerreotypes are an early type of photograph, created by exposing
an image onto a silver-plated copper plate. You can create a similar vintage
look by painting a picture frame border on glass and placing family photos
behind them. Match the painted mats to a decorative element in the room,
to your favorite color, or to one another.

PROJECT SUPPLIES Basic Supplies (page 226; use enamel oil paint), acid-free board,
templates (page 385), copper tape, velvet ribbon, contact cement glue

HOW-TO 1. Have a piece of glass cut to the same size or slightly larger than your
photograph. To keep the paint from rubbing off onto your photos, cut a "mat" of
acid-free board to sandwich between the painted glass and the photo, just large
enough so that it won't show when the picture is in place. Using the templates
copy the outline of the decorative mat opening, enlarging or reducing as needed,
onto decal paper. Affix this paper to the glass. Using a craft knife, trace over the
central outline, then peel away the portion that will become the border. **2.** Paint
this area using your desired enamel oil color. Once the paint has dried, peel away
the decal paper. With a thin brush, paint a strip of gold, freehand, along the inner
edge of the mat, and let it dry thoroughly. **3.** Place the photo between the mat
and the painted side of the glass. Use copper tape (available from stained-glass
suppliers) to seal the package together around the outside edge, then cover that
with a velvet ribbon, gluing it in place with contact cement glue.

PROJECT: "painted" mirror

An abstract wreath of leaves and berries appears to float in front of a second identical wreath. The illusion comes from setting a painted pane of glass against a mirror—in this case an antique one with a pleasingly clouded finish.

PROJECT SUPPLIES Basic Supplies (page 226; use a mirror and clear glass cut to same size as mirror), templates (page 385), wide velvet ribbon

HOW-TO Copy the template, reducing or enlarging it as desired, and copy it onto decal paper. Affix the decal paper to the pane of glass, centering it carefully. With the tip of a craft knife, score the outline of the design into the decal; peel off leaves and berries where you'll apply the paint. Smooth the decal against the glass to eliminate air bubbles, and paint over the exposed areas. Let paint dry, then carefully peel away the rest of the decal. Press the painted side of the glass against the mirror, and then frame the pieces together. Attach a length of wide velvet ribbon (in a color that complements the paint) for hanging.

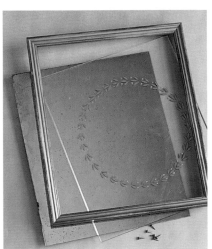

PROJECT: *painted cabinet*

A geometric pattern painted on the inside of this glass cabinet door draws attention away from the bathroom staples within. Creating a pattern as detailed as this is time-consuming, although no more difficult than the other painted-glass projects in this section.

PROJECT SUPPLIES Basic Supplies (page 226), cabinet, kraft paper, scissors, double-sided tape, templates (page 386), large brush, 3/16-inch (5mm) wide masking tape, razor blade (optional)

HOW-TO 1. Prepare the cabinet door by cutting an oval or a circle out of kraft paper. Use double-sided tape to affix it to the center of the glass on the inside of the door. Copy the pattern template, reducing or enlarging it as desired, and then copy it onto enough sheets of decal paper to cover the exposed glass. Affix the decals to the glass, framing the paper oval and lining up the pattern at the seams where the decals meet. Carve the outline of the design with a craft knife, and peel away the area around the diamond shapes and the lines where you'll apply the paint. Smooth the remaining decals against the glass, making sure to eliminate air bubbles. **2.** Using a large brush, apply paint over the entire area, filling in all cut-outs. Let dry. To add borders on side panels, apply 3/16-inch (5mm) wide masking tape around the inside of the glass where it meets the wood. Apply a second border inside the first, leaving 1/8-inch (3mm) wide space; fill the space with paint. **3.** Let it dry, and remove all tape and decals. Scrape off errant paint spots with a razor blade, if necessary. When cleaning the inside, gently go over the glass with a clean, barely damp cloth, but do not rub.

From a painting by Walter Biggs

PAPER CUTTING AND PUNCHING

It's not as difficult a leap as you might think from a child's folded-and-cut-paper snow-flakes to intricate artwork that appears to have been drawn with scissors. The materials required for even the most elaborate cutouts are simple and inexpensive—paper and pencil, scissors and knife—and for this reason, paper cutting has a long history as a folk art. At least since the time of the Chinese Sung dynasty, around 1100 A.D., people have been using cut paper for decoration. The earliest paper cutouts were religious in character, but soon enough the practice extended to secular life. By the time *scherenschnitte* (German for "scissors cutting") came to full flower in Austria in the seventeenth century, whole traditions of cut-paper craft had evolved around the world, including the shadow puppets of Indonesia and the tissue-paper flags known as *papel picado* in Mexico. In seventeenth-century European homes, *scherenschnitte* pictures often were made to be framed and proudly displayed alongside other works of art. The same techniques used centuries ago were used to create the projects on the pages that follow, along with projects that were made with paper punches, a new take on a time-honored tradition. Use old techniques—or new—to craft beautiful paper-cutout cards for your family and friends, and don't be surprised if your work is given similar pride of place.

ABOUT THE MATERIALS

PAPER Be creative with your paper choices; consider parchment, newspaper, brightly colored origami paper, pages from magazines, gift wrap, or handsomely printed text photocopied from old books. Lightweight papers work best for folded cutwork (although tissue is too delicate); heavier papers are best for cutting out a single image in a continuous line. If you intend to display your cutouts, be sure to make them out of nonyellowing, acid-free white and nonfading color papers.

OPPOSITE **Charming paper-cutout greeting cards and envelopes display a variety of blooms. One continuously cut image, such as the salmon-pink carnation, provides flowers for cards and envelopes—negative and positive images. Several papers were used to compose the daffodil.**

SCISSORS Look for very sharp scissors with fine points; embroidery and cuticle scissors work well (though you'll need a separate pair for paper). Pierce the paper with scissor tips or a pin to gain entry into small spaces. Choose scissors over a craft knife when cutting out large shapes and outer edges.

CRAFT KNIFE A craft knife is ideal for cutting central and small areas. To eliminate the chance of a tear, you'll need to change the knife blade whenever the paper starts to pull as you try to cut.

CRAFT PUNCHES Popular among scrapbook enthusiasts, craft punches allow you to punch almost any shape into every kind of paper. A series of related punches—such as flowers in different sizes and shapes—lets you create a theme.

BASIC SUPPLIES

transfer paper

paper

pencil

scissors

craft knife and replacement blades

self-healing mat

bone folder

white craft glue

fine-tipped paintbrush

paper clips or staples

PROJECT: pop-up party supplies

With some clever cutting, rubber-stamped party accessories come to life. A tasteful decorative theme can be a lovely addition to a grown-up gathering.

PROJECT SUPPLIES Basic Supplies (page 233), rubber stamps, ink pad, note cards, fine-tip glue pen, glitter, patterned paper, screw punch, ribbon, adhesive foam dots

HOW-TO For an invitation, stamp a bird (the one pictured also has a branch and berries) onto a blank card, off-center. Using a fine-tip glue pen, apply glue to details such as berries. Sprinkle with glitter (in this case, red), and tap off excess. (For more information on rubber stamping and glittering, see chapters beginning on pages 298 and 142.) Make place cards by stamping the same image on a piece of patterned paper, with the top half above the center of the sheet. Trim around the top half with a craft knife; fold the paper (but not the cut portion) in half so the top stands up. To top a favor bag with a stamped and cut card, punch aligning holes with a screw punch. Thread ribbon through the holes from front to back, cross the ends behind, and thread from back to front. To create napkin rings, stamp the same image on double-sided paper and cut it out completely. Make a ring using the reverse pattern of the same paper, and attach it with an adhesive foam dot.

PROJECT: punched-flower cards and wrapping

Add new dimension to gift wrap and cards with these simple cutouts.

PROJECT SUPPLIES Basic Supplies (page 233; use card stock or wrapping paper), template (page 389), double-sided tape (optional), paper cards (optional)

HOW-TO Photocopy the template, enlarging or reducing it as desired; cut out. Using a pencil, trace around the template onto the card stock or wrapping paper. Carefully cut along the traced lines with a craft knife, leaving gaps between the petals. For gifts, wrap the item with paper in a contrasting color before covering it with a cutout layer. For cards, use double-sided tape to attach a cutout card to a second card in a contrasting color. To add dimension to the petals, gently curl them up with your finger, shaping them as you work.

SILHOUETTES

BASIC SUPPLIES

camera

fine-tipped paintbrush

white acrylic or tempera paint

heavy black permanent paper

fine-gauge felt-tip pen

black or colored acid-free paper

small, sharp scissors

craft knife and replacement blades

spray-mount adhesive

Black-paper silhouettes featuring dignified people in profile were all the rage in eighteenth-century France. This project takes an old idea and makes it new. Instead of adopting those staid poses, the people pictured here took a stance—palming a basketball, playing an instrument, whisking eggs—that better captured their personality. After the photographs were taken, they were turned into one-of-a-kind showpieces. Consider throwing a picture-taking party for friends and family members so that you'll end up with a wall full of people you adore.

taking photographs

Ordinary snapshots are the first step in creating a venerable visual record of the company you keep. Once your subjects have picked their poses, it's time to set up your photo shoot. Here are some helpful recommendations for getting crisp shots: Choose a plain, uncluttered background. For further contrast, your subject should be backlit, as shown above. Don't use a flash—it may cause shadows. The subject should pose in profile.

When your series of silhouettes is complete, arrange the portraits together on a wall. Use spray adhesive to mount your silhouettes on acid-free paper. Center the silhouette in a frame. Use same-color frames to display a series of silhouettes; this will give a unified feel to the grouping. Black silhouettes in red frames have a sophisticated look, while color designs in white frames are playful and modern.

HOW TO MAKE SILHOUETTES

Blanket the background of a photo with white acrylic or tempera paint, then fill in the image with a heavy black permanent marker. Add or exaggerate lively details like cowlicks, eyelashes, hats, and jewelry with a fine-gauge felt-tip pen. For true silhouettes, photocopy the doctored photo, then cut out the blackened part of the photo to use as a template. Trace the template onto black or colored acid-free paper, cut out the image, and affix the image to a background with spray-mount adhesive, working in a well-ventilated area. You can achieve a similar effect by simply photocopying the doctored photos onto quality art paper—glossier papers will print best; rougher paper may need some reinking.

PAPER PUNCHING

BASIC SUPPLIES
craft paper
craft punches

It's possible to cut intricate designs into paper without ever picking up a pair of scissors: Craft punches allow you to create detailed shapes by simply lowering and lifting your hand. These punches (similar in nature to the basic hole punch used to wrangle paper into three-ring binders) come in every shape imaginable. You'll also find corner and edging punches, which add decorative punched borders—and sometimes embossing—to stationery and paper.

PROJECT: flowery favor boxes

A shower of punched cherry blossoms dresses up plain favor boxes. The little parcels are inexpensive—and easy to turn out en masse.

PROJECT SUPPLIES Basic Supplies (above; use flower punches in 4 different shapes and sizes, and white card stock), mini pinking shears, rubber stamp, ink pad, ink, fine-tipped markers, favor boxes, double-sided glue dots, adhesive foam disks

HOW-TO Punch flowers from white card stock; trim the edges of the largest blooms with mini pinking shears so the flowers resemble cherry blossoms. Use a small flower-shaped rubber stamp and different-colored ink pads to add patterns to the centers of the largest and second-largest flowers; you could also draw in a design with fine-tipped markers. Attach 2 or 3 flowers to each box. Some are affixed flat to the box using double-sided glue dots; others are attached with adhesive foam disks so they're raised.

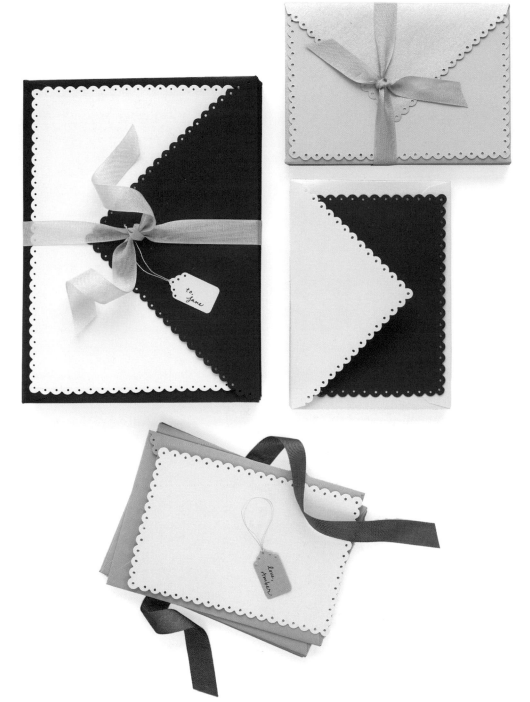

PROJECT: **dot-edged stationery**

Give your correspondence a flourish: Trim the edges of standard note cards and envelopes with a decorative rotary cutter and a micro hole punch.

PROJECT SUPPLIES note cards, ruler, pencil, envelopes, decorative rotary cutter, micro hole punch

HOW-TO Draw a line ⅛ inch (3mm) from the edge of the note card or envelope flap with a ruler and a pencil; cut along the line using a decorative rotary cutter. Next, make a dot inside each scallop with a pencil, then use the marks as a guide to punch out circles with a micro hole punch.

PROJECT: **gift toppers**

With help from craft punches, plain bits of paper become pretty toppers, making small gifts even more precious.

PROJECT SUPPLIES Basic Supplies (page 240; use punches in the shape of leaves and an edging punch), small boxes, adhesive foam dots, ribbon, white craft glue, small round sticker

HOW-TO Make lace-edged bands by using an edging punch on both edges of a strip of paper. Wrap around boxes singly or layered with contrasting strips of paper. To make a wreath, attach the punched leaves around the outside edge of a punched circle, and a small piece of ribbon to the back; attach the leaves with white craft glue, the ribbon with a sticker. To make the leaf topper, attach two punched leafy branches and assorted leaves to a box with adhesive foam dots. Join the branches' stems with a knotted piece of ribbon.

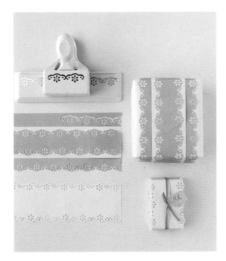

PROJECT: **bell gift toppers**

Bells have long been used to "ring in" new marriages. Set a lovely tone for a wedding with punched bell–topped favor boxes.

PROJECT SUPPLIES Basic Supplies (page 240; use punches in the shape of bells), scissors, vellum, box, double-sided tape, origami paper, micro hole punch, satin cord

HOW-TO Cut vellum to wrap the lid of a favor box; the box pictured is 3 ½ inches (9cm) square and 2 inches (5cm) high. The vellum should be the same width as the lid and long enough to fold down both sides of the lid and partly up the inside; the piece here is 5 ½ by 3 ½ inches (14cm x 9cm). Wrap vellum over the lid; secure it with double-sided tape inside. Fill the box with candies or another favor; put the lid on box. Using a small bell-shaped punch, cut out six bells from origami paper in different patterns. Punch a small hole at the top of each bell with a micro hole punch. Thread bells onto a satin cord (the one pictured is 16 inches [40.5cm] long). Wrap the cord around the box and knot it, adjusting the cord so the knot is on the side of the box, and slide bells so they're on top.

PAPER FLOWERS AND BIRDS

In their traditional roles, crepe paper and tissue paper can be easily overlooked: Crepe paper streamers tend to blend in with party décor, and tissue paper isn't usually as exciting as the gifts tucked inside it. With a few snips and folds and a bit of floral tape, however, both papers can be transformed into exuberant flowers with real staying power. (Crepe paper—more durable and textured—can also be fashioned into decorative birds. See one example on pages 256-257.) The examples on these pages easily lend themselves to wedding displays: Flower for flower, faux floral arrangements are less expensive than those made with live blooms, plus they'll last for decades—not just days—if properly preserved. These projects were inspired by nature, although curly petaled and cone-shaped flowers are decidedly otherworldly. You can mix and match shapes and colors to create, say, pink daffodils or green warblers, or render your crafts to mimic Mother Nature's work. Either way, the finished pieces promise to be memorable.

ABOUT THE MATERIALS

CREPE PAPER Most people are familiar with crepe paper streamers, which are sold in rolls and often draped across doorways during celebrations. Crepe paper is also sold in long sheets, called folds, which were used for the projects on the following pages. When working with crepe paper, keep in mind that its creases, or "grain," should run up and down (not across) the item you're sculpting; this will keep the crepe paper rigid. Double-check the position of your templates to ensure that they're aligned properly with the grain before tracing and cutting.

OPPOSITE **Easy-to-make crepe paper flowers—like the ones pictured in a bouquet here—are sweet and pretty. They have a long history as decorations at festivities.**

TISSUE PAPER Tissue paper more closely resembles the translucence of fresh flower petals. It can be found in a wider range of colors than crepe paper, and is readily available at any store that stocks gift wrap. It is more delicate than crepe paper, and will not recover as well if crushed.

FLORAL WIRE Floral wire comes in several gauges; the higher the gauge, the thinner and more flexible the wire will be. The bouquets on the following pages were made using 18-gauge cloth-wrapped floral wire.

FLORAL TAPE Floral tape, which is sold in rolls, is used to join the petals and stamen of each flower to its stem. When pulled taut and wrapped around the length of a stem, green floral tape stretches and conforms to the shape of the stem, holding everything together tightly.

PROJECT: bridal bouquet

Making a bouquet's worth of flowers can provide you with many quiet moments of escape during the hectic months of wedding planning.

PROJECT SUPPLIES Basic Supplies (page 246), wide satin ribbon, decorative straight pins

HOW-TO Assemble crepe-paper flowers (the bouquet shown has 16) following the instructions beginning on page 246; make a few leaves to fill out the bouquet. Arrange the flowers and leaves. Once you're satisfied with the arrangement, tightly wrap the stems in floral tape to keep them in place. Trim the ends of the stems, as needed. Wrap the stems in a piece of wide satin ribbon to finish, if desired; flip the exposed raw edge under, and pin it in place with decorative straight pins.

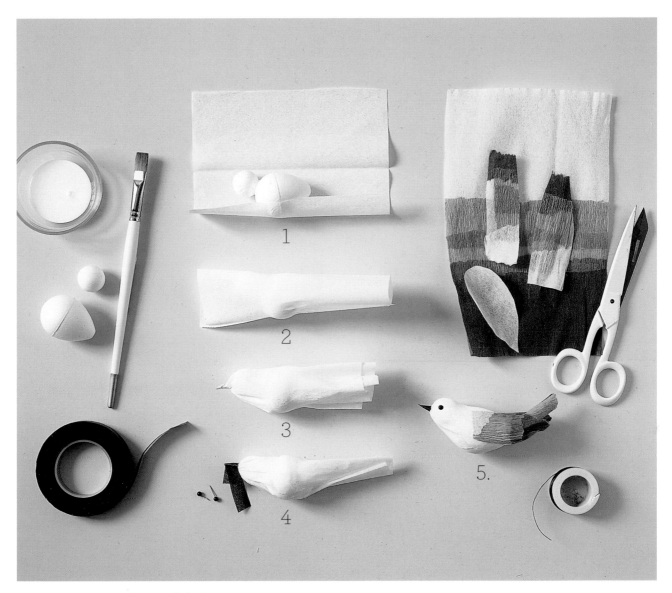

PROJECT: crepe paper birds

Dainty crepe paper birds perched atop just-bloomed branches are welcome anytime—indoors or out. The feathered friends pictured here were inspired by the paintings of John James Audubon and other nineteenth-century naturalists. A flock with different postures (vary the placement of the heads and bodies) appears more lifelike. The branch was trimmed from a quince tree; a tiny nest (filled with dyed quail eggs) was tucked between its limbs.

PROJECT SUPPLIES hot-glue gun, polystyrene balls, polystyrene eggs, scissors, crepe paper, paintbrush, tacky glue, brown floral tape, map tacks, awl, floral wire (optional), branch (optional)

HOW-TO 1. Make the head and body: Use a glue gun to affix a small polystyrene ball to the rounded end of a larger polystyrene egg; let dry. Cut a 7-inch (18cm) square of colored crepe paper. Lay the body near the bottom edge of the paper. **2.** Beginning at the breast, wrap the body, stretching the paper to fit the contours as you go. Brush the inside of the paper with tacky glue. Taper the back end to create the tail. **3.** Twist the front end to create a beak; brush both ends with glue. Trim the ends with scissors while the paper is wet; let it dry. **4.** Wrap the beak in brown floral tape; trim. For eyes, press in map tacks. Make wings: Tear strips of crepe paper in desired hues. **5.** Overlap strips to create a color gradient, and glue. Cut out 2 rectangles; glue 1 to each side of the bird. Taper ends to form wing shapes. For the breast, cut a paper oval in a contrasting color, and glue. To attach the bird to a branch: Use an awl to create a small hole in the base of a finished bird's body. Thread a 3-inch (7.5cm) length of floral wire through the hole, securing it with a dab of hot glue. Wrap the wire around a branch to attach the bird.

TISSUE PAPER

BASIC SUPPLIES
tissue paper
cloth-wrapped floral wire
floral tape
scissors
white craft glue

Let sheer sheets of tissue paper blossom into beautiful flowers and decorations for a wedding or any big day. Although these blooms are less true-to-life (and slightly more fragile) than those crafted from crepe paper, they're every bit as lovely (not to mention inexpensive and simple to create). They can be made in endless colors and will remain fresh long after they are made.

PROJECT: tissue paper bouquet

The luscious blooms in this bouquet were fashioned from tissue paper in various shades of pink, but you could make them in any color.

PROJECT SUPPLIES Basic Supplies (above), wide satin ribbon, decorative straight pins

HOW-TO Making the bouquet takes only an afternoon. Assemble 25 flowers following the instructions on the pages that follow; make a few leaves to fill out the bouquet. Arrange the flowers. Once you're satisfied with the arrangement, tightly wrap the stems in floral tape to keep them in place. Trim the ends of the stems as needed. Wrap the stems in a piece of wide satin ribbon to finish; flip the exposed raw edge under, and pin it in place with decorative straight pins.

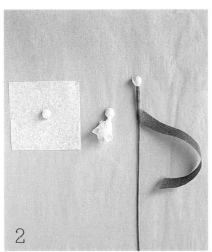

PROJECT: **folded-petal flower**

PROJECT SUPPLIES Basic Supplies (opposite)

HOW-TO 1. Cut 1 3/4-by-2 3/4-inch (4.5cm x 7cm) and 1 1/4-by-2-inch (3cm x 5cm) rectangles from tissue paper. (The flower above has 8 small and 10 large petals.) Fold each rectangle in half lengthwise; cut 1 end of each to be rounded, and twist the other end to shape. **2.** For the center, roll tissue paper in a contrasting color into a tiny ball; cut out a square from tissue paper, and wrap it around the ball, twisting the tissue paper at its base. Attach the twist to a piece of floral wire by wrapping both with floral tape. **3.** Add petals one at a time (start with small petals and end with large ones), taping twisted ends of the petals to the floral wire, then wrapping the floral tape to the bottom of the stem. Trim the floral tape; spread out the petals.

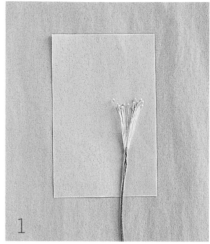

PROJECT: bubble petal flower

PROJECT SUPPLIES Basic Supplies (page 258), store-bought stamens, polystyrene ball

HOW-TO 1. For each flower, attach 12 stamens (or 6 double-ended stamens) to floral wire with floral tape. Cut five 4-by-2 ¼-inch (10cm x 5.5cm) pieces of tissue paper. **2.** For each petal, wrap tissue halfway around 1 ½-inch (3.8cm) polystyrene ball, forming a half-sphere; twist both ends of the tissue paper, and remove the ball. **3.** Attach one end of a petal to the base of the stamens with floral tape. Add the other petals one at a time. Wrap the floral tape to the bottom of the stem. Trim floral tape and the petals' twisted ends. Gently pull the petals away from the center.

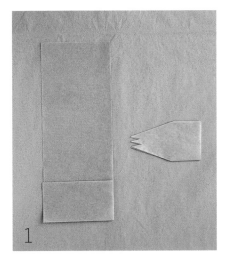

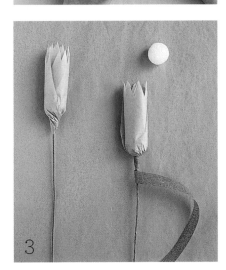

PROJECT: **rolled petal flower**

PROJECT SUPPLIES Basic Supplies (page 258), polystyrene ball

HOW-TO 1. Cut a 16-by-3 ½-inch (40.5cm x 9cm) strip of tissue paper; make 2-inch (5cm) accordion folds by first folding paper behind the strip, then folding paper in front of it. Trim and notch one end of the tissue paper through all the layers, as pictured; unfold. **2.** Insert floral wire into a 1-inch (2.5cm) polystyrene ball; place the ball near the bottom of the tissue paper strip. Roll the tissue around the ball; twist the bottom. **3.** Remove the ball with tweezers. Wrap floral tape around the twisted tissue and wire, then to the end of the stem. Trim the floral tape.

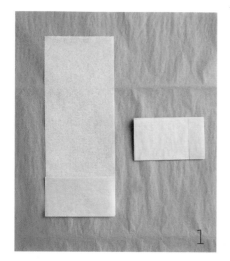

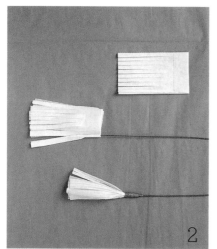

PROJECT: **curly petal flower**

PROJECT SUPPLIES Basic Supplies (page 258)

HOW-TO 1. Cut a 16-by-3 ½-inch (40.5cm x 9cm) strip of tissue paper; make 2-inch (5cm) wide accordion folds by first folding the paper behind the strip, then folding the paper in front of it. **2.** Make 3-inch (7.5cm) deep snips in the tissue paper to create fringe. Wrap unfringed end around floral wire. Secure tissue paper to the stem with floral tape, then wrap floral tape to the bottom of the stem; trim floral tape. **3.** Run a scissors blade along the pieces of fringe to curl; fluff.

PROJECT: **double leaves**

PROJECT SUPPLIES Basic Supplies (page 258)

HOW-TO To make 3 double leaves, stack tissue paper in 3 shades of green. Cut 2-by-3-inch (5cm x 7.5cm) rectangles through all the layers; fold them in half. Trim the tips into points, as pictured; unfold and unstack the tissue. Twist 1 piece at its center. Fold an 18-inch (45.5cm) length of floral wire in half, slip it over the center of the leaf, and twist the wire to secure the tissue. Fold leaves' tips toward each other, and curl them into their finished shape with your fingers. Repeat to finish the remaining double leaves.

PROJECT: **long leaf**

PROJECT SUPPLIES Basic Supplies (page 258)

HOW-TO Stack tissue paper in 2 shades of green. Cut 2-by-3-inch (5cm x 7.5cm) rectangles through both layers. Apply white glue along the upper third of a 9-inch (23cm) piece of floral wire; sandwich the wire between the tissue paper layers. Let dry. Cut a leaf shape; bend wire slightly. Separate the layers of tissue paper.

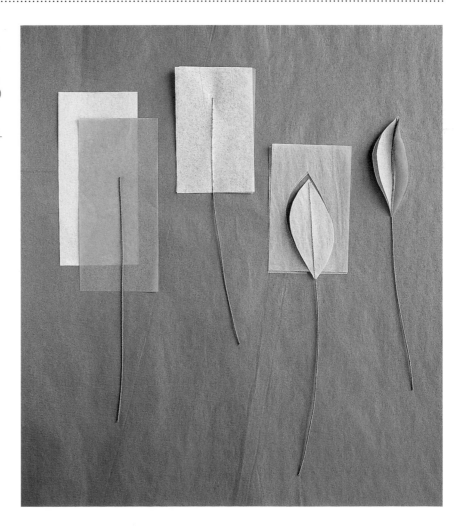

For festive party decorations, construct pom-poms in various colors. Trim some smaller for different-size puffs, and make petals in various shapes. Hang them from monofilament at different heights, leaving at least a foot (30.5cm) of space between pom-poms and candles.

PROJECT: **paper flower pom-poms and puffs**

These joyous bursts of color can be made in all shapes and colors. The giant ones shown opposite are great for hanging above a table. Mini versions adorn napkin holders (below).

PROJECT SUPPLIES Basic Supplies (page 258), monofilament

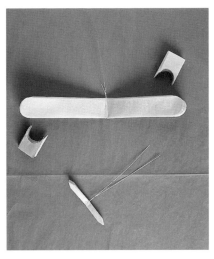

HOW-TO 1. Stack tissue paper (eight 20-by-30-inch [51cm x 76cm] sheets for each large pom-pom; four 10-by-5-inch [25.5cm x 12.5cm] pieces for a smaller puff). Accordion-fold the paper (1 ½-inch [3.8cm] wide folds for large pom-pom; ⅜-inch [10mm] wide folds for puff.

2. Fold an 18-inch (45.5cm) piece of cloth-covered floral wire in half, and slip it over the center of the folded tissue; twist. With scissors, trim the ends of tissue into rounded or pointy shapes.

3. Separate the layers of tissue paper, pulling them away from the center one at a time. For a pom-pom, tie a length of monofilament to floral wire for hanging. For a napkin ring puff, bend the wire into a loop to fit around a rolled napkin, and twist the ends around the loop to secure.

Echoing the vibrant hanging pom-poms, paper-puff napkin rings in citrus shades adorn each place setting. Square glass vessels in various sizes line tables. Covered in sunset-hued tissue (cut to size and secured with double-sided tape), they cast a soft glow and harmonize the party setting.

PROJECT: **photo-printed pillows**

You can easily print photos onto fabric by purchasing printer-ready fabric sheets at a quilting or fabric store, or by creating your own printer-ready fabric (right). The photos in this project were altered on the computer to look as if they were printed in cyanotype—a photo-printing technique developed in the mid-1800s that gives pictures a cyan-blue color. Changing the color of your images to sepia tone or black and white would also look nice printed on white or off-white fabric. The instructions that follow create a 15 ¾-inch (40cm) square washable pillowcase, one featuring twelve photos, and another with four images.

PROJECT SUPPLIES Basic Supplies (page 267), 16-inch (40.5cm) pillow insert, treated fabric (see "Creating Your Own Printer-Ready Fabric," right) or store-bought fabric sheets for ink-jet printers, scissors, fabric glue, sewing machine, thread, ⅜-inch (10mm) twill tape, fabric for pillowcase backing

HOW-TO 1. Upload or scan 12 photographs onto your computer; resize the photos to 4 by 6 inches (10cm x 15cm), and adjust the color to blue. If not using printer-ready fabric, treat your fabric with a bonding agent, as described at right. Print 2 photos per piece of fabric, leaving a ¼-inch (6mm) space between them. **2.** Arrange your prints into 4 rows of 3. Trim the butting edges of the photo pieces, leaving a ¼-inch (6mm) border (leave exterior borders wider). Glue the photos together, overlapping the borders as shown. Machine-sew ⅜-inch (10mm) twill tape over the borders, sewing on both sides. Trim the photo grid to 16 ¾-inch (42.5cm) square. Cut a 16 ¾-inch (42.5cm) square of fabric for the back of the pillow. Lay the photo fabric right-side up. Then lay the plain piece, wrong-side up, on the printed fabric, and pin the 2 pieces together. Machine-sew 3 sides with ½-inch (13mm) seam allowance. Remove the remaining pins, turn the pillow right-side out, and slip the pillow insert into the case. Fold the edges of the opening toward the inside of the pillow and hand-stitch the opening shut.

VARIATION To make a 4-photo pillow, as pictured at left, follow the same instructions for the 12-photo pillow, but print 8-inch (20.5cm) square images, 1 photo per page. Trim the edges, leaving a ¼-inch (6mm) border on each side. When sewing the pillow, you may stitch into some of the edges of the images; just account for this when you're deciding how to lay out the grid of pictures.

creating your own printer-ready fabric

Although it's easiest to purchase fabric sheets, they generally come only in bright white. These sheets are also expensive. Creating your own printer-ready fabric allows you to use whatever color you want, and will be more economical in the long run if you do many projects. Use smooth, natural-fiber fabrics, such as cotton or fine linen; images will print better on smoother fabric and natural fiber will hold up better to the heat of the iron. Cut several pieces of fabric into 9-by-12-inch (22.5cm x 30cm) rectangles, then treat them with a bonding agent (such as Bubble Jet Set 2000), following the manufacturer's instructions. Generally, you'll soak your fabric in the solution, allow it to dry, and then iron the fabric to the shiny side of a piece of freezer paper. Carefully trim the paper-backed fabric with a rotary cutter (on a self-healing mat) and straightedge to fit your printer (usually 8½ x 11 inches [21.25cm x 27.5cm]). After printing onto the fabric, you'll wash it in the second part of a bonding agent (such as Bubble Jet Rinse) to set the ink. Before treating and printing all of your fabric, you may want to test a small swatch, printing onto the fabric to make sure that the images show up to your liking.

PROJECT: **mail organizers**

Printing photos onto magnetic paper allows you to display them on any metal surface you want. Here magazine holders act as mail slots, with images of family members stuck to the fronts.

PROJECT SUPPLIES Basic Supplies (page 267), magnetic paper, craft knife, metal magazine holders

HOW-TO Print pictures onto magnetic paper. Use a craft knife to cut them out to desired size to fit the recessed windows on each metal magazine holder.

 To conserve paper, crowd pictures when laying them out on the page. After printing, cut the pictures out (with white borders, if desired) using a craft knife and a ruler or a straightedge.

PROJECT: **photo-flag cake toppers**

Simple cupcakes become personalized and party-ready when topped with photo flags. This idea could be modified for any occasion—use wedding photos for an anniversary gala, photos of the couple for a bridal shower, or pictures of friends for a birthday party.

PROJECT SUPPLIES Basic Supplies (page 267), heavyweight photo paper or white card stock, paper cutter (or a craft knife and a straightedge), double-sided tape, coffee stirrers or large toothpicks

HOW-TO Print out or copy images onto heavyweight photo paper or card stock, two images for each photo flag. Cut photos with a paper cutter or a craft knife and a straightedge, leaving a white border. Affix the squares back to back with double-sided tape around coffee stirrers or large toothpicks.

PROJECT: picture tins

Brighten your desktop by slipping a picture of a familiar face into the lid of a round tin. The tin also serves as a storage container for small office supplies and can even be magnetized to stick to a metal surface. Small tins also work for this project, such as those pictured on the bulletin board above the mail organizers (opposite).

PROJECT SUPPLIES Basic Supplies (page 267), ink-jet paper, tin with a glass or Plexiglas® lid, pencil, scissors, tape, white craft glue (optional), small magnet (optional)

HOW-TO Print photos onto ink-jet paper. Center the lid of the tin on the photo and trace with a pencil. Cut along the inside of the traced line. Place the photo in the lid, and tape it to the lid's inner rim. To magnetize, glue a magnet to the bottom of the empty container.

PROJECT: bottle-cap frames

Metal bottle caps can frame small black-and-white pictures for novel thumbtacks or magnets. Clear resin is poured into the caps to seal the photos and give them an appealing glossy finish. Twist-off caps are better than conventional ones because they don't bend when they're removed. For appropriately small images, try cutting details from large photos. Or, if your software has a contact-sheet mode, use it to reduce pictures drastically.

PROJECT SUPPLIES Basic Supplies (page 267), ink-jet paper, 1-inch (2.5cm) circular craft punch, white craft glue, metal twist-off bottle caps, clear casting resin, bonding cement, small magnets or thumbtacks

HOW-TO Using the craft punch, cut out pictures. Using white craft glue, attach 1 picture to the inside of each bottle cap. Let it dry. Cover a work surface to protect it from spills, and lay caps on top of it. Following manufacturer's instructions for clear casting resin, fill each bottle cap to the rim. Let them dry overnight. Using bonding cement, attach magnets or thumbtacks to the backs of the bottle caps. Let them dry overnight before using.

POM-POM ANIMALS

With only a ball of yarn and a little imagination you can create a menagerie of fuzzy pom-pom animals. Some of these cuddly creatures are remarkably lifelike; others—like the tickly, oversize caterpillar shown on page 275—are pure whimsy. The ones on these pages were inspired by the woolen miniatures, also known as pom-poms, made by the renowned Steiff Company starting in the 1930s. Prized for their uncanny resemblance to their real-world counterparts, Steiff toys were fashioned from a variety of fabrics, textures, and colors, each carefully chosen to capture the spirit and appeal of a particular small animal. Before you begin, you'll want to carefully study the characteristics and postures of the animals you plan to make. There are many sources at hand for information and inspiration—online image searches, wildlife magazines, encyclopedias, field guides, and even a trip to the zoo. Children's books, with their colorful illustrations, are a particularly rich resource. Use them to help you capture important details of the animal—its color, shape, and coat, feathers, or fuzz. Since the pom-pom parts are simply joined with a needle and thread, it's easy to experiment until you get the shape and expression you want. The resulting palm-size treasures make delightful keepsakes and gifts.

ABOUT THE MATERIALS

POM-POM MAKER Pom-pom makers are plastic, horseshoe-shaped templates with interlocking feet. (You can make one out of cardboard, but commercial versions are inexpensive and easier to work with.) Choose a kit with several sizes, ranging from 1¼ inches to 3½ inches (3-9cm), to make a variety of animals.

YARN Yarn is available at fabric and crafts stores, packaged in balls, pull skeins, spools, and hanks. The label describes the yarn's fiber content, weight, and amount in yards and ounces (and sometimes in meters and grams). The animals on these pages are fashioned out of merino wool or mohair, but you can use any leftover yarn from your knitting basket, including cotton, silk, or blended fibers—let the look and feel of the yarn suggest the animal it might become. Use a few yarns in different colors to make multicolored pom-poms. You can add single threads to your pom-poms for pattern or texture, or to create facial features, as in the ladybug (page 278) and caterpillar (page 275).

SCISSORS Small scissors, such as cuticle scissors, are ideal for trimming pom-poms.

EMBROIDERY FLOSS OR THREAD To join two pom-poms, thread a needle with embroidery floss or thread, and knot one end. Pass the needle through both pom-poms, and knot the other end, trimming off the excess. You can also use embroidery floss to make eyes: Thread a needle with embroidery floss, thread, or beading cord, and knot one end. Draw the needle through the pom-pom; cut and knot the floss near the center of the pom-pom, so it doesn't show.

BASIC SUPPLIES

pom-pom makers

yarn

scissors

embroidery floss or thread

OPPOSITE **This captivating mohair goldfinch's distinct markings are made using yarn in different colors and textures.**

HOW TO WEAVE AND KNOT

Inspired by sailors' knots, these projects involve tying and weaving ropes to make more elaborate designs.
The napkin rings (page 290) require just one simple knot, while the doormat (page 294) features woven swirls of rope.

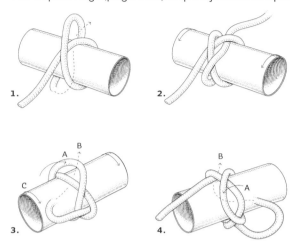

PROJECT: knotted napkin rings

Turk's head, a sailing and scouting knot, is used to form the napkin rings on page 290. They're made with 6-millimeter-thick camping cord. Make the rings on a cardboard tube with a length of rope nine times the tube's circumference.

PROJECT SUPPLIES Basic Supplies (page 291; use about 60 inches [152.5cm] of 6mm-thick camping cord), cardboard tube, needle and thread, lighter

HOW-TO 1. Loop cord as shown. **2.** Rotate the tube toward you 120 degrees. **3.** Pull the slack end down and out of the way. Push the left loop over the right (A). Thread the slack end under and then over as shown (B). Rotate the tube toward you by one third (C). **4.** Push the right loop over to the left (A); thread the slack end under, over, and under as shown (B). Follow the rope's pattern a second time (keep to the right of the initial pattern). Continue until the pattern has been woven twice. Remove the ring. Finish the ends (see "Finishing Ends," below), then sew them to the underside.

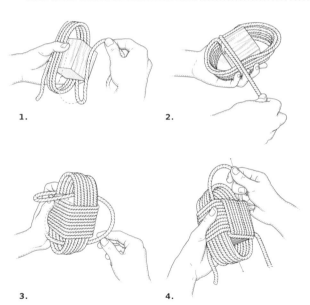

PROJECT: sailor's knot bookends

These clean, bright bookends, woven around wood cubes, are made using a variation of a sailing knot called the monkey's fist.

PROJECT SUPPLIES Basic Supplies (page 291; use 35 feet [10.5m] of ½-inch [13mm] thick twisted rope for each large cube; 35 feet [10.5m] of ¼-inch [6mm] thick rope for each small cube), wood, sandpaper or a file, paint (in same color as rope) and paintbrush, masking tape, permanent craft glue

HOW-TO 1. Ask a lumberyard to cut a 4-by-4 into a pair of 3 ½-inch (9cm) cubes and a pair of 2 ½-inch (6.5cm) cubes. Smooth the edges and corners with sandpaper or a file. Paint cube and let dry. Using masking tape, secure the rope to one side of the cube. Wrap as shown. (As you work, tape down the loops to hold them temporarily in place.) Continue until the front and back of block are fully covered. **2.** Tape at the corner. Give the cube a quarter-turn; wrap it in opposite direction to cover the sides. (Remove the tape from step 1 as loops stay in place.) **3.** Wrap remaining sides by threading through the open loops. (Remove tape from step 2.) **4.** Pull each loop from the first round until the rope is flush with the cube. Trim ends and secure them to cube with permanent craft glue.

finishing ends

You will need to finish a nylon rope's ends to keep them from fraying (the photo shows blue thread for illustrative contrast, but you should use thread that matches your rope): Using a needle, sew through the rope just below any frayed ends; tightly wrap the thread around the rope a couple of times (skip this step when using very thin cord, as in the coasters on page 296). Sew through several more times to secure. Cut off the end of the rope just above the thread. Singe the frayed ends with a lighter to seal.

These textural bookends add style to a host of interior settings.

HOW TO COIL AND GLUE

These projects use a simple and straightforward technique: Just form a length of rope into a coil and glue it in place. Beyond the ideas given here, you can use this method to cover a variety of items, such as an elegant picture frame or a tabletop—round objects work best, as they allow for even coils. To keep nylon rope from fraying, finish the ends with a needle and thread, and singe with a lighter (see "Finishing Ends," page 292).

PROJECT: rope coasters

Coiled-rope coasters are easy to make; patterned cord adds visual interest. Make a dozen for a nautical-themed party, or for everyday use around the house.

PROJECT SUPPLIES Basic Supplies (page 291; use 9 feet [274cm] of 3mm-thick cord for each 4-inch coaster), lighter, corkboard, compass or large round cookie cutter, straight pins, pencil

HOW-TO Using a compass or a large round cookie cutter, trace a 4-inch (10cm) diameter circle onto a sheet of cork-board; cut out with scissors. Singe one end of the cord with a lighter to seal. Apply a bead of permanent craft glue in the center. Arrange the singed end on top, coiling it in place. Continue gluing and coiling to cover; use pins to keep the cord in place. Cut any excess cord and singe the end; glue the end in place. Remove the pins when glue has dried.

A bunch of plain wooden seats gets a new look from simple coils of rope.

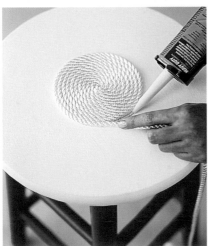

PROJECT: rope-seat stool

For these sturdy stool coverings, plain nylon rope is elevated from trusty standby to elegant trim. Durable rope is ideal for seats at a busy kitchen counter.

PROJECT SUPPLIES Basic Supplies (page 291; use nylon or rock-climbing rope and construction adhesive), wooden stool, caulking gun (for adhesive), needle and thread, lighter, semigloss acrylic paint and paintbrush (optional)

HOW-TO The width of your rope will determine how much you need. For a 13 ½-inch (34.5m) stool, you'll need about 75 feet (23m) of ¼-inch (5mm) thick rope. If desired, paint the stool. Finish the rope end to prevent fraying, as described on page 292. Mark the center of the seat, using a caulking gun; apply a 3-inch (7.5cm) circle of construction glue. Spiral the rope on top, starting at the center, and glue it down by holding it for a few seconds until it's secure. Continue coiling and gluing until the seat's top and side are covered. Cut off any excess rope. Finish the end and glue it under the seat.

RUBBER STAMPING

A rubber stamp is like your own portable print shop. Surprisingly versatile (not to mention affordable), this small-scale crafting tool can be used to create designs that bear an uncanny resemblance to silk-screening, stenciling, or typesetting. Although they're not complicated to use, there are some tricks for achieving sophisticated results. Combine different stamps in a single design or repeat one stamp multiple times. Layer one color on top of another, creating "shadows" and highlights that give depth and dimension. Play with scale by using big stamps on small surfaces and small stamps on big surfaces. You'll end up with original motifs that suggest intricate craftsmanship but are really the result of nothing more than the lowering of a stamp and a little downward pressure. Images can be applied to almost any surface—not just the expected paper but also fabric and objects found in nature, such as stones, seashells, and leaves. You can also stamp on walls and wood, so take a look around the house and imagine adding a pattern to a stairwell, a table, or a chair. Getting started is easy. All you need are a few stamps, ink or paint, and the urge to make your mark.

ABOUT THE MATERIALS

RUBBER STAMPS You'll find a wide array of rubber stamps in crafts stores and a seemingly endless selection online. Rubber stamps are also sometimes sold at office-supply stores. Any simple graphic design (such as line art) or text can be made into a one-of-a-kind rubber stamp; look in the phone book for a vendor, or search for online sources. Try clip art or your own artwork, or have stamps made in your handwriting or a favorite font.

OPPOSITE They can be stamped in minutes, but these gift tags are as beautiful as fine wallpaper and as personal as a handwritten note. For allover designs, use patterned stamps that have a greater surface area than the tag. For initials, apply letters after stamping the tag with a decorative motif. Text can be customized (as with the "Happy Birthday" tag) using special multiletter stamp mounts from office-supply stores.

For customizable designs, you can also buy a kit that includes a stamp mount and a set of letters, numbers, and symbols. Arrange the stamps to spell out your message, then attach them to the mount: some are magnetic, some use self-adhesive letters, and some have raised bars that the letters snap on to. You can remove and rearrange the letters as many times as you like. You can also use a stamp rolling pin to cover larger areas in a continuous pattern, such as when making wrapping paper.

INK PADS AND PAINT Ink pads can be found in crafts stores, online, and at office-supply and stationery stores. The type of ink you need will depend on what you're stamping. Pigment inks—suitable for stamping paper and wood—are thicker and create more opaque images; they were used for most of the projects on the following pages. Dye-based inks are translucent, dry quickly, and can produce sharp detail. They work well on paper, but the stamped image may bleed slightly on very porous papers. Fabric inks, as the name implies, are used on fabric. Some fabric inks need to be set to prevent the stamped design from fading; read the instructions on the package, as the process varies from brand to brand. Permanent ink won't run after it dries. It is suitable for use on glass, paper, and wood, and is ideal for party goods (such as paper napkins and cups) that are likely to get wet. Latex paint, available at crafts and hardware stores, is available in every shade imaginable, and can be mixed in custom colors; use it to stamp walls and furniture.

BASIC SUPPLIES

rubber stamps

ink pads or latex paint

paper, fabric, or other appropriate surface for stamping

HOW TO RUBBER STAMP

RUBBER STAMPING, WITH INK Practice on scrap paper: With some stamps, the edge picks up ink and leaves a mark. If this is the case, wipe that area clean with a baby wipe or damp paper towel each time before stamping. On curved surfaces, use a rolling motion, stamping a portion of the design before gently lowering the rest of the stamp onto the surface. Tightly close ink pad cases after each use.

RUBBER STAMPING, WITH FABRIC INK Purchase fabric ink pads—special sponges that are saturated with permanent ink. Test a fabric swatch before stamping a garment;

wipe the rubber stamp with a baby wipe each time after inking before stamping. Testing will give you a sense of how much ink and pressure to use. After stamping the fabric, follow the manufacturer's instructions on the ink pad to set the design.

RUBBER STAMPING, WITH LATEX PAINT Before applying the design on a painted surface—such as a wall or a piece of furniture—practice on a sheet of kraft paper. Use a paintbrush to apply paint to the stamp. Mistakes made on slick surfaces, such as glossy paint, can be cleaned up right away with a damp paper towel.

PROJECT: monogrammed paper goods

Design and stamp your own stationery set (opposite) for a fraction of the price of custom-printed versions. Or make a set to give to a friend, complete with a blank book in a matching motif.

PROJECT SUPPLIES Basic Supplies (page 299; use a cloth-covered journal)

HOW-TO To make letterhead, computer-print a name (and address, if desired) on a sheet of paper. For the flourish, use two stamps, overlaying the markings: an artistic background design, plus a bold monogram or initial. Repeat the design on a cloth-covered journal using fabric-ink pads.

caring for rubber stamps

A properly cared-for stamp should last for years. Once you finish a stamping project, clean each stamp thoroughly by pressing it into a paper towel dampened with water. You can also use baby wipes. Some inks may stain the rubber, but the stamp is still usable, as long as it's properly cleaned. Never leave mounted stamps submerged in water for an extended period. Store clean stamps in a cool, dry place away from sunlight.

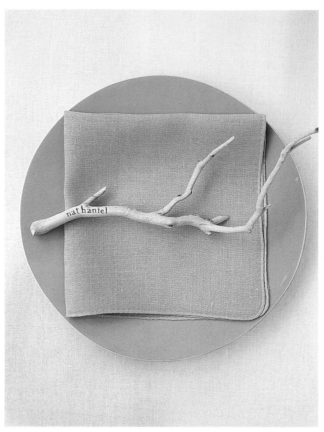

PROJECT: rubber-stamped place cards

Found objects like these are perfect to weight place cards at the table—or become the place markers themselves. Clockwise from above left: Use letter stamps to spell out a guest's name on driftwood. Stamp an egg with a hen, and rest it in a store-bought nest. Use white ink to create contrast on green leaves. Adorn a seashell with a sea horse. Stamp initials on river rocks, which double as chopstick rests. Mark places with stamped-initial feathers.

PROJECT SUPPLIES Basic Supplies (page 299)

HOW-TO Stamp the objects in colors that will show up on their surfaces. On a curved surface such as the clamshell or the egg, gently rock the stamp—the smaller the stamp, the better.

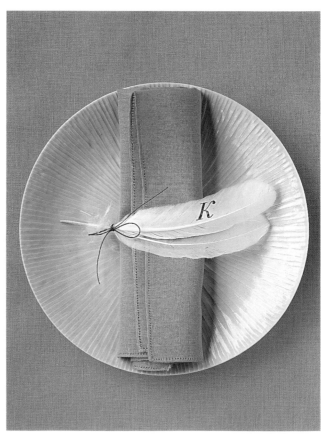

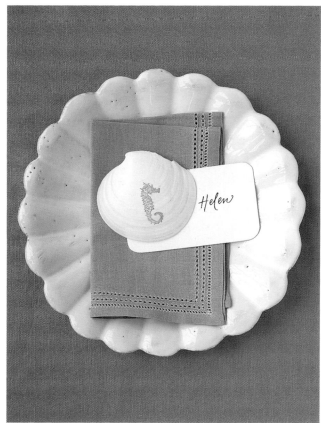

PROJECT: stamped-edge books

A good read always makes a nice gift, but why not make it good-looking, too? Stamped designs add a personal touch to any tome.

PROJECT SUPPLIES Basic Supplies (page 299), books

HOW-TO Use rubber stamps to decorate a book's edges with an image, pattern, or message. For the most clean designs, hold the pages together tightly as you stamp.

PROJECT: **stamped stationery**

Let the beauty of seasons inspire a stationery suite. This grass-covered set is perfect for sending springtime greetings.

PROJECT SUPPLIES Basic Supplies (page 299), glue stick (optional), perforated stamp paper

HOW-TO Design invitations and thank-you notes using plain store-bought cards; a rubber-stamped notepad makes a nice gift. Place stationery on a large piece of scrap paper. Stamp the grass motif across the base of the stationery, overlapping imprints if necessary. Add flower and butterfly accents. To create envelope seals, stamp rows of perforated stamp paper. Punch out designs, and affix to an envelope with a glue stick.

PROJECT: party supplies

The surfaces of plain-paper (not glossy) cups, small bags, and other such items readily absorb ink, making them ideal to convert into a matching set of party goods.

PROJECT SUPPLIES Basic Supplies (page 299), nontoxic ink pads, plain-paper party supplies

HOW-TO Stamp cups, fans, and napkins with green leaves; let dry, then add peonies in 2 shades of pink, which gives the effect of dimension. Embellish mini favor bags with a floral pattern, and invitations and wrapping paper with leaves.

PROJECT: hand-stamped wrapping paper

Enclose petite gifts or party favors in handmade wrapping paper covered in impressions made with a square rubber stamp or stamped rolling pin.

PROJECT SUPPLIES Basic Supplies (page 299), stamped rolling pin (optional)

HOW-TO Start with a large piece of paper. For a uniform pattern, stamp repeatedly with the same square stamp, leaving a small space between each impression. Or cut the paper to fit the box and stamp in the center: If your box and stamp are the same size, the pattern will fall on the top of the box. If the box is larger than the stamp, the pattern can trail down the sides. A miniature stamped rolling pin, which creates a texture as you roll it, also makes an attractive pattern. For this project, several different colors were applied to a sheet of white paper to create a muted design. Store stamped pages flat.

PROJECT: rubber-stamped hat

Freshen a plain canvas hat with a spray of leaves and a brightly colored bird.

PROJECT SUPPLIES Basic Supplies (page 299), canvas hat

HOW-TO Follow general instructions for fabric stamping (page 300). To begin, place the hat on a kraft-paper-covered table, then stamp, using bird and leaf stamps and a fabric-ink pad.

PROJECT: spot-on stationery

Plain-paper products become much more presentable when rubber-stamped with dotty designs. The eraser of a new pencil is the perfect tool for creating the bright spots. You can also trim a pencil eraser with a craft knife to make petal shapes.

PROJECT SUPPLIES Basic Supplies (page 299), nontoxic ink pads, pencils

HOW-TO Use different erasers to apply multiple colors of stamp-pad ink. This project shows decorated stationery, and cards and wrapping paper. For dots, use an uncut round pencil eraser. Cut the eraser down the middle and remove one half to make half-circle petals. For thinner petals, cut into a sliver shape. Draw stems with a thin marker or colored pencil.

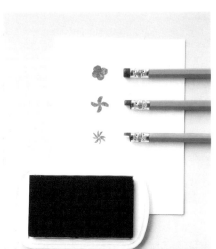

SOAP MAKING

Pretty and practical, handmade soaps make lovely home accents and excellent hostess gifts and thank-yous. Making soap from scratch—a painstaking procedure of combining fat and lye—was once on the list of everyday household chores. Today, you can skip that process. Begin with glycerin soap, melt it down, and reshape it in molds. Pantry staples add spice and texture; essential oils impart fragrance. You might also mix in natural exfoliants, which gently scrub away dirt, excess oil, and dry skin. Make a few batches and you'll have the perfect gifts and home accents on hand. Also on the pages that follow: other comforting bath and body treatments to make and to share, including soothing salts, aromatic teas, and invigorating fizzies. Although it may be tempting to save these homemade treats for display purposes, make sure you put them to work. After all, they'll make the biggest splash when mixed with water.

ABOUT THE MATERIALS

MOLDS You can buy soap or candle molds meant for the task (the two are interchangeable), but plenty of household items, such as baking molds, plastic containers, and empty cartons, will work just as well. If you plan to reuse the molds for food, be sure to wash them thoroughly. Biscuit and cookie cutters can also be used to cut different soap shapes.

GLYCERIN SOAP These projects start with solid blocks of white and translucent glycerin soap, humectants that gently soften skin; the amount of each you'll use is dictated by the degree of translucency you're trying to achieve.

BENCH SCRAPER A bench scraper, a commonly used baking tool, is perfect for cleanly cutting through bars of glycerin soap.

OPPOSITE **Show off gifts of handmade soaps in unexpected little dishes, including patterned eggcups and scallop-edged saucers. To finish each package, secure with a strip of glassine or waxed paper and a satin ribbon.**

FOOD COLORING Once melted, glycerin soap can be tinted most any shade using the common colorings available at any grocery store.

ESSENTIAL OILS Natural essential oils can add aroma to homemade soaps. Popular favorites include balsam (redolent of Christmas greenery), bergamot (with an invigorating woodsy scent), peppermint (tingly on the skin), orange (with a zesty aroma), and eucalyptus (known for its healing qualities). Be aware that essential oils are potent and should be handled with care; pregnant women should speak to a doctor before working with them. Some oils are more potent than others; peppermint oil, for example, is strongly scented, while grapefruit oil is milder. Add oils a drop at a time to avoid overdoing it.

ADDITIVES You also might add fresh ginger for zest or oatmeal to soothe hardworking hands; ground loofah and cranberry seeds will scrub away dirt and dry skin as the soap cleans. Natural clays are absorbent and cut grease. Additional ideas for additives are found on pages 320 and 323.

BASIC MATERIALS

molds

nonstick cooking spray or petroleum jelly

liquid-measuring cup

glycerin soap

bench scraper

spoon

toothpick

food coloring

essential oils

additives (such as natural clays or exfoliators)

rubbing alcohol (in a spray bottle)

HOW TO MAKE SOAP

The following steps are for general soap making. For specific mold and add-in instructions, refer to the individual project how-tos.

1. Coat molds evenly with nonstick cooking spray or petroleum jelly; wipe out any excess.

2. To determine how much glycerin soap you'll need, fill the molds with water, then pour the water into a liquid-measuring cup. Note the amount, then pour out the water. Chop the glycerin soap into ½-inch (13mm) chunks with a bench scraper; place the chunks in the measuring cup and microwave the glycerin soap, covered with a paper towel, on medium for 30-second intervals until it is melted but not boiling. Add chunks of glycerin soap, as needed, between intervals until the amount of melted glycerin soap in the measuring cup equals the amount of water you measured earlier. (You can also use a double boiler to melt the glycerin soap chunks.)

3. Remove glycerin from the microwave, and stir with a spoon until it's smooth. Skim off any bubbles with the spoon. Use a toothpick to add food coloring, stirring until the desired color is reached. Reheat the mixture for 15 seconds to fully incorporate the color.

4. Mix in any oils or other additives, if using. (Use oils sparingly: 4 or 5 drops per 1 cup [200ml] of soap mixture.)

5. Pour the melted soap mixture into the prepared molds. Let them harden for 2 hours. Release the soap from the molds.

BENCH SCRAPER, CLEAR GLYCERIN, WHITE GLYCERIN, AND MEASURING TOOLS

ESSENTIAL OILS

PROJECT: pantry soaps

Yogurt and cottage cheese containers make round or oval-shaped bars of soap. These soaps are enhanced with ingredients you probably have in your pantry, such as oatmeal, honey, and ground spices, for added texture, color, and mild fragrance. For a themed present, put a few earth-tone soaps and a bath mitt, facecloth, or scrub brush together in a plain wooden box.

PROJECT SUPPLIES Basic Supplies (page 319), honey, ground ginger, cinnamon, ground cloves, oatmeal, chamomile tea, plastic yogurt or cottage cheese containers

HOW-TO The long, thin box (bottom right) holds a number of delectable bars. Follow instructions for "How to Make Soap" (left), and add extra ingredients to make (from top) honey-ginger (this bar uses more white glycerin soap than clear), cinnamon-clove, oatmeal-honey, honey-ginger (this bar uses more clear glycerin soap than white), and chamomile soap. Fill containers 1 ¼ inches (3cm) deep. After each soap has set, press on the sides of the mold to loosen the soap and on the bottom to release it.

After pouring the melted glycerin mixture into the mold, spray the liquid's surface with rubbing alcohol, which will eliminate any bubbles from the soap. To stamp messages in soap, tape together metal letter stamps to spell out your message, then imprint the soap using light, even pressure.

PROJECT: tin-mold soaps

Small baking molds and cookie cutters make soaps in delightful shapes. The scalloped-edge round soaps on page 318 were made with a biscuit cutter; most of the other soaps were made in tartlet molds. The heart-shaped ones (above) were made with a cookie cutter and stamped with Valentine messages.

PROJECT SUPPLIES Basic Supplies (page 319), 9-by-9-inch (23cm x 23cm) baking pan, scalloped biscuit cutter or heart-shaped cookie cutter, chocolate-egg mold, metal letter stamps (optional), tartlet molds

HOW-TO Follow instructions for "How to Make Soap" (page 320). To make cutout soaps, pour the glycerin soap mixture to desired depth in baking pan; let harden. Remove the block of soap from the pan, and cut out soaps with a biscuit cutter or cookie cutter (scraps can be remelted and used again). For egg-shaped soap, fill half of a chocolate-egg mold with glycerin soap mixture; let it set 2 hours, and re-move. Grease egg mold again and pour more mixture into the mold; immediately top with the set half. Press the halves together and smooth the seam with your fingers. For tartlet soaps, follow "How to Make Soap," pouring the glycerin into tartlet molds.

PROJECT: exfoliating soaps

Miniature loaf pans turn out perfectly shaped full-size bars of exfoliating soap; these can be used whole, or sliced to make mini bars. For a gift of mixed soaps, attach a label detailing the contents to the underside of the box.

PROJECT SUPPLIES Basic Supplies (page 319); natural exfoliants, such as crushed apricot seeds, cranberry seeds, ground loofah, and strawberry seeds; mini loaf pan; knife (optional)

HOW-TO Follow instructions for "How to Make Soap" (page 320), and add extra ingredients to make (in open box, from top): apricot, cranberry, loofah, and strawberry-seed soaps. Add essential oils for fragrance if you like. After adding the exfoliant, scent, and coloring, as desired, to the melted glycerin, stir the mixture until it is the consistency of glue to keep the seeds from settling. Pour the mixture into mini loaf pans. Let set for 2 hours. For metal molds, freeze the molds for 20 minutes (to help release the bars). Invert a frozen mold, pry the soap from the sides, and press the bottom of the mold to free the soap. If needed, trim the edges of the soap with a knife.

PROJECT: natural clay soaps

Clay, such as fuller's earth or French green clay, does double duty in this project: It tints the soap and cuts grease. Fill an empty milk or juice carton with the glycerin soap mixture and then slice bars from the hardened block, or use smaller juice box containers to make a single large bar.

PROJECT SUPPLIES Basic Supplies (page 319), French green clay, fuller's earth, dry milk, honey, cardboard milk or juice cartons, fine-mesh sieve

HOW-TO Follow instructions for "How to Make Soap" (page 320). Fuller's earth makes bars in shades of brown; for bars in a lighter shade of brown, use more white glycerin than clear. French green clay makes bars in gradations of green. For bars in a lighter shade of green, use more white glycerin than clear; for a darker green, use more clear glycerin, more clay (up to 1 tablespoon [15ml]), or green food coloring. Ivory bars are infused with dry milk and honey. Pour the glycerin soap mixture into a thoroughly cleaned and dried cardboard milk or juice carton through a fine-mesh sieve to strain out clumps. To unmold the hardened soap, rip away the carton. Use a bench scraper to cut a large block into smaller bars.

BATH AND BODY

Homemade bath and body treatments are almost as fun to make as they are to use. They're also great gifts for friends who need a little pampering. The best part? These indulgent treats are easy to turn out en masse, so there will be plenty to give—and keep.

PROJECT: bath salts

Bath salts look even more appealing when you layer several salts with different-size grains in a glass jar. Add a few drops of essential oil— in this case, lavender—for fragrance.

PROJECT SUPPLIES essential oil, dendritic salt, lidded glass jar, Epsom salt, coarse gray salt, Dead Sea salt, extra-large sea salt, label, thin ribbon

HOW-TO Mix 3 to 5 drops of essential oil with 1 cup (200ml) of dendritic salt, which has star-shaped, rather than flat-sided, crystals. Place a layer of the scented salt in the bottom of a jar. In the jar pictured at left, the dendritic salt is topped with layers of Epsom salt, coarse gray salt, Dead Sea salt, and extra-large sea salt. Add a label identifying the mixture, and tie to the lid with thin ribbon.

PROJECT: **tub teas**

Nothing soothes like a good long soak, especially one coupled with a heady infusion of calming scents. Give a few small bags in different scents, so bathers can customize each soak.

PROJECT SUPPLIES heat-sealable tea bags or muslin circles and waxed twine; dried aromatics such as lemon verbena, lavender, peppermint, or chamomile

HOW-TO For larger bags, fill heat-sealable tea bags (perfect for 1 bath) with ¼ cup (50ml) lemon verbena, lavender, peppermint, or chamomile. For smaller bags, top 5 ¼-inch (6mm) starched muslin circles with 1 tablespoon (15ml) of botanicals; tie tightly with waxed twine and knot to close.

PROJECT: bath fizzies

Effervescent bath fizzies scent water as they bubble, turning the tub into a relaxing retreat. Fill cellophane bags with the colorful blocks to give as gifts.

PROJECT SUPPLIES baking soda, citric acid, cornstarch, spritzer bottle, food coloring, essential oil, small baking molds (such as tarlet tins)

HOW-TO Sift 1 ¾ cup (350ml) of baking soda, 1 cup (200ml) of citric acid, and 2 cups (400ml) of cornstarch into a bowl. To add color, fill a small spritzer bottle with water and add about 6 drops of food coloring. Pour 1 cup (200ml) of the powdered mixture into a glass bowl. Lightly spritz with colored water, stirring after each spritz, until the powder packs tightly. Add water slowly, so the mixture does not fizz. Check the consistency of the powder with your fingers; when it can be tightly packed or shaped, stop spritzing (this may take a little while). Add 5 or 6 drops of essential oil. Mix well. Firmly pack the mixture into small baking molds. Each of these tablets uses ¼ cup (50ml) of the powdered mixture, which is good for one bath. Repeat with the remaining powdered mixture, using different essential oils and colors of water for variety. Allow the tablets to set for 2 hours, then carefully pop out the tinted tablets.

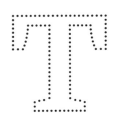

TIN PUNCHING

The first time you set a pointed tool to tin and hit it with a hammer, you might be surprised by the loud snap that echoes back. But don't be surprised when, a few punches later, you find yourself addicted to the craft; the methodical act of hammering designs into thin metal is simple and therapeutically satisfying. At one time, the perforations on punched, or pierced, tin served a practical purpose. In colonial America, the holes that made the pattern in a tin lantern allowed light to shine through but were small enough to shield the candle inside from drafts. Similarly, the punched tin panels in pie safes, predecessors to iceboxes, let air circulate around food but prevented pests from doing the same. Although punched tin is no longer a household necessity, its decorative potential makes it a welcome addition to almost any room. Using geometric patterns instead of the original rustic designs—flowers and birds were popular—results in a more modern look. Punched circlets, for example, give personality to a plain metal lamp. A crosshatch pattern can bring new life to an old pie tin, which can become a piece worthy of display. These designs might be noisy to create, but the effect they have is quietly charming.

ABOUT THE MATERIALS

METAL SHEETS Despite the name of the craft, the projects here use 28- to 30-gauge sheets of nickel silver and tin plate; you can also try other metals, such as brass or copper. Gauge refers to the thickness of the metal; the higher the number, the thinner the metal; 28- to 30-gauge is ideal for punching. Look for the metal sheets at jewelry-making-supply stores, some crafts stores, and online.

PARTICLEBOARD You'll want to protect your work surface with a piece of particleboard, a composite of wood shavings and sawdust. You can buy particleboard at home centers and hardware stores.

METAL-WORKING TOOLS
Use tin-punching tools (available from specialty dealers) to make dots, lines, curves, teardrops, and other shapes in metal sheets. With just a few of these implements, you can create an abundance of patterns. A hammer is ideal for pounding the ends of the punching tools as they pierce the metal. Use metal-cutting scissors for trimming the sheets to size, and a metal file to smooth rough edges.

BASIC SUPPLIES

paper

ruler

pencil

clear tape

28- to 30-gauge metal sheets

particleboard

tin-punching tools

hammer

rawhide mallet

metal-cutting scissors

metal file

OPPOSITE **Sheets of metal are easy to pierce with decorative holes in a diamond or swirled pattern.**

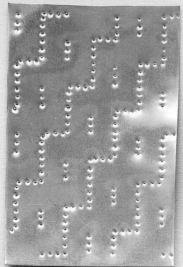
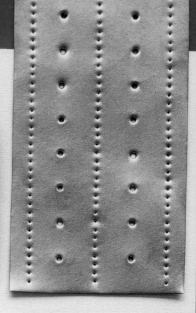

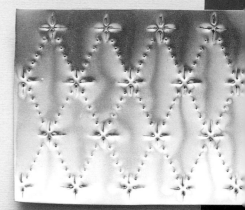

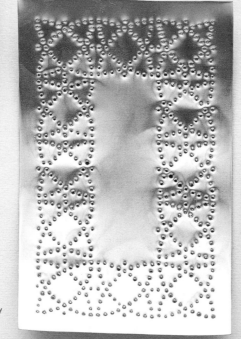

TIN PUNCH TYPES

Sheets of metal used to make thicker objects, like the vintage tray on top, require more elbow grease. It's not hard to design appealing patterns; working on a grid, just repeat lines and basic shapes. You can vary the effects by using different tin-punching tools. The basic punch makes circular holes. The plug removes a round of the metal, rather than just punching through, leaving less of a raised mark on the back. Tools that make lines, teardrop shapes, and crescents offer additional design opportunities.

HOW TO PUNCH TIN

This process isn't difficult, but it's still a good idea to practice on a scrap of metal before starting a project.

  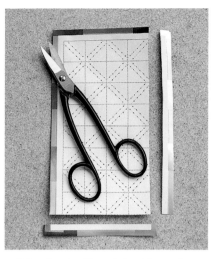

1. On a piece of paper, draw a grid using a ruler; plot dots where you'll want to punch (or photocopy the templates on page 390). Tape the paper to the metal, and place the metal on a piece of particleboard. Position the punching tool on one of the dots. Tap the end lightly with a hammer to make a groove in the metal; then tap again, more forcefully, to pierce. Repeat, making more holes to complete your design.

2. The metal will be slightly warped. With a rawhide mallet, pound gently on the back to flatten.

3. Trim sheet with metal-cutting scissors to the size you need. Smooth any rough edges with a metal file.

PROJECT: spice safe

Update a cupboard with a punched-tin front, which will lighten the look of a plain wooden box. This former medicine chest now houses spices.

PROJECT SUPPLIES Basic Supplies (page 329), wooden cupboard, molding, handsaw, latex paint, sandpaper (optional), ⅜-inch (10mm) nails

HOW-TO Punch a pattern, such as these rows of double diamonds, as described above. Trim the metal sheet with metal-cutting scissors to fit the front of the cupboard. Cut the molding to frame the metal insert; paint it to match the cabinet, and distress it with sandpaper, if desired. Tack the panel and molding in place using ⅜-inch (10mm) nails all the way around.

PROJECT: salt and pepper shakers

Transform plain, small lidded jars into retro salt and pepper shakers with punched lids. Use a plug punch to make larger holes for red-pepper flakes, grated cheese, or dried herbs.

PROJECT SUPPLIES Basic Supplies (page 329), S or P template (page 391), lidded jars, table salt, ground pepper

HOW-TO Tape an S or a P template to the lid, or work freehand. Place lids on a sheet of particleboard. With a delicate hand, so as not to collapse the lids, use the basic punch to tap small dots to form letters.

PROJECT: recipe box

This idea isn't just for recipes—you can label any wooden storage box with a metal tag to denote what's inside.

PROJECT SUPPLIES Basic Supplies (page 329), "recipes" template (page 391), wooden box, ⅜-inch (10mm) nails

HOW-TO Use the template, or print your own from a computer—you can use any word or phrase you want as a label. Make sure the letters are well spaced from one another; the letters' dots, on the other hand, should be close together for best readability. Tape the template to the metal, then punch, following the instructions on page 331. Use ⅜-inch (10mm) nails to secure the label to the box.

PROJECT: pie-plate sconce

A vintage pie plate will reflect the flame of a candle beautifully—and look lovely even when the candle isn't lit.

PROJECT SUPPLIES Basic Supplies (page 329), tin pie plate, template (page 390), clip-on candleholder, candle, adhesive plate hanger

HOW-TO Trace the bottom of the pie plate onto a piece of paper to determine the size of the template you'll need; cut out the paper, and lay out your pattern. Tape the paper inside the pan, and punch your design, following the instructions on page 331. Add a clip-on candleholder (available at antiques stores and online) to the rim. Mount punched plate on the wall with an adhesive plate hanger.

PROJECT: stamped pendant lamp

Dress up a simple metal pendant lamp with a pattern of overlapping circles that evokes the shape of the lamp and lets pinpricks of light gleam through. The ice method described for the lamp shade can also be used to punch tin and aluminum boxes and cans.

PROJECT SUPPLIES Basic Supplies (page 329), metal pendant lamp, duct tape

HOW-TO Remove the socket from the lamp. To punch a pattern in the shade without crushing or bending it, seal the hole at the top with duct tape. Fill the shade with water to 1 inch (2.5cm) from the rim, and freeze, creating a firm backing for hammering. Punch a design of overlapping circles. Replace the lamp socket after the ice has melted and the shade is completely dry.

PROJECT: **punched tartlet-tin magnets**

Diminutive tartlet tins come in shapes worth showing off; delicate punched patterns make them even more charming. Here they've been turned into magnets and mounted on an enameled-metal tray that's suspended on the wall to double as a bulletin board.

PROJECT SUPPLIES Basic Supplies (page 329), magnets, epoxy

HOW-TO Cut paper to fit inside the tartlet tins and map out uncomplicated patterns on them (or work freehand). Place the tartlet tins flat-side down on particleboard and punch the design into the bottoms of the tins. Add small magnets to the backs with beads of epoxy.

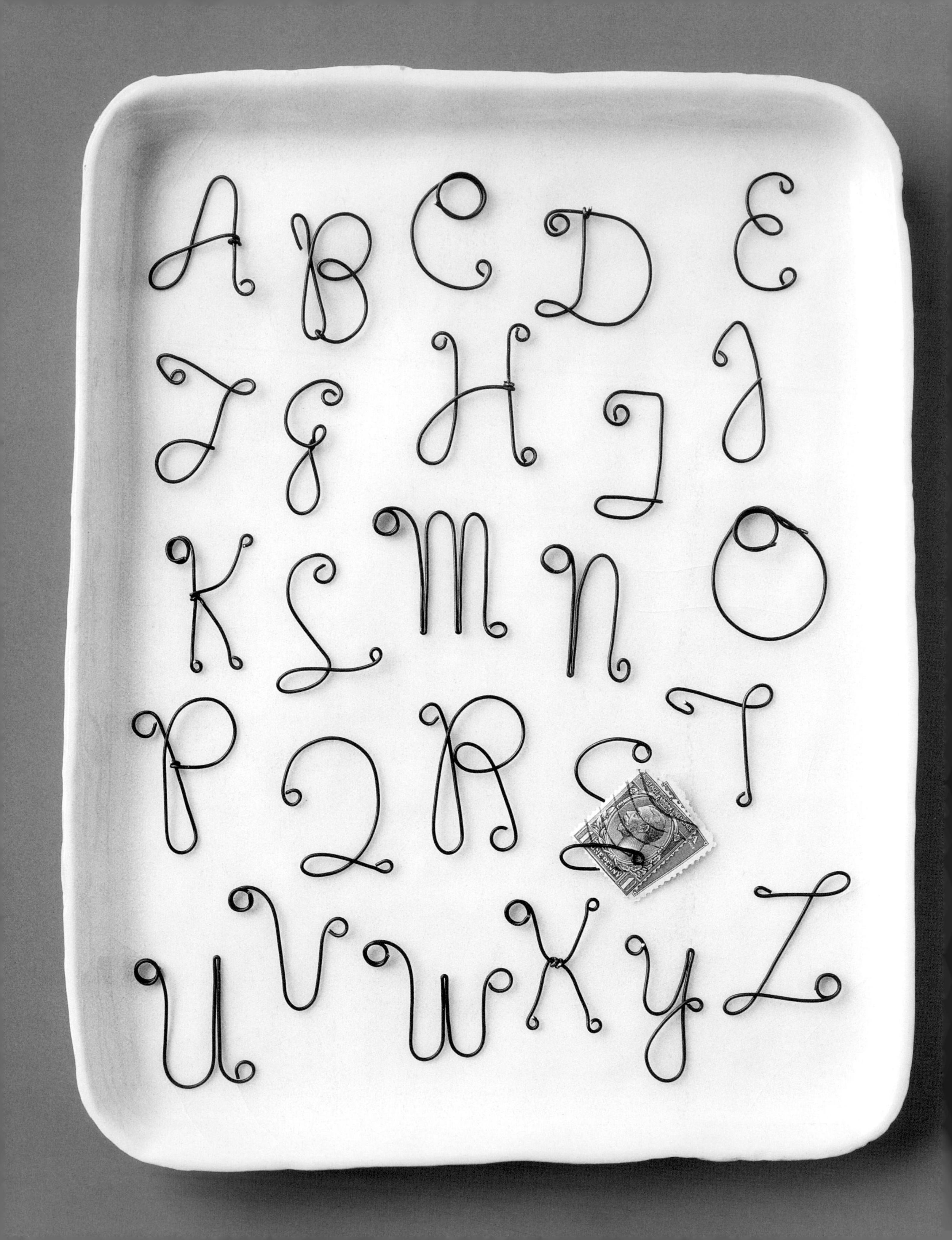

W WIREWORK

Think of working with wire as drawing with a pencil—in three dimensions. Each graphite-colored line (or length of wire) is guided into curves, coils, and bends until a design emerges. The resulting objects can't help but be a celebration of movement. Wirework's filigreed appearance is a product of centuries-old techniques; the objects can be soldered, but are usually secured with just a series of twists and cinches. For that reason, the only tools you'll need to create them are pliers, wire cutters, and the wire itself. Wirework dates to seventeenth-century Slovakia, where tinkers, who repaired broken pottery objects with iron wire, transformed their practical trade into an artistic profession. Traveling and selling their wares in Europe and, later, the United States, these early wireworkers are credited with inspiring a dizzying array of kitchen tools, tabletop items, and even chandeliers. By the early 1900s, at the height of wirework's popularity, there were an estimated ten thousand tinkers working in Europe and the United States. Wire tools were coveted not only for their beauty, but also their functionality: Wire was used to make such practical items as spatulas, colanders, trivets, eggcups, and salad spinners. Eventually, though, the advent of new materials that didn't rust (such as plastic and stainless steel) relegated wirework to the realm of nostalgia. Its beauty, however, has never gone out of style. The pieces have a graphic appearance that allows them to easily blend into both modern and rustic settings. The projects that follow offer a new twist on an old craft. Don't be surprised if after making a monogram paper clip or a looped organizer you find yourself designing projects of your own. Something about the pliability of the wire inspires the imagination to bend and curl and coil right along with it.

ABOUT THE MATERIALS

WIRE Wire is measured by gauge (thickness). The higher the number, the thinner the wire. These projects use 16-, 18-, 20-, and 28-gauge wire. Annealed steel wire, which has been heated and then cooled to make it more pliable, works best. You'll find it at crafts and hardware stores. You can let it oxidize, to produce an antiqued appearance, or apply a spray-on lacquer if you wish to preserve its dark color.

PLIERS With different kinds of pliers, or even your fingers, you can bend, twist, and loop wire into an endless variety of shapes. Use flat-nose, round-nose, and needlenose pliers to achieve different effects.

DOWELS Wrap wire around dowels or other round household objects, such as a dowel or mop handle, to make even loops.

WIRE CUTTERS Hardened tempered-steel jaws let you snip wire effortlessly. Smaller ones are more comfortable to work with.

OPPOSITE **You can form a whole alphabet of wire paper clips, or perfect your technique with just your initials. See instructions on page 339.**

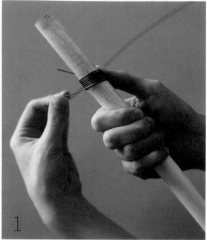

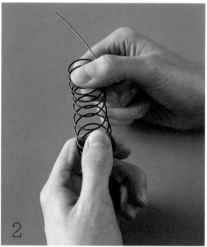

PROJECT: looped organizers

Use your fingers and a dowel to make even, perfectly rounded loops. Tack one or several of these simple organizers near a desk or inside a kitchen cabinet to corral wayward notes, recipes, or mementos.

PROJECT SUPPLIES wire cutters, 16-gauge wire, 1-inch (2.5cm) dowel, ¾-inch (2cm) dowel, mop handle and/or wooden spoon handle, round-nose pliers, nails or tacks

HOW-TO 1. To make the example shown on the door above, cut a piece of 16-gauge wire twice as long as the organizer you want to make. Starting 2 to 3 inches (2.5–7.5cm) from one end, gently but firmly wrap the wire around the dowel with one hand, holding the coils in place with the other. **2.** Slip the coils off the dowel, and flatten them, spreading them evenly with your fingers. Use round-nose pliers to create a loop at each end for hanging. Hang the organizer with nails or tacks.

VARIATIONS You can vary the basic technique by forming different-size coils and leaving more space between them. To make an organizer with large-spaced double coils (pictured on door, far left), use a 1½-inch (3.8cm) diameter mop handle, and loop wire around it twice to form a double coil. Remove that coil from the handle, move down the wire 2 inches (5cm), and create another double loop. Repeat, evenly spacing the coils and removing each one after forming it. For smaller double coils (on the door, center), use the same technique with a ¾-inch (2cm) dowel or a wooden spoon handle, alternating sides as you form each loop. Leave about 1 inch (2.5cm) between coils.

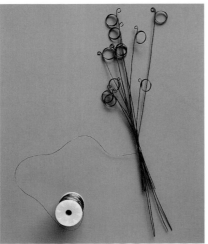

PROJECT: peacock photo display

Show off postcards and pictures in style, tucked into the loops of this fan-shaped photo holder. Using varying lengths of wire adds visual interest to the arrangement, and allows you to see more photos at once.

PROJECT SUPPLIES wire cutters, 18-gauge wire, ⅝-inch (16mm) dowel, needle-nose pliers, 28-gauge wire

HOW-TO Snip 18-gauge wire into 11 pieces: two 16-inch (10.5cm), two 15-inch (38cm), three 14-inch (35.5cm), and four 15 ¾-inch (40cm). Starting ½ inch (13mm) from the end of each wire, coil the wire around a ⅝-inch (16mm) dowel, making a loop; with needle-nose pliers, make a tiny loop from the excess ½ inch (13mm). Bundle all but the 15 ¾-inch (40cm) wires together, bottom ends aligned. Add the 15 ¾-inch (40cm) wires, extending their ends 4 ½ inches (11.5cm) below the others. Wrap about 1 ½ inches (3.8cm) of the bundle with 28-gauge wire, ending where the shorter wires end. Use needle-nose pliers to make a small loop at the end of each 15 ¾-inch (40cm) wire. Bend the longer wires into a base and fan out the holders.

WIRE AND TWIG FORM WREATHS

BASIC SUPPLIES

wreath form (wire or twig, depending on project)

floral wire (usually 26-gauge)

small wire cutters

hand pruners

Perfect for heavier materials, such as evergreen branches, wire forms allow you to densely pack twigs, boughs, leaves, and other decorative objects so that they entirely cover the framework and create a uniformly thick and dense wreath. Twig forms, on the other hand, tend to create a much airier appearance because they cannot be packed so densely. They are wonderful for materials that you want to give room to breathe, like clusters of dried berries or delicate blossoms, such as those of the dogwood tree.

PROJECT: Eastern juniper wreath

A coating of white floral spray and clear glitter gives this Eastern juniper wreath an icy effect; silver balls and crystals add sparkle. Cedar boughs would also work well for this project. When spraying paint and adhesive, be sure to work in a well-ventilated area.

PROJECT SUPPLIES Basic Supplies (above; use 20-inch [51cm] double-wire form), Eastern juniper branches, white floral spray, spray adhesive, large cardboard box, clear plastic glitter, spoon, 26-gauge silver wire (for crystals), clear glass or plastic beads, different-size wired silver balls, 2¾-inch (7cm) wide double-face satin ribbon, appropriate hanging hardware, monofilament

HOW-TO 1. Cut branches into 4- to 6-inch (10–15cm) long pieces. Gather the pieces into thick bundles; secure them with wire individually. Attach 1 end of wire to the wreath form. Lay a bundle on the form, and tightly wrap it with wire; the wire should go halfway up the bundle. Without cutting the wire, add another bundle, so its top overlaps the bottom half of the previous one; wire, and repeat to cover the form.
2. Coat the front of the wreath with white floral spray, covering as much greenery as possible; let it dry for 20 minutes. Coat the back of the wreath with floral spray, let it dry, then repeat front and back. Coat both sides with spray adhesive. Place the wreath in the cardboard box and sprinkle with clear plastic glitter. Shake off the excess, and flip. Spoon excess glitter from the box, and sprinkle it over the back of the wreath. Glitter front and back again (do not add a second coat of spray adhesive). Let it dry overnight. For crystal decorations, slide a length of silver wire through a glass or plastic bead. Twist the wire around itself to secure the bead. Repeat with different-size beads. Twist beads and silver-wired balls into clusters. With ribbon, make a sash bow (see below). Shake the wreath to remove excess glitter. Wire the ribbon to the bottom of the wreath. Carefully attach the bead and ball clusters, wiring as necessary. Hang with monofilament, as described opposite.

how to tie a bow

SASH BOW To make a bow with extra-long tails, start with three pieces of satin ribbon: one 20 inches (50cm) long, one 16 inches (40cm), and one that's about 2 yards (1.8m) for the tails (you can make this shorter, depending on your preference). Make loops of the 20-inch and 16-inch ribbons; fold the ends toward the center, overlapping them, and secure with fabric glue. Stack the loops, the shorter on top of the longer.

Lay the 2-yard ribbon across the center of the loops, and knot. Rotate the knot to the back of bow. Slide 26-gauge wire through the knot and hang.

DOUBLE BOW For a double bow, such as for the gumdrop wreath on page 351, follow the same instructions as for the sash bow, but use two equal lengths of ribbon (two pieces of 20-inch-long ribbon, for example), and a third that is longer to create tails.

how to hang a wreath

WALL Attach a wire loop to the back of the form; wrap floral wire around the back of wire and twig forms, or pin into straw or Styrofoam® forms. Hang the wreath on a sturdy nail or hook.

DOOR OR MOLDING To avoid creating unsightly holes in walls or woodwork, suspend wreath from the top of a door or molding with either a length of sturdy ribbon or monofilament (the monofilament's packaging should list how much weight it will support). To hang, cut a piece of ribbon (at least 3-inches [7.5cm] wide) or monofilament long enough so that, when the ribbon or monofilament is doubled, the wreath will hang at the desired height. Loop the ribbon or monofilament around the back of the wreath form (or pin it, in the case of Styrofoam or straw forms). If using ribbon, fold the edges over ½ inch (1.25cm), and secure to the top of the door or molding with a few flat, heavy-duty thumbtacks (available at hardware stores). If using monofilament, knot the ends of the doubled-up string and use a heavy-duty tack to secure the string to the top of the door or the molding. To hang particularly heavy wreaths with ribbon, first hang with monofilament to support the bulk of the weight, then attach the ribbon as a decorative detail.

MIRROR A mirror provides an elegant, reflective backdrop for wreaths. Wrap metal wreath forms with floral tape to prevent them from scratching mirrors on which they're hung. To hang, use the same technique as for hanging at the top of a door or molding, but tack the ribbon or monofilament to the back of the mirror's frame.

PROJECT: **cedar and arborvitae wreath**

Fragrant branches of cedar and arborvitae make wonderful holiday wreaths for either indoor or outdoor use because they are less likely to shed than traditional pine boughs.

PROJECT SUPPLIES Basic Supplies (opposite; use 16-inch [40.5cm] double-wire form), cedar and arborvitae boughs, 3-inch (7.5cm) wide ribbon for hanging

HOW-TO Cut cedar and arborvitae boughs to 4- to 6-inch (10–15cm) lengths; make small bunches of cedar, and add 1 sprig of arborvitae to each. Attach 1 end of the wire to the wreath form. Lay the first bunch on the form. Wrap floral wire around the stems three times to secure them. Do not cut the wire. Continue adding bunches around the wreath form, overlapping each bundle by half. When finished, secure the floral wire with a knot and create a hanging loop on the back of the frame. See above for hanging instructions.

PROJECT: "sugared fruit" wreath

The lure of fruit as decoration has a venerable history, but apples, grapes, and pears have never stood up to long display. One good solution is to use artificial fruit. Traditionally, the fruit was crafted from pressed and painted cotton. More familiar to us is the modern synthetic variety, made from materials such as plastic and polystyrene. Coated with glass glitter to resemble a dusting of sugar, these look as tempting as the real thing.

PROJECT SUPPLIES Basic Supplies (page 344; use an 18-inch [45.5cm] double-wire form and 26-gauge brass wire), artificial fruit (such as grapes, apples, lemons, and pears), U pins, hot-glue gun and glue sticks, white craft glue, gold acrylic paint, paintbrush, clear glass glitter, medium cardboard box, silk grape leaves

HOW-TO 1. Begin by attaching 26-gauge brass wire to the bottoms of the fruit. For the grapes, simply wrap the wire around their stems. For other fruit, such as apples and lemons, insert a U pin and apply a dab of hot glue to keep it in place, then wrap the wire through the pin. Mix white craft glue with gold acrylic paint and then paint the wired fruit with the mixture. While they're still wet, cover each piece of fruit with a thick layer of glass glitter (too little glitter will leave the fruit looking dull). Apply the glitter while working over the cardboard box, to keep your work area clean. Wrap wire around the stems of the grape leaves, paint them with the glue mixture, and dust them lightly with the glitter. **2.** Once dry, wire the fruits directly to the wreath form. The fruit will shift when the wreath is moved or hung, so you may wish to affix them to their neighbors with discrete applications of hot glue. Wire on the grape leaves. See page 345 for hanging instructions.

prewrapping bunches

You can assemble a cedar and arborvitae wreath (page 345) either by wrapping loose bunches of boughs or other foliage directly onto your form, or by prewrapping the bases of the bunches before attaching them to the form. The advantage of prewrapping the bunches is that it may be easier to gauge how many you need before wiring them to the form. Yet, some people prefer not to prewrap, because it requires one extra step. Ultimately, to prewrap or not is a matter of preference; experiment with both techniques to determine which you like best.

PROJECT: dogwood wreath

A collection of branches and blooms comprises this ephemeral wreath. Flowering dogwood grows across the continent, but it is endangered or threatened in parts of the country. Check with your local extension office or the USDA's plants website (plants.usda.gov) to see if you can collect the branches and blooms in your area. Dry fresh blooms between heavy boxes or in a plant press (see Botanical Pressing, page 46).

PROJECT SUPPLIES Basic Supplies (page 344; use an 18- or a 20-inch [45.5cm or 51cm] twig form), deciduous branches (including dogwood), hot-glue gun, glue stick, dried white dogwood blooms

HOW-TO 1. Cut about 75 deciduous branch tips and strip them of the leaves, cutting them into 6-inch (15cm) lengths. Cutting this many branches from one tree could shock the plant, so take them from multiple trees. Use some dogwood branches; their buds will add detail. Secure floral wire to the twig form. Lay a bundle of 6 or 8 branch tips on the form. Wrap floral wire around the stems and wreath form 3 times. Do not cut the wire. Continue adding bundles of tips, overlapping the previous ones by half, all the way around. Cut the wire and secure. **2.** Use a hot-glue gun to attach about 60 dried white dogwood blooms to the branches. Humidity will cause the blooms to wilt, so make, hang, and store the wreath in a dry environment. See page 345 for hanging instructions.

STRAW, FOAM, AND WOOD FORMS

Straw, Styrofoam®, and floral foam wreath forms differ from wire and twig forms in that you can add decorations not just to the fronts, but also to the sides for a full, deep wreath. Medium-density fiberboard (MDF) wood wreaths have the advantage that they are quite durable. Decorations are generally glued or stuck directly into these forms, so you probably won't need floral wire.

PROJECT: harvest wreath

Inexpensive husks are available at many large grocery stores year-round, so you can make this wreath in any season. Dried corn husks are attached to a straw form with U pins. Pairing this wreath with a collection of gourds, berries, and candles makes a lovely autumnal display.

PROJECT SUPPLIES four to five 8-ounce (227g) bags of dried corn husks, 18-inch (45.5cm) straw wreath form, U pins, 3-inch (7.5cm) wide ribbon for hanging

HOW-TO Soak husks in water until pliable, about 10 minutes, then tear them into 2-inch (5cm) wide strips. Bend 1 strip in half, and attach it to the wreath form with a U pin. Working from the inside of the wreath form outward, create rows of 4 or 5 strips. Circle the wreath form as you go, overlapping rows so that the pinned edges stay hidden. Let dry overnight. See page 345 for hanging instructions.

PROJECT: gumdrop wreath

Layers of gumdrops are used here to create a particularly enticing holiday decoration. With nothing but toothpicks, white gumdrops, and a Styrofoam form you can easily make this whimsical creation. You can make a gumdrop wreath with any size form—the most important thing is to make it in even rows. Of course, the wreath can also be as colorful as you choose by using a variety pack of gumdrops.

PROJECT SUPPLIES floral wire, toothpicks, 2-inch [5cm] Styrofoam wreath form, gumdrops, 3-inch (7.5cm) wide satin ribbon for hanging

HOW-TO Wrap enough floral wire around the wreath form to leave a large loop for hanging. Break toothpicks in half. Lay the wreath form flat. Begin a short row: Place the pointed end of a few toothpick halves into the Styrofoam, following the form's curve from inside to outside; push one gumdrop onto the broken end of each toothpick. After a row is a few inches (6–8cm) long, make a parallel row on each side until the section is covered. Repeat until the wreath is complete. (Note: If you try to complete an entire ring of gumdrops before moving to the next row, it will be very difficult to create a uniform pattern.) See page 345 for hanging instructions.

PROJECT: carnation wreath

Carnations are wonderfully romantic when bunched and made into a wreath. Using a floral foam form will allow you to keep the flowers fresh for weeks.

PROJECT SUPPLIES about 84 carnations, floral shears or scissors, 12-inch [30.5cm] floral-foam wreath form with plastic backing, wired glass balls, 2 yards (183cm) of 3-inch (7.5cm) wide ribbon

HOW-TO To ensure that flowers stay fresh for the longest amount of time, purchase them when they're still partially closed and then condition them by cutting the stems at an angle above or below (but not on) a swollen node, 2 to 3 inches (5-7.5 cm) from the head, and submerging in clean water for at least 12 hours. After soaking, drain the flowers. Immerse the form in water for 20 minutes; let drain. Push the stems into the foam, starting on the top, and then the sides, spacing them evenly and clustering them together. Push the wired glass balls in randomly among the flowers. Hang the wreath from a nail attached to the wall or a door (there should be a place for a nail on the back of the wreath form); monofilament is generally not sturdy enough to hang this type of wreath. Then add a decorative ribbon with four long tails: Tie the ribbon into a bow, adding another length of ribbon through the knot before tightening. Slip wire through the back of the bow and hang above the wreath. Tuck 2 tails from the bow behind the wreath so that the ribbon appears to be supporting the wreath. To keep the flowers fresh, remove the wreath from its display every 3 days and soak for 3 minutes; let it drain, and dry the plastic back with a towel before rehanging.

PROJECT: black rose wreath

This Halloween-ready wreath is made with an MDF form and inexpensive silk flowers. Respray when it begins to look dull, and you can use it from year to year. It's sturdy enough to be hung outside, but may show wear, depending on exposure to the elements. You could make this wreath for a different time of year by spray-painting the flowers a different color.

PROJECT SUPPLIES twenty-five to thirty 4-inch (10cm) wide red silk roses, 16-inch (40.5cm) MDF frame, hot-glue gun and glue sticks, newspaper, black floral spray, scissors, 54 inches (137cm) of 3-inch (7.5cm) wide black taffeta ribbon (plus extra for hanging), flat thumbtacks

HOW-TO Remove the stems from the roses, and then attach the blooms to the wreath form with a hot-glue gun. Lay the wreath on a piece of newspaper in a well-ventilated area, and spray it with black floral spray. Let the wreath dry for 30 minutes. Cut about 54 inches (1.34cm) of the ribbon, and make a large bow; affix it to the top of the wreath with the glue gun. See page 345 for hanging instructions.

BASIC TECHNIQUES

The skills you'll need to master vary based on the type of projects you create. The seven below, however, should be part of every crafter's repertoire.

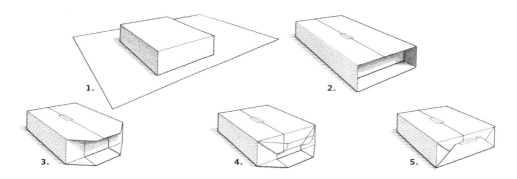

WRAPPING A GIFT BOX

The secret behind the perfect presentation? Clean creases, hidden seams, and pretty paper. **1.** Place the box facedown on wrapping paper. **2.** Bring the wrapping paper around the box. Pull it taut, and tape. (For extra-neat packages, use double-sided tape to secure paper from below.) **3.** Fold in the sides, creasing along the top and bottom flaps. **4.** Working with one side at a time, fold down the top flap, creasing along the edge of the box. Fold over a small bit of the bottom flap to make a clean edge. **5.** Bring up the bottom flap, and tape it shut. Repeat on other side. Finish with a bow.

TYING A BOW

To create an attractive bow that has even loops and tails—and unties with a tug—follow these steps. Place the box facedown on the ribbon, positioning it so the ribbon runs the length of the box. Draw the ribbon ends up, and tie—don't knot—pulling the ribbon taut. Turn the box right-side up. Wrap the ribbon around the width of the box. **1.** Cross the ribbon. **2.** Create two loops that are equal in size. **3.** Cross the right loop over the left. **4.** Bring it under and through the hole. **5.** Pull the knot tight. **6.** Adjust the loops and the tails, and trim the ends of the tails until they are the same length. Notch the ends, if desired, or trim them with pinking or scalloping shears (both will prevent fraying).

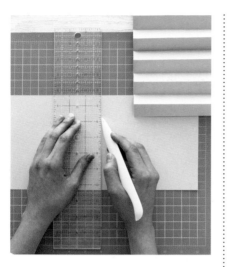

USING A BONE FOLDER

Perfectly fold scrapbook pages, artful letters, origami boxes, and more. Place a ruler on the paper where you want the fold. Hold the ruler firmly in place with one hand. Run the pointed tip of a bone folder along the length of the ruler, pressing it firmly down as you go. Remove the ruler and fold the paper along the scored line.

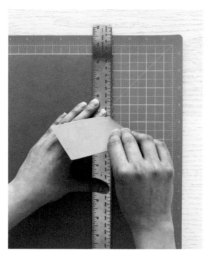

MAKING A DECKLE EDGE

Edges that are torn but neat and straight give cards a charming, handmade look. Place a sheet of paper or card stock facedown on a flat surface. Align a metal ruler parallel to one side, about an inch (2.5cm) in. Pressing firmly on the ruler, rip the edge of the paper along the length of the ruler. Repeat on the remaining three sides to create the desired size.

USING A SCREW PUNCH

Traditional hole punches only work around the edges of a sheet of paper. To make a hole at any point, use a screw punch (sometimes called a Japanese hole punch). Cover your work surface with a self-healing mat. Place paper on top. Insert the desired tip in the punch (most come with several sizes). Place the tip of the punch on the paper. Press down on the punch firmly until you can't push any more, then release.

BRUSHING ON GLUE

To keep paper from buckling, glue should be applied in a thin, even coat. Squeeze glue into a small bowl. Use a paintbrush to spread glue over the appropriate area. When you're finished gluing, clean the bowl and brush with warm water before the glue dries.

CUTTING WITH A CRAFT KNIFE

Cover your work surface with a self-healing mat. Place paper or card stock on top, and place a ruler where you'd like to cut. Hold the ruler firmly in place with one hand. Run the pointed tip of a craft knife along the length of the ruler, dragging it very gently down as you go. This will lightly score the paper (you're not trying to cut through it yet), and leave a "path" for the blade to follow. While continuing to hold the ruler in place, draw the blade down the scored line, pressing a little harder to cut through the paper. Ignore your instincts: Pressing hard and dragging the knife will lead to crooked cuts and broken blades. If the paper starts to bunch and tear under the blade, it's time to replace your blade.

Adorn the blank cover of an oversized scrapbook with a custom label (template opposite) to make a family album.

TEMPLATES

Unless otherwise noted, copy the templates at 100 percent, or size to your project as needed. Go to www.marthastewart.com/craft-book-templates to download these templates, or search our archives for other examples.

ALBUMS, SCRAPBOOKS, AND MEMORY BOXES
generations album label, page 21

ALBUMS, SCRAPBOOKS, AND MEMORY BOXES
postcards scrapbook label, page 23

ALBUMS, SCRAPBOOKS, AND MEMORY BOXES
postcards scrapbook border, page 23

S	M	T	W	Th	F	Sa
—	—	—	—	—	—	—
—	—	—	—	—	—	—
—	—	—	—	—	—	—
—	—	—	—	—	—	—
—	—	—	—	—	—	—
—	—	—	—	—	—	—

BOTANICAL PRINTING
calendar grid, pages 72-73 (enlarge 125%)

A B C D

E F G H I

J K L M

N O P Q

R S T U V

W X Y Z

BEADING
beaded letters, page 37 (enlarge 275%)

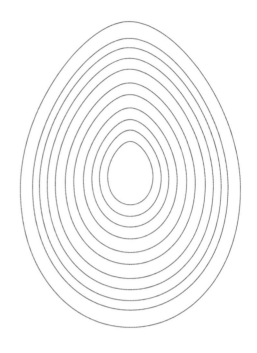

BLOCK PRINTING
designs, pages 42–43

CALLIGRAPHY
guidesheet, page 76

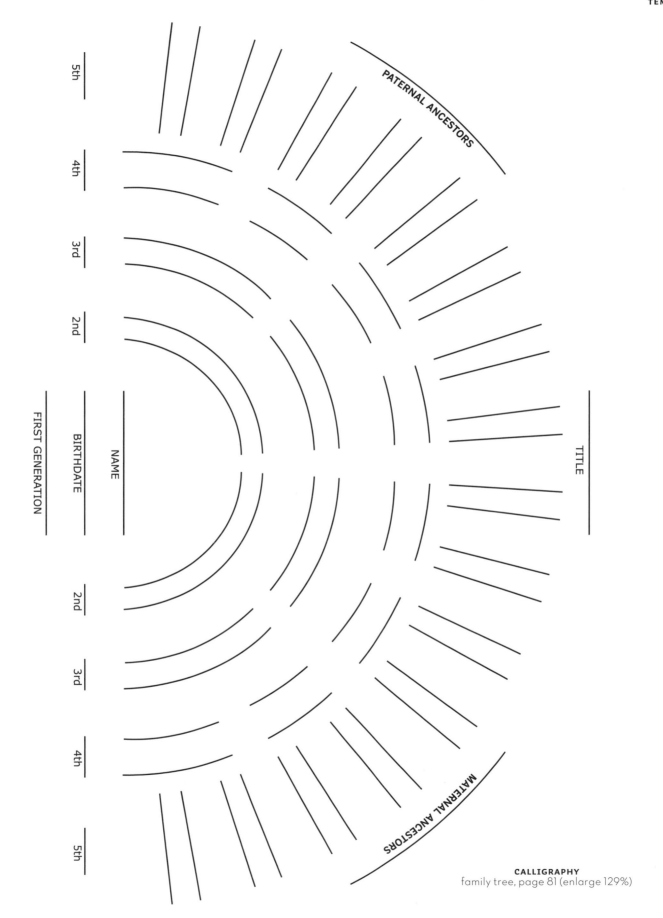

PATERNAL ANCESTORS

MATERNAL ANCESTORS

5th

4th

3rd

2nd

FIRST GENERATION

BIRTHDATE

NAME

2nd

3rd

4th

5th

TITLE

CALLIGRAPHY
family tree, page 81 (enlarge 129%)

DECOUPAGE
animals

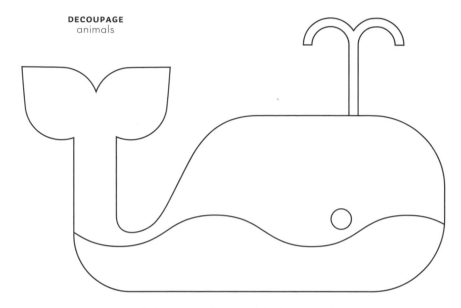

whale step stool, page 121 (enlarge 113%)

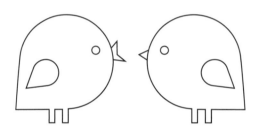

bird dresser decals, page 120

three bears clothes hangers, page 120

dog and cat chair backs, page 121

GLITTERING
snowflake ornaments, page 146 (enlarge 150%)

ETCHING GLASS
etched glasses, page 126

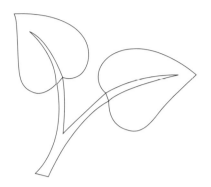

ETCHING GLASS
etched mirror, pages 124–125

a b c d
e f g h i
j k l m n
o p q r
s t u v w
x y z

ETCHING GLASS
kitchen canisters, page 122

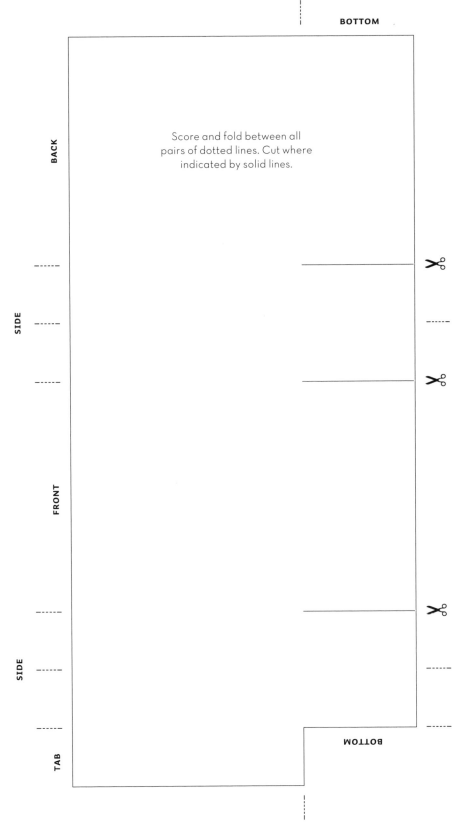

BOTTOM

BACK

Score and fold between all
pairs of dotted lines. Cut where
indicated by solid lines.

SIDE

FRONT

SIDE

TAB

BOTTOM

ORIGAMI AND PAPER FOLDING
mini shopping bag, page 218

ORIGAMI AND PAPER FOLDING
custom envelopes, page 219

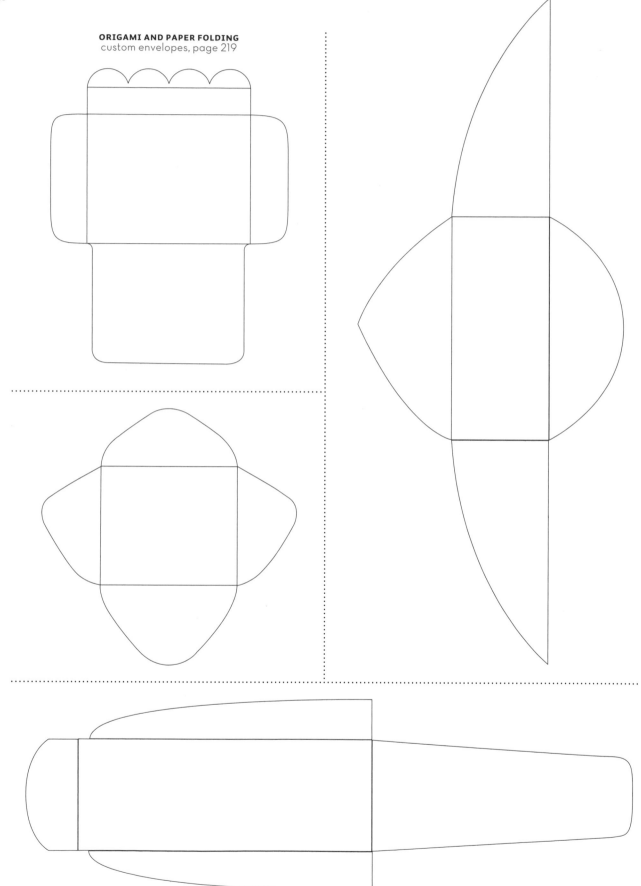

PAINTING CHINA AND GLASS
painted plates, page 222; embellished tea set, page 224

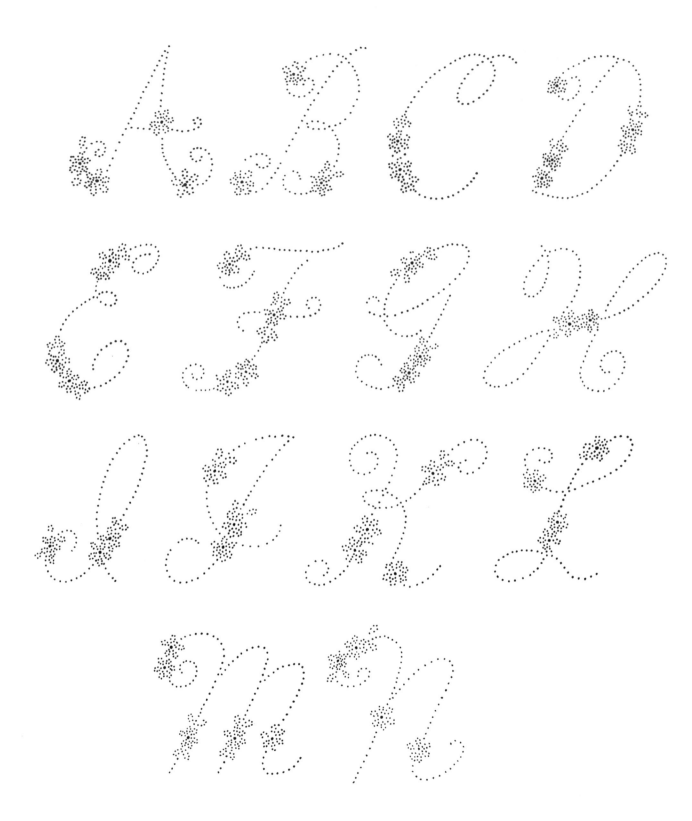

PAINTING CHINA AND GLASS
dot-painted bathroom accessories, page 225

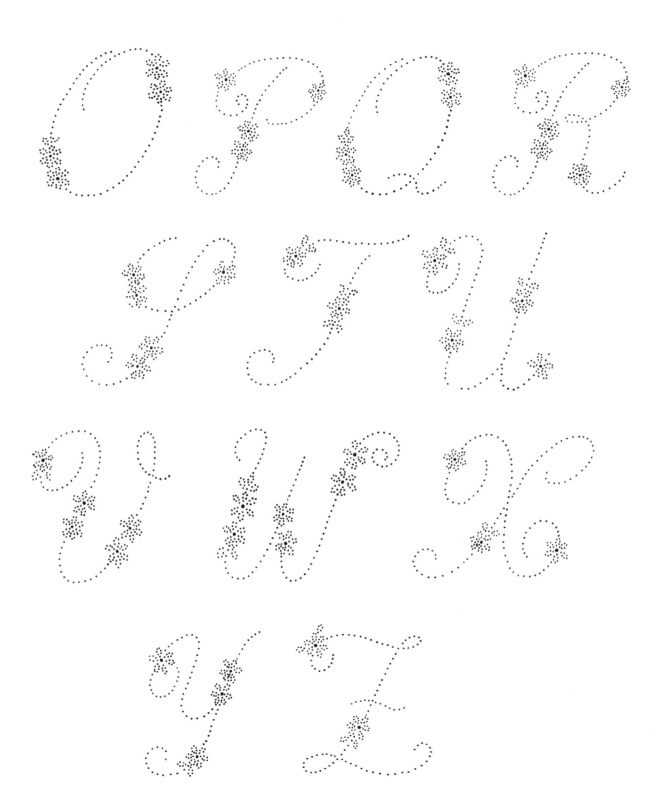

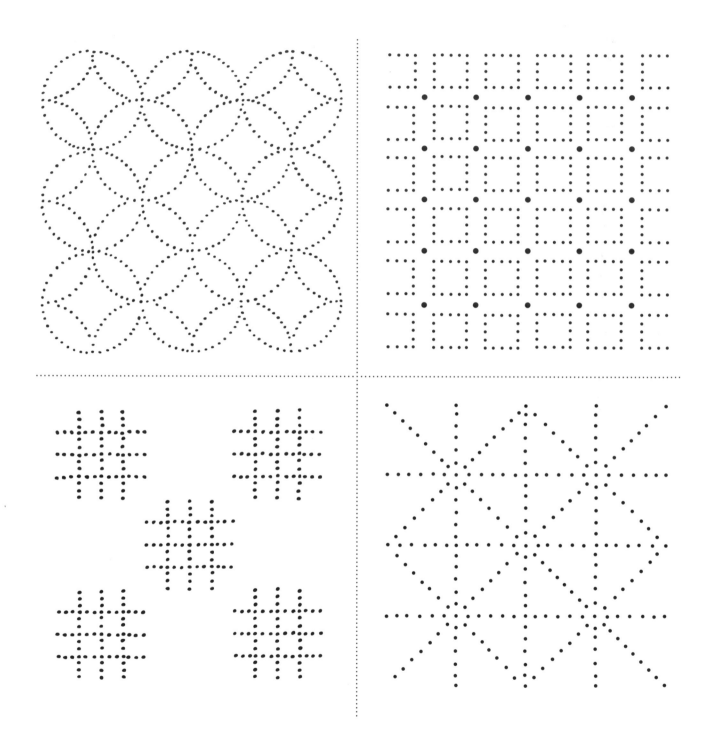

PAINTING CHINA AND GLASS
painted-tile coasters, page 225 (enlarge 175%)

PAINTING CHINA AND GLASS
painted mirror, page 229

PAINTING CHINA AND GLASS
painted picture-frame border, page 228

PAINTING CHINA AND GLASS
bathroom tiles, page 225

PAINTING CHINA AND GLASS
painted cabinet, page 231

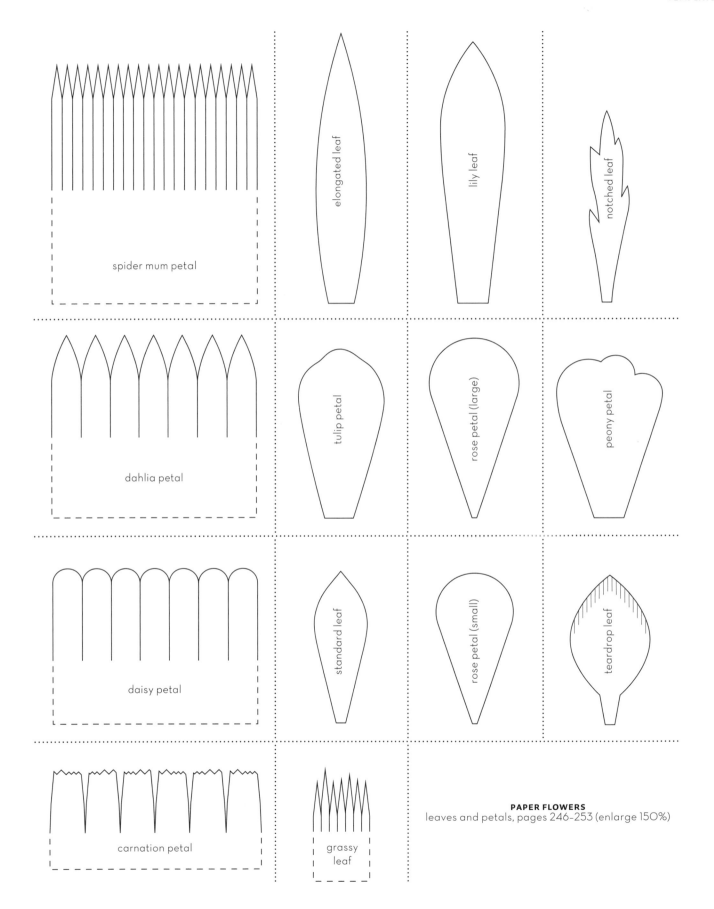

spider mum petal

elongated leaf

lily leaf

notched leaf

dahlia petal

tulip petal

rose petal (large)

peony petal

daisy petal

standard leaf

rose petal (small)

teardrop leaf

carnation petal

grassy leaf

PAPER FLOWERS
leaves and petals, pages 246–253 (enlarge 150%)

PAPER CUTTING AND PUNCHING
cut-flower projects, pages 232–235

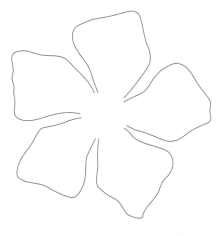

PAPER CUTTING AND PUNCHING
punched-flower cards and wrapping, page 237

RUBBER STAMPING
double cornucopia, page 311

SILKSCREENING
director's chair, runner, and napkins, page 317 (enlarge 122%)

SILKSCREENING
custom t-shirts, page 316

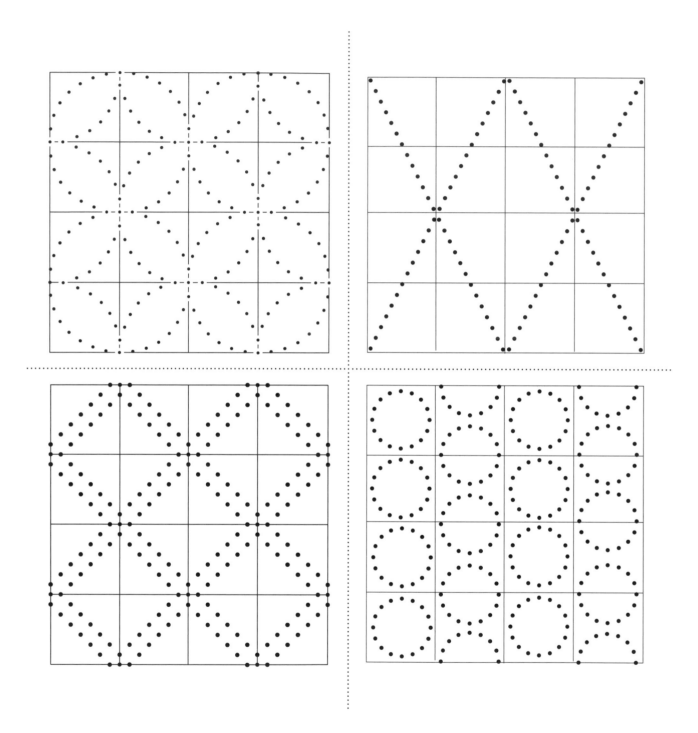

TIN PUNCHING
patterns, pages 330, 331, 333

TIN PUNCHING
alphabet, page 332

SOURCES

The following is a list of addresses that we hope will prove useful as you source the tools, materials and general craft supplies that you will need to complete the projects in this book. Many of the contacts provided are for suppliers of general equipment relating to the crafts featured in the book. However, wherever possible, we have provided contacts for specific project products. If you cannot find the exact product we have used, be flexible and adapt the project idea to suit the products available to you.

Note: All addresses, phone numbers and websites were verified at the time of publication, although, naturally, this information is subject to change.

adhesives and glues

CRAFT CREATIONS
Ingersoll House
Delamore Road
Cheshunt
EN8 9HD
tel: 01992 781900
email:
enquiries@craftcreations.com
www.craftcreations.co.uk

HOBBYCRAFTS
Visit the website or phone for details of your nearest store.
tel: 0800 0272387
www.hobbycraft.co.uk

HOMECRAFTS DIRECT
Homecrafts Direct
PO Box 38
Leicester

LE1 9BU
tel: 0116 2697733
email: info@homecrafts.co.uk
www.homecrafts.co.uk

albums and scrapbooks

CALICO CRAFTS
tel: 01353 624100
www.calicocrafts.co.uk

THE CRAFTZ BOUTIQUE
Unit 15
Whitehill Ind Estate
Whitehill Lane
Wootton Bassett
Swindon
SN4 7DB
tel: 01793 859977/01793 790919
email:

sales@thecraftzboutique.com
www.thecraftboutique.com

beads

BEADS DIRECT
tel: 0870 086 9877
email:
service@beaddirect.co.uk
www.beadsdirect.co.uk

THE BEAD SCENE
PO Box 6351
Towcester
NN12 7YX
tel: 01327 353639
email:
stephanie@thebeadscene.com
www.thebeadscene.com

GUTERMANN
Perivale-Gutermann Ltd
Bullsbrook Road
Hayes
UB4 OJR
tel: 020 8589 1600
email:
perivale@guetermann.com

KARS
PO Box 272
Aylesbury
HP18 9FH
tel: 01844 238080
email: info@kars.nl
www.kars.biz

KERNOWCRAFT ROCKS &
GEMS
Bolingey
Perranporth
TR6 ODH
tel: 01872 573888
email: info@kernowcraft.com
www.kernowcraft.com

RUCRAFT
tel: 0844 8805852
www.rucraft.co.uk

THE SPELLBOUND BEAD
COMPANY
45 Tamworth Street
Lichfield
WS13 6JW

tel: 01543 417650
email:
info@spellboundbead.co.uk
www.spellboundbead.co.uk

block printing supplies

LONDON GRAPHIC CENTRE
tel: 020 7759 4500
email:
info@londongraphics.co.uk
www.londongraphics.co.uk

botanical pressing supplies

FRED ALDOUS LTD
37 Lever Street
Manchester
M1 1LW
tel: 0161 236 4224
www.fredaldous.co.uk

botanical printing
see light sensitive printing

calligraphy supplies

SCRIBBLERS
www.scribblers.co.uk

candlemaking supplies

CANDLE MAKERS
SUPPLIERS
28 Blythe Road
London
W14 OHA
tel: 020 7602 4031 or
020 7602 4032
email:
mail@candlemakers.co.uk
www.candlemakers.co.uk

FULLMOONS CAULDRON
PO Box 2173
Ascot
SL5 OPQ
tel: 01344 627 945
www.fullmoons-cauldron.co.uk

china and glass paints

HOBBYCRAFTS
Visit the website or phone for details of your nearest store.
tel: 0800 0272387
www.hobbycraft.co.uk

LAINE'S FLORAL ART &
HOBBY CRAFTS
60 Commerce Street
Insch
AB52 6JB
tel: 01464 820335
www.lainesworld.co.uk

PORCELAINE PAINTS
43 Old School Close
Codicot
Hitchin
SG4 8YJ
email:
sales@porcelainpaint.co.uk
www.porcelainpaint.co.uk

clay (including polymer clay)

KARS
PO Box 272
Aylesbury
HP18 9FH
tel: 01844 238080
email: info@kars.nl
www.kars.biz

clear iron-on vinyl

see vinyl, clear iron-on

clip art

THE CLIP ART WAREHOUSE
www.clipart.co.uk

cookie cutters and molds

For biscuit cutters and mini loaf pans

DE CUISINE
Spion House
Rushall Lane
Lytchett Matravers
Poole
BH16 6AJ
tel: 01202 620097
www.decuisine.co.uk

For molds and bakeware
LAKELAND
Visit the website or phone for details of your nearest store.
tel: 015394 88100
www.lakeland.co.uk

cutting tools

CRAFT CREATIONS
Ingersoll House
Delamore Road
Cheshunt
EN8 9HD
tel: 01992 781900
email:
enquiries@craftcreations.com
www.craftcreations.co.uk

fabric paints

DYLON
Spotless Punch Limited
Knowles House
Cromwell Road

Redhill
RH1 1RT
tel: 01737 742020
email: info@dylon.co.uk
www.dylon.co.uk

fabric supplies

JOHN LEWIS
Visit the website or phone for details of your nearest store.
tel: 08456 049 049
www.johnlewis.com

floral supplies

see nature crafts

frames and framing materials

For framing materials
HOBBYCRAFTS
Visit the website or phone for details of your nearest store.
tel: 0800 0272387
www.hobbycraft.co.uk

For frames
IKEA
Visit the website for details of your local store.
www.ikea.com

furniture and accessories

For wooden furniture, desk tidies and wooden hangers ideal for decorating
IKEA
Visit the website for details of your local store.
www.ikea.com

For a range of high-quality furniture and accessory blanks
SCUMBLE GOOSIE
Griffin Mill
London Road
Thrupp
Stroud
GL5 2AZ
tel: 01453 731305
www.scumble-goosie.com

gilding supplies

ALEC TIRANTI LTD
3 Pipers Court
Berkshire Drive
Thatcham
RG19 4ER
tel: 0845 123 2100
email: enquiries@tiranti.co.uk
www.tiranti.co.uk

glass etching

HOBBY'S
W Hobby Limited
Knight's Hill Square
London
SE27 0HH
tel: 020 8761 4244
www.hobby.uk.com

glitter

THE CRAFT BARN
9 East Grinstead Road
Lingfield
RH7 6EP
tel: 01342 836398
www.craftbarnonline.co.uk

CRAFTS U LOVE
Westcoats Farm
Stan Hill
Charlwood
Horley
RH6
tel: 01293 863 576
www.craftsulove.co.uk

jewellery making supplies

THE BEAD SHOP
21a Tower Street
Covent Garden
London

WC2H 9NS
tel: 020 7240 0931
email: sales@beadworks.co.uk
www.beadworks.co.uk

CREATIVE BEADCRAFT LTD
Unit 2
Asheridge Business Centre
Asheridge Road
Chesham
HP5 2PT
tel: 01494 778 818
www.creativebeadcraft.co.uk

RUCRAFT
tel: 0844 8805852
www.rucraft.co.uk

journals and notebooks

PAPERCHASE
213–215 Tottenham Court
Road
London
W1T 7PS
tel: 020 7467 6200
www.paperchase.co.uk

light sensitive printing

For light sensitive (blue print) fabric
RAINBOW SILKS
6 Wheelers Yard
High Street

Great Missenden
HP16 0AL
tel: 01494 862111
email:
caroline@rainbowsilks.co.uk
www.rainbowsilks.co.uk

*For light sensitive (sunprint)
paper*
HAWKIN'S BAZAAR
*Visit the website or phone for
details of your nearest store.*
tel: 0844 557 5261
www.hawkin.com

marbleizing

FRED ALDOUS LTD
37 Lever Street
Manchester
M1 1LW
tel: 0161 236 4224
www.fredaldous.co.uk

memory foil tape

CHEDDAR STAMPER
14 Mansfield Lane
Calverton
Nottingham
NG14 6HL
tel: 0115 938 4711
www.cheddarstamper.co.uk

mosaics supplies

MOSAIC TRADER UK
Unit 14b
Barton Business Park
New Dover Road
Canterbury
CT1 3AA
tel: 01227 781601
email:
info@mosaictraderuk.co.uk
www.mosaictraderuk.co.uk

nature crafts

*For dried and decorative
materials for floral
arrangements including
wreaths and pine cones*
THE ESSENTIALS COMPANY
tel: 01379 608899
email:
info@essentialscompany.co.uk
www.theessentialscompany.co.uk

*For pressed flowers and
leaves*
CROFT PETALS
The Old Dairy Barn
Dunmow Road
Beauchamp Roding
Nr Ongar
CM5 0PF
tel: 01279 876542

email: sales@croftpetals.co.uk
www.croftpetals.co.uk

For shells
EATON'S SEASHELLS
tel: 01279 410284
www.eatonsseashells.co.uk

paper

*For a wide range of
decorative papers*
THE PAPER WAREHOUSE
Grosvenor House Papers Ltd
Westmorland Business Park
Kendal
LA9 6NP
tel: 01539 726161
email: info@ghpkendal.co.uk
www.ghpkendal.co.uk

PAPERCHASE
213–215 Tottenham Court
Road
London
W1T 7PS
tel: 020 7467 6200
www.paperchase.co.uk

RUCRAFT
tel: 0844 8805852
www.rucraft.co.uk

For card blanks and stationery
THE CRAFT BARN
9 East Grinstead Road
Lingfield
RH7 6EP
tel: 01342 836398
www.craftbarnonline.co.uk

For Japanese and origami papers
JAPAN CENTRE
212 Piccadilly
London
W1J 9HG
tel: 020 7439 8035
email: info@
japancentrebookshop.co.uk
www.japancentre.com

For wood veneer paper
CRAFTY COMPUTER PAPER
Woodhall
Barrasford
Hexham
NE48 4DB
tel: 01434 689 153
email: sales@
craftycomputerpaper.co.uk

paper punches

THE ART OF CRAFT
101 Lynchford Road
North Camp
Farnborough
GU14 6ET
tel: 01252 377677
email: info@art-of-craft.co.uk
www.art-of-craft.co.uk

RUCRAFT
tel: 0844 8805852
www.rucraft.co.uk

photo craft supplies

For magnetic paper
MAGNETICK MAGNETIC
MATERIALS
Unit 3b
Sopwith Crescent
Wickford Business Park
Wickford
SS11 8YU
tel: 01268 768 768
www.magnetick.co.uk

For photo paper
FOTOSPEED
Unit 6
Park Lane Industrial Estate
Corsham
SN13 9LG
tel: 01249 555
email: info@fotospeed.com
www.fotospeed.com

For printer-ready fabric sheets
CRAFTY COMPUTER PAPER
Woodhall

Barrasford
Hexham
NE48 4DB
tel: 01434 689 153
email: sales@
craftycomputerpaper.co.uk
www.craftycomputerpaper.co.uk

plate hangers

WARES OF KNUTSFORD LTD
PO Box 321
Knutsford
WA16 8YQ
tel: 08456 121273
email:
sales@waresofknutsford.co.uk
www.waresofknutsford.co.uk

polymer clay
see clay

polystyrene shapes

LAINE'S FLORAL ART &
HOBBY CRAFTS
60 Commerce Street
Insch
AB52 6JB
tel: 01464 820335
www.lainesworld.co.uk

pom-pom maker

SEW AND SO
tel: 01453 889988
email:
salesteam@sewandso.co.uk
www.sewandso.co.uk

quilling

EVIE'S CRAFTS
79 Dale Street
Milnrow
Rochdale
OL16 3NJ
tel: 01706 712489
www.eviescraftsltd.co.uk

FRED ALDOUS LTD
37 Lever Street
Manchester
M1 1LW
tel: 0161 236 4224
www.fredaldous.co.uk

JANE JENKINS QUILLING
DESIGN
33 Mill Rise
Skidby
Cottingham
HU16 5UA
tel: 01482 843721
www.jjquilling.co.uk

ribbon and cord

CRAFTS U LOVE
Westcoats Farm
Stan Hill
Charlwood
Horley
RH6
tel: 01293 863 576
www.craftsulove.co.uk

CRAFTY RIBBONS
3 Beechwood Clump Farm
Tin Pot Lane
Blandford
DT11 7TD
tel: 01258 455889
www.craftyribbons.com

rope

ROPE LOCKER
Mylor Yacht Harbour
Falmouth
TR11 5UF
tel: 0117 230 8525
www.ropelocker.co.uk

rub-on letters and borders

LETRASET LTD
Kingsnorth Industrial Estate
Wotton Road
Ashford

TN23 6FL
tel: 01233 624421
email: enquiries@letraset.com
www.letraset.com

rubber stamping supplies

THE CRAFT BARN
9 East Grinstead Road
Lingfield
Surrey
RH7 6EP
tel: 01342 836398
www.craftbarnonline.co.uk

PERSONAL IMPRESSIONS
Curzon Road
Chilton Industrial Estate
Sudbury
CO10 2XW
Visit the website for details of local stockists.
tel: 01787 375241
email: customerservices@
personalimpressions.com
www.personalimpressions.com

RUCRAFT
tel: 0844 8805852
www.rucraft.co.uk

WHICHCRAFT
The Corn Exchange
Craft Gallery

Doncaster
DN1 1QZ
tel: 01302 369666
email: info@whichcraftuk.co.uk
www.whichcraft.co.uk

silkscreening supplies

LONDON GRAPHIC CENTRE
tel: 020 7759 4500
email:
info@londongraphics.co.uk
www.londongraphics.co.uk

soap making supplies

SOAP BASICS
Mail order only:
23 Southbrook Road
Melksham
SN12 8DS
tel: 01225 899286
email: info@soapbasics.co.uk
www.soapbasics.co.uk

tin punching

For 28-gauge (0.3mm)
metal sheets
THE CRAZY WIRE
COMPANY
Unit 18
Lake Enterprise Park
Caton Road

Lancaster
LA1 3NX
tel: 01524 848777
www.crazywireco.co.uk

vinyl, clear iron-on

*Distributors of HeatnBond
iron-on vinyl (for stockists see
website)*
F W BRAMWELL & CO LTD
Old Empress Mills
Empress Street
Colne
BB8 9HU
email:
info@bramwellcrafts.co.uk
www.bramwellcrafts.co.uk

wirework

THE SCIENTIFIC WIRE
COMPANY
18 Raven Road
London
E18 1HW
tel: 020 8505 0002
www.wires.co.uk

yarns

DESIGNER YARNS LTD
Units 8–10 Newbridge
Industrial Estate

Pitt Street
Keighley
BD21 4PQ
tel: 01535 664222
www.designeryarns.uk.com

INDEX

Y

Z

PHOTOGRAPHY CREDITS

WILLIAM ABRANOWICZ 84, 92, 93, 94, 95, 114, 116, 117, 118, 119, 127, 181, 347

ANTONIS ACHILLEOS 120, 121, 308, 309, 310, 311

SANG AN 24, 30, 32 (photos), 33, 34, 36, 38 (photos), 39 (photos), 96, 97, 98 (bottom), 99, 102 (left), 108, 109 (top), 110, 111, 112, 113, 146, 147, 149, 162, 206, 207 (bottom), 218, 289 (top), 318, 320, 321, 323, 324, 325, 326, 327

BURCU AVSAR 166, 167

ERIC AXENE 26, 27

JAMES BAIGRIE 4, 66, 67, 208 (right), 240, 258, 259, 260, 261, 262, 263, 264, 265, 304

CHRISTOPHER BAKER 46, 54, 55, 56, 57, 192, 194 (photo), 195, 196, 197, 210

HARRY BATES (illustrations) 32, 38, 39, 156, 157, 194, 292, 294, 366

ROLAND BELLO 290, 292 (photo), 293, 295, 296, 297

LUIS BRUNO 232, 234, 235

GEMMA COMAS 14, 17, 19, 20, 21 (top), 22, 23 (bottom 2), 298, 300, 301, 302, 303, 306 (top), 307 (top)

JIM COOPER 40, 42

CARLTON DAVIS 37

FORMULA Z/S 98 (right)

JÜRGEN FRANK 207 (top 3)

LAURIE FRANKEL 243 (bottom 2)

DANA GALLAGHER 23 (top), 50, 352, 353 (top)

GENTL & HYERS 35, 58, 60, 61, 62, 63, 64, 65, 100, 138, 139, 140, 145, 204, 205, 216, 217, 219, 226, 227, 228, 229, 230, 231, 280, 282, 283, 285, 286, 287, 288, 346, 348, 349, 351, 353 (bottom 2)

JOHN GRUEN 209, 292

FRANK HECKERS 44, 45, 272, 274, 275, 276, 277, 278, 279

RAYMOND HOM 5, 107, 356 (bottom right), 360 (middle and right columns), 364 (bottom right)

GRACE HUANG 53

LISA HUBBARD 70 (right), 71, 72, 73, 307 (bottom 2), 322, 328, 330, 331, 332, 333, 334, 335, 350 (left)

GABRIELLA IMPERATORI-PENN 128, 130, 131, 132, 133

YOKO INOUE 270 (right)

DITTE ISAGER front cover, 2, 6

THIBAULT JEANSON 124, 125, 134, 136, 137, 238, 239

ERIK JOHNSON 176, 179, 182 (top)

KARL JUENGEL 163, 180 (left)

RICK LEW 189, 191

STEPHEN LEWIS 25, 52, 68 (bottom), 101, 141

SIVAN LEWIN 312, 314, 315

JONATHAN LOVEKIN 168, 170, 171, 172, 173, 174, 175

CHARLES MARAIA 306 (bottom)

MAURA MCEVOY 74, 76, 77, 78, 79, 80, 81

JOSHUA MCHUGH 28, 29

DAVID MEREDITH 155, 158-159, 160, 161, 266, 268, 269, 270 (left), 271 (left)

JAMES MERRELL 271 (right)

ELLIE MILLER 180 (right), 237

JOHNNY MILLER 1, 18, 21 (bottom), 43, 48 (left, center), 70 (left), 85, 86, 87, 88, 89, 90, 91, 98 (left), 103, 104, 106, 109 (bottom), 126 (bottom right), 142, 144, 150, 151, 152, 178, 182 (bottom), 184, 185, 208 (left), 213 (photo), 215 (photo), 241, 345, 354, 355, 356 (except bottom right), 357, 358, 359, 360 (left column), 361, 362, 363, 364 (except bottom right), 365, 367

LAURA MOSS 182

AMY NEUNSINGER 244, 247, 248, 249, 250, 251, 252, 253

HELEN NORMAN 122, 126 (bottom left), 316 (top), 317

ERIC PIASECKI 148, 183, 342, 344

CON POULOS 102 (right), 105

DAVID PRINCE 350 (right)

MARIA ROBLEDO 82

ALEXANDRA ROWLEY 220, 222, 223, 224, 225, 305

DAVID SAWYER 48 (right), 49, 336, 338, 339, 340, 341

VICTOR SCHRAGER 51, 126 (top)

KATE SEARS 164, 165, 236, 242, 243 (top two)

KIRSTEN STRECKER 198, 199, 200, 201, 202, 203

SIMON UPTON 8, 10, 13, back cover

SIMON WATSON 68 (top 3), 69

ANNA WILLIAMS 186, 188, 190, 214 (photo), 254, 255, 256, 257, 284, 289 (bottom)